SC

1·9

U.S. Pocket

Stamp
Catalogue

D1269752

PRESIDENT	Wayne Lawrence
VICE PRESIDENT/PUBLISHER	Stuart J. Morrissey
EDITORIAL DIRECTOR	Richard L. Sine
EDITOR	William W. Cummings
ASSISTANT EDITOR	William H. Hatton
VALUING EDITOR	Martin J. Frankevicz
NEW ISSUES EDITOR	David C. Akin
COMPUTER CONTROL COORDINATOR	Denise Oder
VALUING ANALYSTS	Jose R. Capote, Roger L. Listwan
EDITORIAL ASSISTANTS	Judith E. Bertrand, Beth Brown
ART/PRODUCTION DIRECTOR	Edward Heys
PRODUCTION COORDINATOR	Janine Skinn Apple
DIRECTOR OF MARKETING & SALES	Jeff Lawrence
SALES MANAGER	Mike Porter
ADVERTISING MANAGER	David Lodge

Copyright© 1991 by

Scott Publishing Co.

911 Vandemark Road, Sidney, Ohio 45365

A division of AMOS PRESS INC., publishers of
Linn's Stamp News, Coin World, Cars & Parts magazine and *The Sidney Daily News.*

2A

CONTENTS

4A

7A

8A

9A

10A

11A

Don't forget to update these Scott Albums with yearly supplements

Scott Minuteman Album
Scott National Album
Scott American Album

Published in November every year.

15A

17A

INTRODUCTION
TO STAMP COLLECTING

A fascinating hobby, an engrossing avocation and a universal pastime, stamp collecting is pursued by millions. Young and old, and from all walks of life, stamp collectors all are involved in that kind of indoor sport: "the paper chase."

It was 150 years ago that Rowland Hill's far-reaching postal reforms became a reality and the world's first adhesive postage stamp was placed on sale at post offices in Great Britain. The date was May 6, 1840. Not too long thereafter a hobby was born that has continued to grow ever since.

Although for the next seven years there were only four stamp issues in England, the Penny Black, two types of the 2-penny blue and the 1-penny red, there were people who saved them. One story has it that a woman covered a wall in a room of her home with copies of the Penny Black.

As country after country began to issue postage stamps, the fraternity of stamp collectors flourished. Today, their numbers are in the millions while the number of stamp-issuing countries has exceeded 650.

The hobby of stamp collecting may take many forms. There are those people who collect the stamps of a single country. Others collect a single issue, i.e., the U.S. Transportation Coils that are current. Others specialize in but a single stamp, with all its nuances and variations. Some collect a type of postage stamp, such as air mails, commemoratives, etc. Another type of collection would consist only of covers (envelopes) bearing a stamp with a postal marking from the first day of that stamp's issue.

Most popular, however, is collecting by country, especially one's own country. This catalogue is designed to aid in forming just such a collection. It lists the postage stamps of the United States and is a simplified edition of information found in Volume 1 of the *Scott Standard Postage Stamp Catalogue.*

20A

How to use this book

The number (1811) in the first column of the example below is the stamp's identifying Scott number. Each stamp issued by the United States has a unique number. The letter-number combination in the second column (A964) indicates the design and refers to the illustration with the same designation. Following in the same line are the denomination of the stamp, its color or other description along with the color of the paper (in italic type) if other than white, and finally the catalogue value both unused and used.

Scott Number	Illustration Design No.	Denomination	Color or Description	Color of the Stamp paper	Unused Value	Used Value
1811	A984	1c	dark blue, *greenish*		15	15

About this edition

Two new sections and a new minimum value for single stamps greet you in this edition. New to this book are specific sections for Computer Vended Postage and Special Printings.

The former is more popularly known in the United States as "Autopost," a test situation using only a few machines in Washington, DC, and one of its Maryland suburbs. As of the publication date of this book, the test has been concluded and there are no announced plans for continuation of the approach . . . which is used quite a bit elsewhere in the world.

Special Printings is a section made up of stamps which had appeared elsewhere in this catalogue. None of the items listed in this section were issued for postal purposes. A notation appears in the text where each of the items had appeared, along with a lengthier explanation at the beginning of the section itself. Items included in this section are among the most valued in U.S. philately.

The minimum value for a stamp has been raised this year, which reflects what you can expect to pay for an item, as well as the handling costs for a dealer. The lower the catalogue value of an item, the higher the percentage of that "value" that should be attributed to dealer handling costs.

Therefore, you may find the total purchase price of a set of stamps to be considerably below the total catalogue value for the individual items within that set. Likewise, the catalogue value of a se-tenant block or pair may well be less than the catalogue value of the individual increments — that is not to suggest that you should separate your blocks or pairs into individual items to show a value increase. Rather, it is very possible that the demand for the individual items will be far less than that for the se-tenant item.

Further, given that the Scott Catalogue values stamps on the basis purchasing them individually, you will find packets, mixtures and collections where the unit cost of the material will be substantially less than the total catalogue value. Such situations, again, are a function of the cost of selling.

Catalogue Value

The Scott Catalogue Value is a retail price, what you could expect to pay for the stamp in a grade of Fine-Very Fine. The value listed is a reference which reflects recent actual dealer selling prices.

Dealer retail price lists, public auction results, published prices in advertising, and individual solicitation of retail prices from dealers, collectors, and specialty organizations have been used in establishing the values found in this Catalogue.

Use this Catalogue as a guide in your own buying and selling. The actual price you pay for a stamp may be higher or lower than the Catalogue Value because of one or more of the following: the amount of personal service a dealer offers, increased interest in the country or topic represented by the stamp or set, whether an item is a "loss leader," part of a special sale, or otherwise is being sold for a short period of time at a lower price, or if at a public auction you are able to obtain an item inexpensively because of little interest in the item at that time.

For unused stamps, more recent issues are valued as never-hinged, with the beginning point determined on a country-by-country basis. Notes to show the beginning points are prominently noted in the text.

Grade

A stamp's grade and condition are crucial factors of its value. Values quoted in this Catalogue are for stamps graded at Fine-Very Fine and with no faults. The accompanying illustrations show an example of a Fine-Very Fine grade between the grades immediately lesser and better: Fine and Very Fine.

FINE stamps have the design noticeably off-center to two sides. Imperforate stamps may have small margins and earlier issues may show the design touching one edge of the stamp. Used stamps may have heavier than usual cancellations.

FINE-VERY FINE stamps may be somewhat off-center to

one side, or only slightly off-center to two sides. Imperforate stamps will have two margins at least normal size and the design will not touch the edge. *Early issues of a country may be printed in such a way that the design naturally is very close to the edges.* Used stamps will not have a cancellation that detracts from the design. This is the grade used to establish Scott Catalogue Values.

VERY FINE stamps may be slightly off-center to one side, with the design well clear of the edge. Imperforate stamps will have three margins at least normal size. Used stamps will have light or otherwise neat cancellations.

FINE

Scott Catalogues value stamps in **FINE-VERY FINE** condition

VERY FINE

Condition

The above definitions describe *grade,* which is centering and (for used stamps) cancellations. *Condition* refers to the soundness of the stamp, i.e., faults, repairs, and other factors influencing price.

Copies of a stamp which are of a lesser grade and/or condition trade at lower prices and those of exceptional quality often command higher prices than those shown in this catalogue.

Factors which increase the value of a stamp include exceptionally wide margins, particularly fresh color, and the inclusion of selvage.

Factors other than faults which decrease the value of a stamp include no gum or regumming, hinge remnant, foreign object adhering to gum, natural inclusion, or a straight edge.

Faults include a missing piece, tear, clipped perforation, pin or other hole, surface scuff, thin spot, crease, toning, oxidation or other form of color changeling, short or pulled perforation, stains or such man-made changes as reperforation or the chemical removal or lightening of a cancellation.

Scott Publishing Co. recognizes that there is no formal, enforced grading scheme for postage stamps, and that the final price you pay for a stamp or obtain for a stamp you are selling will be determined by individual agreement at the time of the transaction.

Forming a collection

Methods of collecting stamps are varied and many. A person may begin by attempting to gather a single specimen of every stamp face-different issued by a country. An extension of that approach is to include the different types of each stamp, such as perforation varieties, watermark varieties, different printings and color changes. The stamps may be collected on cover (envelope) complete with postal markings, thus showing postal rates, types of cancellations and other postal information.

Collections also may be limited to types of stamps. The postage stamps issued by most countries are divided into such categories as regular postage (made up of definitives and commemoratives), air mail stamps, special delivery stamps, postage due stamps, and so on. Any of those groups may provide the basis for a good collection.

Definitive stamps are those regular issues used most on mail sent out on a daily basis. They normally are issued in extended sets, sometimes over a period of years. The sets feature a rising series of face values that allows a mailer to meet any current postal rate. Definitive stamps may be printed in huge quantities and often are kept in service by the postal service for long periods of time.

Commemorative stamps meet another need. They are issued to celebrate an important event, honor a famous person or promote a special project or cause. Such stamps are issued on a limited basis for a limited time. They are usually more colorful and often of a larger size than definitives, making them of special interest to the collector.

Although few air mail stamps are issued by the United States, they continue to remain very popular among collectors. Just as with regular issues, air mail stamps are subject to several ways of collecting. In addition to amassing the actual stamps, air mail enthusiasts pursue "first flight covers," "airport dedication covers," and even "crash covers."

Not as popular, but still collected as a unit, are special delivery stamps and postage due stamps. Special delivery stamps insure speedier delivery of a letter once it has reached its destination post office through "normal" postal means. Postage due stamps are used when a letter or parcel did not carry enough postage to pay for its delivery, subjecting the recipient to a fee to make up the difference. The United States no longer issues postage due stamps.

The resurgence of official stamps — those only used by departments and offices of the federal government — in 1983 has also brought about a resurgence of interest in them by stamp collectors. Originally issued between 1873 and 1911, they were stopped then until recently. To be legally used, they must be on cards, envelopes or parcels that bear the return address of a federal office or facility.

"Topical" collecting is becoming more and more prevalent. Here the paramount attraction to the collector is the subject depicted on the stamp. The topics or themes from which to choose are virtually unlimited, other than by your own imagination. Animals, flowers, music, ships, birds and famous people on stamps make interesting collections. The degree of specialization is limitless, leading to such topics as graduates of a specific college or university, type of aircraft, or work of a specific artist. Scott's *"By-Topic" Stamp Annual* divides the stamps of the world, issued over about the period of a year, into more than 80 topical areas.

The album

Stamps, to be displayed at their best, should be housed properly. A good album not only achieves this, but gives protection from dirt, loss and damage. When choosing an album, consider these three points: is it within your means, does it meet your special interests, and is it the best you can afford?

Scott's *Pony Express* and *Minuteman* album are ideal companions to this Catalogue. Scott also publishes the National Album series for United Stamps, with much more specialization.

Loose-leaf albums are recommended for all collectors beyond the novice level. Not only do loose-leaf albums allow for expansion of a collection, but the pages may be removed for mounting stamps onto them as well as for display. A special advantage of a loose-leaf album is that in many cases it may be kept current with supplements published annually on matching pages. All of the Scott albums noted are loose-leaf and supplemented annually.

Mounts and hinges

Mounts and hinges are used to affix stamps to the album page. Most stamp mounts are pre-glued, clear plastic containers that hold a stamp safely and may be affixed to an album page with minimum effort. They are available in sizes to fit any stamp, block or even complete envelope. They are particularly important with unused stamps when there is a desire not to disturb the gum.

Although the mount is important, so is the venerable hinge. Many a stamp in the past was ruined beyond redemption by being glued to an album page. Hinges are inexpensive and effective. Use only peelable hinges. These may be removed from a stamp or album page without leaving an unsightly mark or causing damage to either.

Hinges are perfect for less expensive stamps, used stamps and stamps that previously have been hinged. Using these is simple: Merely fold back about a quarter of the hinge, if it is not pre-folded, adhesive side out. Moisten the shorter side and affix it to the back of the stamp. Then, holding the stamp with a pair of tongs, moisten the longer side of the hinge and place it (with stamp attached) in its proper place on the album page.

Stamp tongs

Noted above, stamp tongs are a simple, but important, accessory and should always be used when handling a stamp. Fingers easily can damage a stamp. Tongs cost little and quickly will pay for themselves. They come in a variety of styles. Beginners should start with tongs having a round end. Those with sharp ends may cause damage to a stamp. With just a little practice, you will find it easier to work with stamps using tongs than using your fingers...and your stamps will be better for it.

Magnifying glass

A good magnifying glass for scrutinizing stamps in detail is another useful philatelic tool. It allows you to see variations in stamps that otherwise are invisible to the naked eye. Also, a glass makes minute parts of a stamp design large enough to see well. Your first glass should be at least 5X magnification, with edge-to-edge clarity. Stronger magnifications are available and may also be useful.

Perforation gauge
and watermark detector

Although many stamps appear to be alike, they are not. While the design may be the same and the color identical, there are two others areas where differences occur and where specialized devices are needed for such identification: perforation measurement and watermark detection. A ruler measuring in millimeters also is useful.

The perforation gauge, printed on plastic, cardboard, or metal, contains a graded scale that enables you to measure the number of perforation "teeth" in two centimeters. To determine the perforation measurement, place the stamp on the gauge and move the former along the scale until the points on one entry of the scale align perfectly with the teeth of the stamp's perforations. A stamp may have different perforations horizontally and vertically.

Watermarks are a bit more difficult to detect. They are a design impressed into the paper at the time of manufacture. Occasionally a watermark may be seen by holding a stamp up to the light, but often a watermark detector is necessary. The simplest of the many types of detectors available consists of a small black tray (glass or hard plastic). The stamp is placed face down in the tray and watermark detection fluid is poured over it. If there is a watermark, or a part of one, it should become visible when the stamp becomes soaked with the fluid.

There are a number of other liquids which, over the years, have been recommended for use to detect watermarks. The currently available fluids made specifically for that purpose are the safest — to the stamp and the collector. We do not recommend anything other than such watermark detection fluids for that use.

1

Benjamin
Franklin
A1

A3

George
Washington
A2

A4

Reproductions (found in Special Printings section). The letters R. W. H. & E. at the bottom of each stamp are less distinct on the reproductions than on the originals.

5c. On the originals the left side of the white shift frill touches the oval on a level with the top of the "F" of "Five." On the reproductions it touches the oval about on a level with the top of the figure "5."

10c. On the reproductions, line of coat at left points to right tip of "X" and line of coat at right points to center of "S" of CENTS. On the originals, line of coat points to "T" of TEN and between "T" and "S" of CENTS. On the reproductions the eyes have a sleepy look, the line of the mouth is straighter, and in the curl of hair near the left cheek is a strong black dot, while the originals have only a faint one.

Franklin
A5

A5

ONE CENT.

Type I. Has complete curved lines outside the labels with "U.S. Postage" and "One Cent." The scrolls below the lower label are turned under, forming little balls. The ornaments at top are substantially complete.

Type Ib. Same as I but balls below the bottom label are not so clear. The plume-like scrolls at bottom are not complete.

A6

Type Ia. Same as I at bottom but top ornaments and outer line at top are partly cut away.

A7

Type II. The little balls of the bottom scrolls and the bottoms of the lower plume ornaments are missing. The side ornaments are complete.

A8

Type III. The top and bottom curved lines outside the labels are broken in the middle. The side ornaments are complete.

Type IIIa. Similar to type III with the outer line broken at top or bottom but not both.

A9

Type IV. Similar to type II, but with the curved lines outside the labels recut at top or bottom or both.

Prices for types I and III are for stamps showing the marked characteristics plainly. Copies of type I showing the balls indistinctly and of type III with the lines only slightly broken, sell for much lower prices.

2

UNITED STATES

Scott No.	Illus. No.	Description	Unused Value	Used Value	//////
1847, July 1					
1	A1	5c red brown, *bluish*	3,500.	425.00	☐☐☐☐☐
1a.		5c dark brown, *bluish*	3,500.	425.00	☐☐☐☐☐
1b.		5c orange brown, *bluish*	4,000.	525.00	☐☐☐☐☐
1c.		5c red orange, *bluish*	*10,000.*	*1,850.*	☐☐☐☐☐
2	A2	10c black, *bluish*.	*15,000.*	1,100.	☐☐☐☐☐
2a.		Diagonal half used as 5c on cover.		*10,000.*	☐☐☐☐☐
2b.		Vertical half used as 5c on cover .		*15,000.*	☐☐☐☐☐
2c.		Horizontal half used as 5c on cover		—	☐☐☐☐☐

Nos. 3 and 4 are now listed in the Special Printings section.

Scott No.	Illus. No.	Description	Unused Value	Used Value	//////
1851-56					
5	A5	1c blue, type I.	*200,000.*	*17,500.*	☐☐☐☐☐
5A	A5	1c blue, type Ib	*8,500.*	*2,500.*	☐☐☐☐☐
6	A6	1c blue, type Ia.	*22,500.*	*6,500.*	☐☐☐☐☐
7	A7	1c blue, type II.	500.00	90.00	☐☐☐☐☐
8	A8	1c blue, type III	*6,500.*	1,500.	☐☐☐☐☐
8A	A8	1c blue, type IIIa	2,500.	600.00	☐☐☐☐☐
9	A9	1c blue, type IV ('52)	350.00	80.00	☐☐☐☐☐
9a.		Printed on both sides, reverse inverted		—	☐☐☐☐☐
10	A10	3c orange brown, type I.	950.00	40.00	☐☐☐☐☐
10a.		Printed on both sides.		—	☐☐☐☐☐
11	A10	3c dull red, type I.	130.00	7.00	☐☐☐☐☐
11c.		Vertical half used as 1c on cover .		*7,500.*	☐☐☐☐☐
11d.		Diagonal half used as 1c on cover.		*7,000.*	☐☐☐☐☐
11e.		Double impression.		—	☐☐☐☐☐
12	A11	5c red brown, type I ('56)	*8,500.*	950.00	☐☐☐☐☐
13	A12	10c green, type I ('55)	*9,000.*	600.00	☐☐☐☐☐
14	A13	10c green, type II ('55).	2,000.	225.00	☐☐☐☐☐
15	A14	10c green, type III ('55)	2,000.	225.00	☐☐☐☐☐

Washington
A10

Thomas Jefferson
A11

A13

Type II. The design is complete at the top. The outer line at the bottom is broken in the middle. The shells are partly cut away.

A10

THREE CENTS.

Type I. There is an outer frame line at top and bottom.

A11

FIVE CENTS.

Type I. There are projections on all four sides.

A14

Type III. The outer lines are broken above the top label and the "X" numerals. The outer line at the bottom and the shells are partly cut away, as in Type II.

A12

A15

Type IV. The outer lines have been recut at top or bottom or both.

Types I, II, III and IV have complete ornaments at the sides of the stamps and three pearls at each outer edge of the bottom panel.

A12

TEN CENTS.

Type I. The "shells" at the lower corners are practically complete. The outer line below the label is very nearly complete. The outer lines are broken above the middle of the top label and the "X" in each upper corner.

A16

4

Franklin
A20

ONE CENT.

Type V. Similar to type III of 1851-56 but with side ornaments partly cut away.

A21

THREE CENTS.

Type II. The outer frame line has been removed at top and bottom. The side frame lines were recut so as to be continuous from the top to the bottom of the plate.

Type IIa. The side frame lines extend only to the top and bottom of the stamp design.

A22

FIVE CENTS.

Type II. The projections at top and bottom are partly cut away.

A22

FIVE CENTS.

Type II. The projections at top and bottom are partly cut away.

A23
(Two typical examples).

TEN CENTS.

Type V. The side ornaments are slightly cut away. Usually only one pearl remains at each end of the lower label but some copies show two or three pearls at the right side. At the bottom the outer line is complete and the shells nearly so. The outer lines at top are complete except over the right " X ".

A17   **A18**

      A19

TWELVE CENTS.

Plate I. Outer frame lines complete.

Plate III. Outer frame lines noticeably uneven or broken, sometimes partly missing.

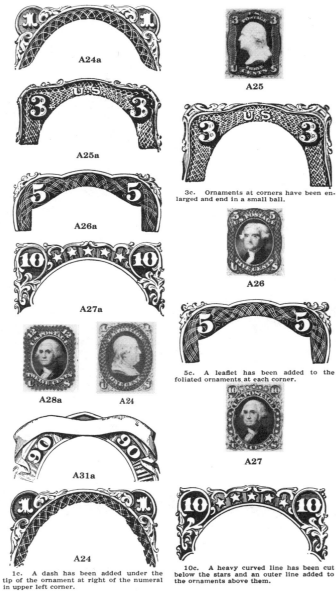

A24a

A25

A25a

3c. Ornaments at corners have been enlarged and end in a small ball.

A26a

A26

A27a

A28a   A24

5c. A leaflet has been added to the foliated ornaments at each corner.

A27

A31a

A24

1c. A dash has been added under the tip of the ornament at right of the numeral in upper left corner.

10c. A heavy curved line has been cut below the stars and an outer line added to the ornaments above them.

6

Scott No.	Illus. No.	Description	Unused Value	Used Value	//////
16	A15	10c green, type IV ('55)	*11,500.*	1,100.	☐☐☐☐☐
17	A16	12c black	2,500.	250.00	☐☐☐☐☐
17a.		Diagonal half used as 6c on cover.		*3,500.*	☐☐☐☐☐
17b.		Vertical half used as 6c on cover .		*8,500.*	☐☐☐☐☐
17c.		Printed on both sides		*3,500.*	☐☐☐☐☐

1857-61

Scott No.	Illus. No.	Description	Unused Value	Used Value	//////
18	A5	1c blue, type I ('61)	750.00	350.00	☐☐☐☐☐
19	A6	1c blue, type Ia.	*11,500.*	2,500.	☐☐☐☐☐
20	A7	1c blue, type II.	450.00	125.00	☐☐☐☐☐
21	A8	1c blue, type III	5,000.	1,400.	☐☐☐☐☐
22	A8	1c blue, type IIIa	750.00	250.00	☐☐☐☐☐
22b.		Horizontal pair, imperf. between .		3,500.	☐☐☐☐☐
23	A9	1c blue, type IV	2,000.	325.00	☐☐☐☐☐
24	A20	1c blue, type V	110.00	22.50	☐☐☐☐☐
24b.		Laid paper	–	–	☐☐☐☐☐
25	A10	3c rose, type I.	675.00	27.50	☐☐☐☐☐
25b.		Vertical pair, imperf. horizontally		*10,000.*	☐☐☐☐☐
26	A21	3c dull red, type II	45.00	2.75	☐☐☐☐☐
26a.		3c dull red, type IIa	110.00	20.00	☐☐☐☐☐
26b.		Horizontal pair, imperf. vertically, type II	–	–	☐☐☐☐☐
26c.		Vertical pair, imperf. horizontally, type II		–	☐☐☐☐☐
26d.		Horizontal pair, imperf. between, type II		–	☐☐☐☐☐
26e.		Double impression, type II		–	☐☐☐☐☐
27	A11	5c brick red, type I ('58)	*8,000.*	750.00	☐☐☐☐☐
28	A11	5c red brown, type I.	1,350.	250.00	☐☐☐☐☐
28b.		bright red brown	1,850.	400.00	☐☐☐☐☐
28A	A11	5c Indian red, type I ('58)	*10,000.*	2,000.	☐☐☐☐☐
29	A11	5c brown, type I ('59).	850.00	200.00	☐☐☐☐☐
30	A22	5c orange brown, type II ('61).	750.00	750.00	☐☐☐☐☐
30A	A22	5c brown, type II ('60).	450.00	175.00	☐☐☐☐☐
30b.		Printed on both sides.	3,750.	3,000.	☐☐☐☐☐
31	A12	10c green, type I.	5,750.	525.00	☐☐☐☐☐
32	A13	10c green, type II.	2,000.	165.00	☐☐☐☐☐
33	A14	10c green, type III	2,000.	165.00	☐☐☐☐☐
34	A15	10c green, type IV	*17,500.*	1,600.	☐☐☐☐☐
35	A23	10c green, type V ('59).	200.00	50.00	☐☐☐☐☐
36	A16	12c black, plate I	375.00	85.00	☐☐☐☐☐
36a.		Diagonal half used as 6c on cover (I)		*15,000.*	☐☐☐☐☐
36b.		12c black, plate III ('59)	350.00	110.00	☐☐☐☐☐
36c.		Horizontal pair, imperf. between (I).		–	☐☐☐☐☐
37	A17	24c gray lilac ('60)	600.00	235.00	☐☐☐☐☐
37a.		24c gray	600.00	235.00	☐☐☐☐☐

Scott No.	Illus. No.	Description	Unused Value	Used Value	//////
38	A18	30c orange ('60)	675.00	300.00	☐☐☐☐☐
39	A19	90c blue ('60)	1,000.	3,500.	☐☐☐☐☐

1861
62B	A27a	10c dark green	6,000.	450.00	☐☐☐☐☐

1861-62
63	A24	1c blue	140.00	15.00	☐☐☐☐☐
63a.		1c ultramarine	250.00	40.00	☐☐☐☐☐
63b.		1c dark blue	190.00	25.00	☐☐☐☐☐
63c.		Laid paper	—	—	☐☐☐☐☐
63d.		Vertical pair, imperf. horizontally		—	☐☐☐☐☐
63e.		Printed on both sides..........	—	2,500.	☐☐☐☐☐
64	A25	3c pink	4,500.	300.00	☐☐☐☐☐
64a.		3c pigeon blood pink	—	1,350.	☐☐☐☐☐
64b.		3c rose pink	300.00	45.00	☐☐☐☐☐
65	A25	3c rose	70.00	1.00	☐☐☐☐☐
65b.		Laid paper	—	—	☐☐☐☐☐
65d.		Vertical pair, imperf. horizontally	1,200.	750.00	☐☐☐☐☐
65e.		Printed on both sides..........	1,650.	1,000.	☐☐☐☐☐
65f.		Double impression.............		1,200.	☐☐☐☐☐
67	A26	5c buff	5,750.	400.00	☐☐☐☐☐
67a.		5c brown yellow..............	5,750.	400.00	☐☐☐☐☐
67b.		5c olive yellow	5,750.	400.00	☐☐☐☐☐
68	A27	10c yellow green	275.00	30.00	☐☐☐☐☐
68a.		10c dark green	290.00	31.00	☐☐☐☐☐
68b.		Vertical pair, imperf. horizontally		3,500.	☐☐☐☐☐
69	A28	12c black	550.00	55.00	☐☐☐☐☐
70	A29	24c red lilac ('62)	650.00	80.00	☐☐☐☐☐
70a.		24c brown lilac..............	550.00	67.50	☐☐☐☐☐
70b.		24c steel blue	4,000.	275.00	☐☐☐☐☐
70c.		24c violet	4,500.	550.00	☐☐☐☐☐
70d.		24c grayish lilac	1,400.	275.00	☐☐☐☐☐
71	A30	30c orange	525.00	70.00	☐☐☐☐☐
71a.		Printed on both sides..........		—	☐☐☐☐☐
72	A31	90c blue	1,450.	250.00	☐☐☐☐☐
72a.		90c pale blue	1,450.	250.00	☐☐☐☐☐
72b.		90c dark blue	1,600.	275.00	☐☐☐☐☐

1861-66
73	A32	2c black ('63)	120.00	22.50	☐☐☐☐☐
73a.		Half used as 1c on cover, diagonal, vertically or horizontally		1,250.	☐☐☐☐☐
73d.		Laid paper	—	—	☐☐☐☐☐
73e.		Printed on both sides..........		4,000.	☐☐☐☐☐

The 3c scarlet is found in the Special Printings section.

8

Scott No.	Illus. No.	Description	Unused Value	Used Value	//////
75	A26	5c red brown ('62)	1,450.	225.00	☐☐☐☐☐
76	A26	5c brown ('63)	375.00	57.50	☐☐☐☐☐
76a.		5c dark brown	425.00	70.00	☐☐☐☐☐
76b.		Laid paper		—	☐☐☐☐☐
77	A33	15c black ('66)	575.00	67.50	☐☐☐☐☐
78	A29	24c lilac ('63)	300.00	50.00	☐☐☐☐☐
78a.		24c grayish lilac	300.00	50.00	☐☐☐☐☐
78b.		24c gray	300.00	50.00	☐☐☐☐☐
78c.		24c black violet	*10,000.*	*600.00*	☐☐☐☐☐
78d.		Printed on both sides..........		3,500.	☐☐☐☐☐
1867					
79	A25	3c rose	2,000.	400.00	☐☐☐☐☐
79b.		Printed on both sides..........		—	☐☐☐☐☐
80	A26	5c brown	*40,000.*	—	☐☐☐☐☐
80a.		5c dark brown		*37,500.*	☐☐☐☐☐
81	A30	30c orange		*32,500.*	☐☐☐☐☐
82	A25	3c rose		*45,000.*	☐☐☐☐☐
83	A25	3c rose	2,000.	400.00	☐☐☐☐☐
84	A32	2c black	4,500.	1,100.	☐☐☐☐☐
85	A25	3c rose	1,750.	450.00	☐☐☐☐☐
85A	A24	1c blue		*450,000.*	☐☐☐☐☐
85B	A32	2c black	1,500.	350.00	☐☐☐☐☐
85C	A25	3c rose	4,500.	950.00	☐☐☐☐☐
85D	A27	10c green	—	*25,000.*	☐☐☐☐☐
85E	A28	12c black	2,000.	575.00	☐☐☐☐☐
85F	A33	15c black		—	☐☐☐☐☐
86	A24	1c blue	900.00	250.00	☐☐☐☐☐
86a.		1c dull blue..................	900.00	250.00	☐☐☐☐☐
87	A32	2c black	400.00	70.00	☐☐☐☐☐
87a.		Half used as 1c on cover, diagonal or vertically.................		*2,000.*	☐☐☐☐☐
88	A25	3c rose	300.00	10.00	☐☐☐☐☐
88a.		3c lake red	350.00	12.50	☐☐☐☐☐
89	A27	10c green	1,650.	175.00	☐☐☐☐☐
90	A28	12c black	1,900.	190.00	☐☐☐☐☐
91	A33	15c black	3,750.	450.00	☐☐☐☐☐
92	A24	1c blue	450.00	100.00	☐☐☐☐☐
92a.		1c pale blue	450.00	100.00	☐☐☐☐☐
93	A32	2c black	150.00	25.00	☐☐☐☐☐
93a.		Half used as 1c on cover, diagonal or vertically.................		*1,250.*	☐☐☐☐☐
93c.		Horizontal half used as 1c on cover		*1,750.*	☐☐☐☐☐
94	A25	3c red	110.00	2.50	☐☐☐☐☐
94a.		3c rose.......................	110.00	2.50	☐☐☐☐☐
94c.		Vertical pair, imperf. horizontally	*1,000.*		☐☐☐☐☐
94d.		Printed on both sides..........	*950.00*		☐☐☐☐☐

9

A28

12c. Ovals and scrolls have been added to the corners.

A29　　　　**A30**

A31　　　　**Grill**

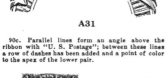

A31

90c. Parallel lines form an angle above the ribbon with "U. S. Postage"; between these lines a row of dashes has been added and a point of color to the apex of the lower pair.

A32　　　　**A33**

A34　　　　**A35**

A36　　　　**A37**

A38　　　　**A39**

A40　　　　**A41**

A42　　　　**A43**

A40

FIFTEEN CENTS.　Type I.　Picture unframed.

A40a

Type II.　Picture framed.

Type III.　Same as type I but without fringe of brown shading lines around central vignette.

10

Scott No.	Illus. No.	Description	Unused Value	Used Value	//////
95	A26	5c brown	1,050.	225.00	□□□□□
95a.		5c dark brown	1,100.	250.00	□□□□□
96	A27	10c yellow green	800.00	110.00	□□□□□
96a.		10c dark green	800.00	110.00	□□□□□
97	A28	12c black	800.00	120.00	□□□□□
98	A33	15c black	800.00	135.00	□□□□□
99	A29	24c gray lilac	1,650.	400.00	□□□□□
100	A30	30c orange	1,900.	350.00	□□□□□
101	A31	90c blue	4,750.	750.00	□□□□□

Nos. 102-111 are found in the Special Printings section.

1869

112	A34	1c buff	225.00	60.00	□□□□□
112b.		Without grill................	*750.00*		□□□□□
113	A35	2c brown	190.00	25.00	□□□□□
113b.		Without grill................	*600.00*		□□□□□
113c.		Half used as 1c on cover, diagonal, vertically or horizontally		—	□□□□□
113d.		Printed on both sides..........		—	□□□□□
114	A36	3c ultramarine	150.00	5.50	□□□□□
114a.		Without grill................	*600.00*	—	□□□□□
114b.		Vertical one third used as 1c on cover.................		—	□□□□□
114c.		Vertical two thirds used as 2c on cover		—	□□□□□
114d.		Double impression............		—	□□□□□
115	A37	6c ultramarine	775.00	100.00	□□□□□
115b.		Vertical half used as 3c on cover .		—	□□□□□
116	A38	10c yellow	850.00	95.00	□□□□□
117	A39	12c green	750.00	90.00	□□□□□
118	A40	15c brown & blue, Type I	1,900.	300.00	□□□□□
118a.		Without grill................	*3,500.*		□□□□□
119	A40a	15c brown & blue, Type II	950.00	150.00	□□□□□
119b.		Center inverted	*145,000.*	17,500.	□□□□□
119c.		Center double one inverted......	—		□□□□□
120	A41	24c green & violet	2,000.	450.00	□□□□□
120a.		Without grill................	*5,000.*		□□□□□
120b.		Center inverted	*125,000.*	16,500.	□□□□□
121	A42	30c blue & carmine	2,250.	225.00	□□□□□
121a.		Without grill................	3,750.		□□□□□
121b.		Flags inverted...............	*120,000.*	45,000.	□□□□□
122	A43	90c carmine & black	6,000.	1,000.	□□□□□
122a.		Without grill................	*13,500.*		□□□□□

1870-71

134	A44	1c ultramarine	575.00	60.00	□□□□□
135	A45	2c red brown	425.00	37.50	□□□□□

A44

A45

A48

A49

A44

A48

A45

A49

A46

A50

A46

A51

A47

A50

A47

A51

Scott No.	Illus. No.	Description	Unused Value	Used Value	//////
135a.		Diagonal half used as 1c on cover.	−		☐☐☐☐☐
136	A46	3c green	325.00	10.00	☐☐☐☐☐
137	A47	6c carmine	1,850.	250.00	☐☐☐☐☐
138	A48	7c vermilion ('71)	1,250.	225.00	☐☐☐☐☐
139	A49	10c brown	1,600.	400.00	☐☐☐☐☐
140	A50	12c dull violet	*13,000.*	1,500.	☐☐☐☐☐
141	A51	15c orange	2,100.	700.00	☐☐☐☐☐
142	A52	24c purple	−	*9,500.*	☐☐☐☐☐
143	A53	30c black	5,000.	825.00	☐☐☐☐☐
144	A54	90c carmine	6,750.	750.00	☐☐☐☐☐
145	A44	1c ultramarine	190.00	7.00	☐☐☐☐☐
146	A45	2c red brown	70.00	5.00	☐☐☐☐☐
146a.		Half used as 1c on cover, diagonal or vertically		−	☐☐☐☐☐
146c.		Double impression.............	−		☐☐☐☐☐
147	A46	3c green	140.00	50	☐☐☐☐☐
147a.		Printed on both sides...........		*1,500.*	☐☐☐☐☐
147b.		Double impression.............		*1,000.*	☐☐☐☐☐
148	A47	6c carmine	250.00	12.00	☐☐☐☐☐
148a.		Vertical half used as 3c on cover .		−	☐☐☐☐☐
148b.		Double impression.............		*1,250.*	☐☐☐☐☐
149	A48	7c vermilion ('71)	365.00	50.00	☐☐☐☐☐
150	A49	10c brown	250.00	12.00	☐☐☐☐☐
151	A50	12c dull violet	575.00	62.50	☐☐☐☐☐
152	A51	15c bright orange...............	550.00	60.00	☐☐☐☐☐
152a.		Double impression.............		−	☐☐☐☐☐
153	A52	24c purple	675.00	80.00	☐☐☐☐☐
154	A53	30c black	1,150.	95.00	☐☐☐☐☐
155	A54	90c carmine	1,500.	175.00	☐☐☐☐☐
1873					
156	A44a	1c ultramarine	62.50	1.75	☐☐☐☐☐
156e.		With grill	*1,200.*		☐☐☐☐☐
156f.		Imperf., pair..................	−	*500.00*	☐☐☐☐☐
157	A45a	2c brown	170.00	7.00	☐☐☐☐☐
157c.		With grill	*850.00*	*600.00*	☐☐☐☐☐
157d.		Double impression.............	−	−	☐☐☐☐☐
157e.		Vertical half used as 1c on cover .		−	☐☐☐☐☐
158	A46a	3c green	52.50	15	☐☐☐☐☐
158e.		With grill	*175.00*		☐☐☐☐☐
158h.		Horizontal pair, imperf. vertically		−	☐☐☐☐☐
158i.		Horizontal pair, imperf. between .		*1,300.*	☐☐☐☐☐
158j.		Double impression.............		*600.00*	☐☐☐☐☐
158k.		Printed on both sides...........		−	☐☐☐☐☐
159	A47a	6c dull pink	225.00	9.50	☐☐☐☐☐
159b.		With grill	*650.00*		☐☐☐☐☐
160	A48a	7c orange vermilion.............	450.00	55.00	☐☐☐☐☐
160a.		With grill	*1,350.*		☐☐☐☐☐

A52

A46a

3c. The under part of the upper tail of the left ribbon is heavily shaded.

A53

A54

A47a

6c. The first four vertical lines of the shading in the lower part of the left ribbon have been strengthened.

A44a

1c. In pearl at left of numeral. "1" is a small crescent.

A48a

7c. Two small semi-circles are drawn around the ends of the lines which outline the ball in the lower right hand corner.

A45a

2c. Under the scroll at the left of "U. S." there is a small diagonal line. This mark seldom shows clearly. The stamp, No. 157, can be distinguished by its color.

A49a

10c. There is a small semi-circle in the scroll at the right end of the upper label.

Scott No.	Illus. No.	Description	Unused Value	Used Value	//////
161	A49a	10c brown	250.00	10.00	□□□□□
161c.		With grill	1,750.		□□□□□
161d.		Horizontal pair, imperf. between .		2,500.	□□□□□
162	A50a	12c black violet	675.00	65.00	□□□□□
162a.		With grill	3,000.		□□□□□
163	A51a	15c yellow orange	650.00	60.00	□□□□□
163a.		With grill	3,000.		□□□□□
165	A53	30c gray black	725.00	60.00	□□□□□
165c.		With grill	3,000.		□□□□□
166	A54	90c rose carmine	1,500.	185.00	□□□□□

Nos. 167-177 are found in the Special Printings section.

1875, June 21

178	A45a	2c vermilion...................	180.00	5.00	□□□□□
178b.		Half used as 1c on cover..........		–	□□□□□
178c.		With grill		300.00	□□□□□
179	A55	5c blue	200.00	9.00	□□□□□
179c.		With grill		350.00	□□□□□

1879

182	A44a	1c dark ultramarine.............	140.00	1.25	□□□□□
183	A45a	2c vermilion...................	65.00	1.25	□□□□□
183a.		Double impression.............	–	500.00	□□□□□
184	A46a	3c green	50.00	15	□□□□□
184b.		Double impression.............		–	□□□□□
185	A55	5c blue	260.00	7.50	□□□□□
186	A47a	6c pink	500.00	12.00	□□□□□
187	A49	10c brown (without secret mark) ...	850.00	14.00	□□□□□
188	A49a	10c brown (with secret mark)	525.00	15.00	□□□□□
189	A51a	15c red orange	190.00	14.00	□□□□□
190	A53	30c full black	525.00	32.50	□□□□□
191	A54	90c carmine	1,150.	150.00	□□□□□

Nos. 192-204 are found in the Special Printings section.

1882, Apr. 10

205	A56	5c yellow brown................	135.00	4.50	□□□□□

No. 205C is found in the Special Printings section.

1881-82

206	A44b	1c gray blue	37.50	40	□□□□□
207	A46b	3c blue green	45.00	15	□□□□□
208	A47b	6c rose ('82)...................	250.00	45.00	□□□□□
208a.		6c brown red	225.00	55.00	□□□□□
209	A49b	10c brown ('82)	85.00	2.50	□□□□□
209b.		10c black brown..............	110.00	6.75	□□□□□
209c.		Double impression............		–	□□□□□

A50a

12c. The balls of the figure "2" are crescent shaped.

A51a

15c. In the lower part of the triangle in the upper left corner two lines have been made heavier forming a "V". This mark can be found on some of the Continental and American (1879) printings, but not all stamps show it.

Secret marks were added to the dies of the 24c, 30c and 90c but new plates were not made from them. The various printings of these stamps can be distinguished only by the shades and paper.

A55   **A56**

A44b

1c. The vertical lines in the upper part of the stamp have been so deepened that the background often appears to be solid. Lines of shading have been added to the upper arabesques.

A46b

3c. The shading at the sides of the central oval appears only about one-half the previous width. A short horizontal dash has been cut about 1mm. below the "TS" of "CENTS."

A47b

6c. On the original stamps four vertical lines can be counted from the edge of the panel to the outside of the stamp. On the re-engraved stamps there are but three lines in the same place.

A49b

10c. On the original stamps there are five vertical lines between the left side of the oval and the edge of the shield. There are only four lines on the re-engraved stamps. In the lower part of the latter, also, the horizontal lines of the background have been strengthened.

Scott No.	Illus. No.	Description	Unused Value	Used Value	//////
1883, Oct. 1					
210	A57	2c red brown	35.00	15	☐☐☐☐☐
211	A58	4c blue green	155.00	7.50	☐☐☐☐☐
1887					
212	A59	1c ultramarine	65.00	65	☐☐☐☐☐
213	A57	2c green	25.00	15	☐☐☐☐☐
213b.		Printed on both sides.		—	☐☐☐☐☐
214	A46b	3c vermilion	50.00	37.50	☐☐☐☐☐
1888					
215	A58	4c carmine	160.00	11.00	☐☐☐☐☐
216	A56	5c indigo	160.00	6.50	☐☐☐☐☐
217	A53	30c orange brown	360.00	75.00	☐☐☐☐☐
218	A54	90c purple	700.00	130.00	☐☐☐☐☐
1890-93					
219	A60	1c dull blue	18.50	15	☐☐☐☐☐
219D	A61	2c lake	150.00	45	☐☐☐☐☐
220	A61	2c carmine	15.00	15	☐☐☐☐☐
220a.		Cap on left "2"	35.00	1.00	☐☐☐☐☐
220.		Cap on both "2"'s	110.00	8.00	☐☐☐☐☐
221	A62	3c purple	50.00	4.50	☐☐☐☐☐
222	A63	4c dark brown	50.00	1.50	☐☐☐☐☐
223	A64	5c chocolate	50.00	1.50	☐☐☐☐☐
224	A65	6c brown red	55.00	15.00	☐☐☐☐☐
225	A66	8c lilac ('93)	40.00	8.50	☐☐☐☐☐
226	A67	10c green	95.00	1.75	☐☐☐☐☐
227	A68	15c indigo	135.00	15.00	☐☐☐☐☐
228	A69	30c black	225.00	20.00	☐☐☐☐☐
229	A70	90c orange	325.00	95.00	☐☐☐☐☐
1893					
230	A71	1c deep blue	18.50	25	☐☐☐☐☐
231	A72	2c brown violet	17.00	15	☐☐☐☐☐
232	A73	3c green	42.50	12.50	☐☐☐☐☐
233	A74	4c ultramarine	62.50	5.50	☐☐☐☐☐
233a.		4c blue (error)	*8,500.*	*3,250.*	☐☐☐☐☐
234	A75	5c chocolate	67.50	6.50	☐☐☐☐☐
235	A76	6c purple	62.50	18.00	☐☐☐☐☐
235a.		6c red violet	62.50	18.00	☐☐☐☐☐
236	A77	8c magenta	50.00	8.00	☐☐☐☐☐
237	A78	10c black brown	100.00	5.50	☐☐☐☐☐
238	A79	15c dark green	170.00	50.00	☐☐☐☐☐
239	A80	30c orange brown	225.00	70.00	☐☐☐☐☐
240	A81	50c slate blue	350.00	120.00	☐☐☐☐☐
241	A82	$1 salmon	1,150.	525.00	☐☐☐☐☐
242	A83	$2 brown red	1,250.	450.00	☐☐☐☐☐

A57   A58   A59

A60   A61   A62

A63   A64   A65

A66   A67   A68   A69   A70

HOW TO USE THIS BOOK

The number in the first column is its Scott number or identifying number. The letter and number that come next (A41) indicate the design and refer to the illustration so designated. Following that is the denomination of the stamp and its color. Finally, the value, unused and used is shown.

18

Scott No.	Illus. No.	Description	Unused Value	Used Value	//////
243	A84	$3 yellow green	2,100.	800.00	☐☐☐☐☐
243a.		$3 olive green..............	2,100.	800.00	☐☐☐☐☐
244	A85	$4 crimson lake	2,500.	1,000.	☐☐☐☐☐
244a.		$4 rose carmine	2,500.	1,000.	☐☐☐☐☐
245	A86	$5 black	2,850.	1,200.	☐☐☐☐☐

1894

Scott No.	Illus. No.	Description	Unused Value	Used Value	//////
246	A87	1c ultramarine	15.00	2.00	☐☐☐☐☐
247	A87	1c blue	37.50	85	☐☐☐☐☐
248	A88	2c pink, Type I..............	12.50	1.50	☐☐☐☐☐
249	A88	2c carmine lake, Type I...........	75.00	95	☐☐☐☐☐
250	A88	2c carmine, Type I.............	14.00	25	☐☐☐☐☐
250a.		Vertical pair, imperf. horizontally	1,500.		☐☐☐☐☐
250b.		Horizontal, pair, imperf. between.	1,500.		☐☐☐☐☐
251	A88	2c carmine, Type II	125.00	1.50	☐☐☐☐☐
252	A88	2c carmine, Type III	70.00	2.00	☐☐☐☐☐
252a.		Horizontal pair, imperf. vertically	1,350.		☐☐☐☐☐
252b.		Horizontal pair, imperf. between .	1,500.		☐☐☐☐☐
253	A89	3c purple	50.00	4.25	☐☐☐☐☐
254	A90	4c dark brown	60.00	1.75	☐☐☐☐☐
255	A91	5c chocolate.................	47.50	2.50	☐☐☐☐☐
255c.		Vertical pair, imperf. horizontally	1,000.		☐☐☐☐☐
256	A92	6c dull brown.................	90.00	12.00	☐☐☐☐☐
256a.		Vertical pair, imperf. horizontally	850.00		☐☐☐☐☐
257	A93	8c violet brown ('95)	80.00	8.00	☐☐☐☐☐
258	A94	10c dark green	115.00	5.00	☐☐☐☐☐
259	A95	15c dark blue	185.00	30.00	☐☐☐☐☐
260	A96	50c orange	225.00	50.00	☐☐☐☐☐
261	A97	$1 black, Type I	500.00	160.00	☐☐☐☐☐
261A	A97	$1 black, Type II	1,200.	325.00	☐☐☐☐☐
262	A98	$2 bright blue.................	1,500.	400.00	☐☐☐☐☐
263	A99	$5 dark green	2,000.	650.00	☐☐☐☐☐

1895

Scott No.	Illus. No.	Description	Unused Value	Used Value	//////
264	A87	1c blue	3.50	15	☐☐☐☐☐
265	A88	2c carmine, Type I.............	18.00	40	☐☐☐☐☐
266	A88	2c carmine, Type II	15.00	1.75	☐☐☐☐☐
267	A88	2c carmine, Type III	3.00	15	☐☐☐☐☐
268	A89	3c purple	22.50	65	☐☐☐☐☐
269	A90	4c dark brown	24.00	75	☐☐☐☐☐
270	A91	5c chocolate.................	22.50	1.20	☐☐☐☐☐
271	A92	6c dull brown.................	42.50	2.50	☐☐☐☐☐
271a.		Wmkd. USIR.................	2,250.	350.00	☐☐☐☐☐
272	A93	8c violet brown	30.00	65	☐☐☐☐☐
272a.		Wmkd. USIR.................	1,100.	110.00	☐☐☐☐☐
273	A94	10c dark green	40.00	80	☐☐☐☐☐
274	A95	15c dark blue	110.00	5.50	☐☐☐☐☐

A71 A72 A73 A74 A75 A76 A77 A78 A79 A80 A81 A82 A83 A84 A85 A86

TWO CENTS.

Type I. The horizontal lines of the ground work run across the triangle and are of the same thickness within it as without.

Type II. The horizontal lines cross the triangle but are thinner within it than without.

Type III. The horizontal lines do not cross the double frame lines of the triangle. The lines within the triangle are thin, as in type II.

20

Scott No.	Illus. No.	Description	Unused Value	Used Value	//////
275	A96	50c orange	160.00	14.00	☐☐☐☐☐
275a.		50c red orange	170.00	16.00	☐☐☐☐☐
276	A97	$1 black, Type I.	375.00	45.00	☐☐☐☐☐
276A	A97	$1 black, Type II	825.00	92.50	☐☐☐☐☐
277	A98	$2 bright blue.	600.00	200.00	☐☐☐☐☐
277a.		$2 dark blue.	650.00	210.00	☐☐☐☐☐
278	A99	$5 dark green	1,350.	275.00	☐☐☐☐☐

1898

Scott No.	Illus. No.	Description	Unused Value	Used Value	//////
279	A87	1c deep green	6.00	15	☐☐☐☐☐
279B	A88	2c red, Type III	5.50	15	☐☐☐☐☐
279c.		2c rose carmine, Type III	120.00	20.00	☐☐☐☐☐
279d.		2c orange red, Type III	6.50	15	☐☐☐☐☐
279e.		Booklet pane of 6.	350.00	*200.00*	☐☐☐☐☐
279f.		2c deep red, Type III	12.50	75	☐☐☐☐☐
280	A90	4c rose brown.	20.00	45	☐☐☐☐☐
280a.		4c lilac brown.	20.00	45	☐☐☐☐☐
280b.		4c orange brown.	20.00	45	☐☐☐☐☐
281	A91	5c dark blue	22.50	40	☐☐☐☐☐
282	A92	6c lake	32.50	1.40	☐☐☐☐☐
282a.		6c purple lake.	35.00	1.65	☐☐☐☐☐
282C	A94	10c brown, Type I	100.00	1.20	☐☐☐☐☐
283	A94	10c orange brown, Type II	60.00	1.00	☐☐☐☐☐
284	A95	15c olive green.	85.00	4.50	☐☐☐☐☐

1898, June 17

Scott No.	Illus. No.	Description	Unused Value	Used Value	//////
285	A100	1c dark yellow green	20.00	3.75	☐☐☐☐☐
286	A101	2c copper red	17.50	1.00	☐☐☐☐☐
287	A102	4c orange	110.00	16.00	☐☐☐☐☐
288	A103	5c dull blue.	80.00	14.00	☐☐☐☐☐
289	A104	8c violet brown	120.00	30.00	☐☐☐☐☐
289a.		Vertical pair, imperf. horizontally *13,500.*			☐☐☐☐☐
290	A105	10c gray violet	125.00	17.50	☐☐☐☐☐
291	A106	50c sage green	400.00	150.00	☐☐☐☐☐
292	A107	$1 black	1,150.	400.00	☐☐☐☐☐
293	A108	$2 orange brown	1,800.	700.00	☐☐☐☐☐

1901, May 1

Scott No.	Illus. No.	Description	Unused Value	Used Value	//////
294	A109	1c green & black	13.50	2.50	☐☐☐☐☐
294a.		Center inverted	*9,000.*	*4,500.*	☐☐☐☐☐
295	A110	2c carmine & black	13.50	75	☐☐☐☐☐
295a.		Center inverted . . . . *35,000.*		*13,500.*	☐☐☐☐☐
296	A111	4c deep red brown & black	70.00	12.50	☐☐☐☐☐
296a.		Center inverted . . . . *10,000.*			☐☐☐☐☐
297	A112	5c ultramarine & black	82.50	11.00	☐☐☐☐☐
298	A113	8c brown violet & black	95.00	45.00	☐☐☐☐☐
299	A114	10c yellow brown & black.	150.00	20.00	☐☐☐☐☐

A87 **A88** **A89** **A90**

A91 **A92** **A93** **A94**

A95 **A96** **A97** **A98**

A99

ONE DOLLAR.

Type I.   The circles enclosing "$1" are broken where they meet the curved line below "One Dollar."   The fifteen left vertical rows of impressions from plate 76 are Type I, the balance being Type II.

Type II.   The circles are complete.

TEN CENTS

Type I.   Tips of foliate ornaments do not impinge on white curved line below "TEN CENTS".

Type II.   Tips of ornaments break curved line below "E" of "TEN" and "T" of "CENTS".

A100 **A101** **A102**

A103 **A104** **A105**

A106 **A107** **A108**

Scott No.	Illus. No.	Description	Unused Value	Used Value	//////
1902-03					
300	A115	1c blue green ('03)	6.50	15	☐☐☐☐☐
300b.		Booklet pane of 6	400.00	250.00	☐☐☐☐☐
301	A116	2c carmine ('03)	7.50	15	☐☐☐☐☐
301c.		Booklet pane of 6	400.00	250.00	☐☐☐☐☐
302	A117	3c bright violet ('03)	30.00	2.00	☐☐☐☐☐
303	A118	4c brown ('03)	30.00	60	☐☐☐☐☐
304	A119	5c blue ('03)	35.00	65	☐☐☐☐☐
305	A120	6c claret ('03)	37.50	1.50	☐☐☐☐☐
306	A121	8c violet black	25.00	1.25	☐☐☐☐☐
307	A122	10c pale red brown ('03)	30.00	70	☐☐☐☐☐
308	A123	13c purple black	25.00	5.00	☐☐☐☐☐
309	A124	15c olive green ('03)	87.50	3.75	☐☐☐☐☐
310	A125	50c orange ('03)	285.00	17.50	☐☐☐☐☐
311	A126	$1 black ('03)	450.00	35.00	☐☐☐☐☐
312	A127	$2 dark blue ('03)	600.00	125.00	☐☐☐☐☐
313	A128	$5 dark green ('03)	1,500.	450.00	☐☐☐☐☐
1906-08					
314	A115	1c blue green	16.00	13.00	☐☐☐☐☐
314A	A118	4c brown ('08)	18,500.	10,000.	☐☐☐☐☐
315	A119	5c blue ('08)	325.00	250.00	☐☐☐☐☐
1908					
316	A115	1c blue green, pair	50,000.	—	☐☐☐☐☐
317	A119	5c blue, pair	5,000.	—	☐☐☐☐☐
318	A115	1c blue green, pair	4,750.	—	☐☐☐☐☐
1903, Nov. 12					
319	A129	2c carmine (I)	4.00	15	☐☐☐☐☐
319a.		2c lake (I)	—	—	☐☐☐☐☐
319b.		2c carmine rose (I)	6.00	20	☐☐☐☐☐
319c.		2c scarlet (I)	4.00	15	☐☐☐☐☐
319d.		Vertical pair, imperf. horizontally	1,750.		☐☐☐☐☐
319e.		Vertical pair, imperf. between	950.00		☐☐☐☐☐
319f.		2c lake (II)	4.50	15	☐☐☐☐☐
319g.		Booklet pane of 6, carmine (I)	90.00	30.00	☐☐☐☐☐
319h.		As g (II)	125.00		☐☐☐☐☐
319i.		2c carmine (II)	17.50	—	☐☐☐☐☐
319j.		2c carmine rose (II)	—		☐☐☐☐☐
319k.		2c scarlet (II)	—		☐☐☐☐☐
319m.		As g, lake (I)	—		☐☐☐☐☐
319n.		As g, carmine rose (I)	—		☐☐☐☐☐
319p.		As g, scarlet (I)	90.00		☐☐☐☐☐
319q.		As g, lake (II)	125.00		☐☐☐☐☐
1906, Oct. 2					
320	A129	2c carmine	17.50	11.00	☐☐☐☐☐

A109

A110

A111

A112

A113

A114

A115

A116

A117

A118

A119

A120

A121

A122

A123

A124

A125

A126

A127

A128

A129

A130

A131

A132

A133

A134

Scott No.	Illus. No.	Description	Unused Value	Used Value	//////
320a.		2c lake (II)	50.00	35.00	☐☐☐☐☐
320b.		2c scarlet.....................	16.00	12.00	☐☐☐☐☐

1908

Scott No.	Illus. No.	Description	Unused Value	Used Value	//////
321	A129	2c carmine, pair...............	—	—	☐☐☐☐☐
322	A129	2c carmine, pair...............	*6,000.*	—	☐☐☐☐☐

1904, Apr. 30

Scott No.	Illus. No.	Description	Unused Value	Used Value	//////
323	A130	1c green	17.50	2.75	☐☐☐☐☐
324	A131	2c carmine	15.00	90	☐☐☐☐☐
324a.		Vertical pair, imperf. horizontally	*6,750.*		☐☐☐☐☐
325	A132	3c violet.....................	60.00	22.50	☐☐☐☐☐
326	A133	5c dark blue	65.00	14.50	☐☐☐☐☐
327	A134	10c red brown	115.00	20.00	☐☐☐☐☐

1907

Scott No.	Illus. No.	Description	Unused Value	Used Value	//////
328	A135	1c green	11.50	1.90	☐☐☐☐☐
329	A136	2c carmine	15.00	1.65	☐☐☐☐☐
330	A137	5c blue	67.50	15.00	☐☐☐☐☐

1908-09

Scott No.	Illus. No.	Description	Unused Value	Used Value	//////
331	A138	1c green	4.50	15	☐☐☐☐☐
331a.		Booklet pane of 6.............	165.00	*35.00*	☐☐☐☐☐
332	A139	2c carmine	4.25	15	☐☐☐☐☐
332a.		Booklet pane of 6.............	100.00	*35.00*	☐☐☐☐☐
333	A140	3c deep violet, Type I	20.00	1.75	☐☐☐☐☐
334	A140	4c orange brown	23.50	55	☐☐☐☐☐
335	A140	5c blue	30.00	1.50	☐☐☐☐☐
336	A140	6c red orange	32.50	3.50	☐☐☐☐☐
337	A140	8c olive green.................	26.00	1.75	☐☐☐☐☐
338	A140	10c yellow ('09)	42.50	1.00	☐☐☐☐☐
339	A140	13c blue green ('09)	25.00	14.00	☐☐☐☐☐
340	A140	15c pale ultramarine ('09)........	40.00	3.75	☐☐☐☐☐
341	A140	50c violet ('09)	175.00	10.00	☐☐☐☐☐
342	A140	$1 violet brown ('09)...........	335.00	50.00	☐☐☐☐☐
343	A138	1c green	4.50	2.75	☐☐☐☐☐
344	A139	2c carmine	6.50	2.00	☐☐☐☐☐
345	A140	3c deep violet, Type I	12.00	10.00	☐☐☐☐☐
346	A140	4c orange brown ('09)	21.00	12.00	☐☐☐☐☐
347	A140	5c blue ('09)	37.50	27.50	☐☐☐☐☐

1908-10

Scott No.	Illus. No.	Description	Unused Value	Used Value	//////
348	A138	1c green	21.00	10.00	☐☐☐☐☐
349	A139	2c carmine ('09)...............	37.50	6.00	☐☐☐☐☐
350	A140	4c orange brown ('10)	80.00	60.00	☐☐☐☐☐
351	A140	5c blue ('09)	90.00	90.00	☐☐☐☐☐

1909

Scott No.	Illus. No.	Description	Unused Value	Used Value	//////
352	A138	1c green	40.00	25.00	☐☐☐☐☐

Scott No.	Illus. No.	Description	Unused Value	Used Value	//////
353	A139	2c carmine	40.00	6.00	☐☐☐☐☐
354	A140	4c orange brown	100.00	45.00	☐☐☐☐☐
355	A140	5c blue	110.00	65.00	☐☐☐☐☐
356	A140	10c yellow	1,500.	600.00	☐☐☐☐☐

1909 Bluish Paper

Scott No.	Illus. No.	Description	Unused Value	Used Value	//////
357	A138	1c green	75.00	65.00	☐☐☐☐☐
358	A139	2c carmine	70.00	55.00	☐☐☐☐☐
359	A140	3c deep violet, Type I	1,500.	1,400.	☐☐☐☐☐
360	A140	4c orange brown	15,000.		☐☐☐☐☐
361	A140	5c blue	2,900.	3,500.	☐☐☐☐☐
362	A140	6c red orange	1,150.	850.00	☐☐☐☐☐
363	A140	8c olive green	15,000.		☐☐☐☐☐
364	A140	10c yellow	1,200.	900.00	☐☐☐☐☐
365	A140	13c blue green	2,000.	1,250.	☐☐☐☐☐
366	A140	15c pale ultramarine	900.00	700.00	☐☐☐☐☐

1909, Feb. 12

Scott No.	Illus. No.	Description	Unused Value	Used Value	//////
367	A141	2c carmine	4.25	1.40	☐☐☐☐☐
368	A141	2c carmine	19.50	15.00	☐☐☐☐☐

1909 Bluish Paper

Scott No.	Illus. No.	Description	Unused Value	Used Value	//////
369	A141	2c carmine	170.00	165.00	☐☐☐☐☐

1909

Scott No.	Illus. No.	Description	Unused Value	Used Value	//////
370	A142	2c carmine	7.00	1.10	☐☐☐☐☐
371	A142	2c carmine	27.50	19.00	☐☐☐☐☐
372	A143	2c carmine	10.00	3.25	☐☐☐☐☐

Imperf.

Scott No.	Illus. No.	Description	Unused Value	Used Value	//////
373	A143	2c carmine	30.00	21.00	☐☐☐☐☐

1910-11

Scott No.	Illus. No.	Description	Unused Value	Used Value	//////
374	A138	1c green	5.00	15	☐☐☐☐☐
374a.		Booklet pane of 6	110.00	30.00	☐☐☐☐☐
375	A139	2c carmine	5.00	15	☐☐☐☐☐
375a.		Booklet pane of 6	95.00	25.00	☐☐☐☐☐
376	A140	3c deep violet, Type I ('11)	11.50	1.00	☐☐☐☐☐
377	A140	4c brown ('11)	17.50	30	☐☐☐☐☐
378	A140	5c blue ('11)	17.50	30	☐☐☐☐☐
379	A140	6c red orange ('11)	24.00	40	☐☐☐☐☐
380	A140	8c olive green ('11)	70.00	8.50	☐☐☐☐☐
381	A140	10c yellow ('11)	65.00	2.50	☐☐☐☐☐
382	A140	15c pale ultramarine ('11)	175.00	11.50	☐☐☐☐☐

1911 Imperf.

Scott No.	Illus. No.	Description	Unused Value	Used Value	//////
383	A138	1c green	2.25	2.00	☐☐☐☐☐
384	A139	2c carmine	3.50	1.75	☐☐☐☐☐

Scott No.	Illus. No.	Description	Unused Value	Used Value	//////

1910 Coil Stamps, Perf. 12 horizontally

Scott No.	Illus. No.	Description	Unused Value	Used Value	//////
385	A138	1c green	18.00	8.00	☐☐☐☐☐
386	A139	2c carmine	32.50	12.50	☐☐☐☐☐

1910-11 Coil Stamps, Perf. 12 vertically

387	A138	1c green	47.50	30.00	☐☐☐☐☐
388	A139	2c carmine	450.00	150.00	☐☐☐☐☐
389	A140	3c deep violet, Type I ('11)	15,000.	6,500.	☐☐☐☐☐

1910 Coil Stamps, Perf. 8½ horizontally

| 390 | A138 | 1c green | 3.00 | 4.00 | ☐☐☐☐☐ |
| 391 | A139 | 2c carmine | 20.00 | 5.75 | ☐☐☐☐☐ |

1910-13 Coil Stamps, Perf. 8½ vertically

392	A138	1c green	12.00	14.00	☐☐☐☐☐
393	A139	2c carmine	24.00	5.50	☐☐☐☐☐
394	A140	3c deep violet, Type I ('11)	32.50	40.00	☐☐☐☐☐
395	A140	4c brown ('12)	32.50	30.00	☐☐☐☐☐
396	A140	5c blue ('13)	32.50	30.00	☐☐☐☐☐

1913

397	A144	1c green	11.00	85	☐☐☐☐☐
398	A145	2c carmine	12.50	28	☐☐☐☐☐
399	A146	5c blue	47.50	6.50	☐☐☐☐☐
400	A147	10c orange yellow	90.00	14.00	☐☐☐☐☐
400A	A147	10c orange	160.00	10.50	☐☐☐☐☐

1914-15

401	A144	1c green	16.00	4.00	☐☐☐☐☐
402	A145	2c carmine ('15)	52.50	1.00	☐☐☐☐☐
403	A146	5c blue ('15)	115.00	11.00	☐☐☐☐☐
404	A147	10c orange ('15)	775.00	42.50	☐☐☐☐☐

1912-14

405	A140	1c green	3.50	15	☐☐☐☐☐
405a.		Vertical pair, imperf. horizontally	650.00	–	☐☐☐☐☐
405b.		Booklet pane of 6	50.00	7.50	☐☐☐☐☐
406	A140	2c carmine, Type I	3.25	15	☐☐☐☐☐
406a.		Booklet pane of 6	60.00	17.50	☐☐☐☐☐
406b.		Double impression	–		☐☐☐☐☐
407	A140	7c black ('14)	60.00	8.00	☐☐☐☐☐

1912 Imperf.

| 408 | A140 | 1c green | 90 | 50 | ☐☐☐☐☐ |
| 409 | A140 | 2c carmine, Type I | 1.00 | 50 | ☐☐☐☐☐ |

1912 Coil Stamps, Perf. 8½ horizontally

| 410 | A140 | 1c green | 4.50 | 3.00 | ☐☐☐☐☐ |
| 411 | A140 | 2c carmine, Type I | 6.00 | 2.50 | ☐☐☐☐☐ |

A135

A136

A137

Franklin
A138

Washington
A139

Washington
A140

Franklin
A148

A141

A142

A143

A144

A145

A146

A147

TYPE I

TYPE I

THREE CENTS.

Type I. The top line of the toga rope is weak
and the rope shading lines are thin. The fifth line
from the left is missing.
  The line between the lips is thin.
  Used on both flat plate and rotary press printings.

28

Scott No.	Illus. No.	Description	Unused Value	Used Value	//////

Coil Stamps, Perf. 8½ vertically

412	A140	1c green	15.00	3.75 ☐☐☐☐☐	
413	A140	2c carmine, Type I.............	24.00	75 ☐☐☐☐☐	

1912-14

414	A148	8c pale olive green.............	25.00	85 ☐☐☐☐☐	
415	A148	9c salmon red ('14)	32.50	9.50 ☐☐☐☐☐	
416	A148	10c orange yellow	26.00	25 ☐☐☐☐☐	
417	A148	12c claret brown ('14)	28.50	3.00 ☐☐☐☐☐	
418	A148	15c gray	47.50	2.00 ☐☐☐☐☐	
419	A148	20c ultramarine ('14)	110.00	9.00 ☐☐☐☐☐	
420	A148	30c orange red ('14).............	80.00	10.00 ☐☐☐☐☐	
421	A148	50c violet ('14)..................	300.00	10.00 ☐☐☐☐☐	

1912, Feb. 12

422	A148	50c violet	160.00	9.50 ☐☐☐☐☐	
423	A148	$1 violet brown	360.00	40.00 ☐☐☐☐☐	

1914-15

424	A140	1c green	1.60	15 ☐☐☐☐☐	
424a.		Perf. 12x10....................	*600.00*	*500.00* ☐☐☐☐☐	
424b.		Perf. 10x12....................		250.00 ☐☐☐☐☐	
424c.		Vertical pair, imperf. horizontally	*425.00*	*250.00* ☐☐☐☐☐	
424d.		Booklet pane of 6...............	3.50	75 ☐☐☐☐☐	
424e.		Vertical pair, imperf. between....		☐☐☐☐☐	
425	A140	2c rose red, Type I.............	1.50	15 ☐☐☐☐☐	
425c.		Perf. 10x12....................		– ☐☐☐☐☐	
425d.		Perf. 12x10....................	–	*600.00* ☐☐☐☐☐	
425e.		Booklet pane of 6...............	12.50	*3.00* ☐☐☐☐☐	
426	A140	3c deep violet, Type I	8.50	90 ☐☐☐☐☐	
427	A140	4c brown	22.00	28 ☐☐☐☐☐	
428	A140	5c blue	18.50	28 ☐☐☐☐☐	
428a.		Perf. 12x10....................		*1,000.* ☐☐☐☐☐	
429	A140	6c red orange	29.00	90 ☐☐☐☐☐	
430	A140	7c black	55.00	2.50 ☐☐☐☐☐	
431	A148	8c pale olive green.............	24.00	1.10 ☐☐☐☐☐	
432	A148	9c salmon red..................	32.50	5.00 ☐☐☐☐☐	
433	A148	10c orange yellow	30.00	18 ☐☐☐☐☐	
434	A148	11c dark green ('15).............	13.50	5.50 ☐☐☐☐☐	
435	A148	12c claret brown	15.00	2.75 ☐☐☐☐☐	
435a.		12c copper red	16.00	2.75 ☐☐☐☐☐	
437	A148	15c gray	72.50	4.50 ☐☐☐☐☐	
438	A148	20c ultramarine	140.00	2.50 ☐☐☐☐☐	
439	A148	30c orange red	190.00	10.00 ☐☐☐☐☐	
440	A148	50c violet ('15).................	500.00	10.00 ☐☐☐☐☐	

1914 Coil Stamps, Perf. 10 horizontally

441	A140	1c green	55	80 ☐☐☐☐☐	
442	A140	2c carmine, Type I.............	6.00	4.50 ☐☐☐☐☐	

TYPE I

TWO CENTS.

Type I. There is one shading line in the first curve of the ribbon above the left " 2 " and one in the second curve of the ribbon above the right " 2."

The button of the toga has a faint outline.

The top line of the toga rope, from the button to the front of the throat, is also very faint.

The shading lines at the face terminate in front of the ear with little or no joining, to form a lock of hair.

Used on both flat and rotary press printings.

TYPE II

TWO CENTS.

Type II. Shading lines in ribbons as on type I.

The toga button, rope, and shading lines are heavy.

The shading lines of the face at the lock of hair end in a strong vertical curved line.

Used on rotary press printings only.

TYPE III

TWO CENTS.

Type III. Two lines of shading in the curves of the ribbons.

Other characteristics similar to type II.

Used on rotary press printings only.

HOW TO USE THIS BOOK

The number in the first column is its Scott number or identifying number. The letter and number that come next (A41) indicate the design and refer to the illustration so designated. Following that is the denomination of the stamp and its color. Finally, the value, unused and used is shown.

Scott No.	Illus. No.	Description	Unused Value	Used Value	//////
Perf. 10 vertically					
443	A140	1c green	14.00	4.00	☐☐☐☐☐
444	A140	2c carmine, Type I..............	19.00	1.00	☐☐☐☐☐
445	A140	3c violet, Type I................	160.00	100.00	☐☐☐☐☐
446	A140	4c brown	82.50	21.00	☐☐☐☐☐
447	A140	5c blue	27.50	17.50	☐☐☐☐☐
1915-16 Coil Stamps, Perf. 10 horizontally					
448	A140	1c green	4.25	2.25	☐☐☐☐☐
449	A140	2c red, Type I..................	1,750.	225.00	☐☐☐☐☐
450	A140	2c carmine, Type III ('16)........	7.00	2.25	☐☐☐☐☐
1914-16 Coil Stamps, Perf. 10 vertically					
452	A140	1c green	7.00	1.40	☐☐☐☐☐
453	A140	2c carmine rose, Type I..........	72.50	3.25	☐☐☐☐☐
454	A140	2c red, Type II.................	70.00	7.50	☐☐☐☐☐
455	A140	2c carmine, Type III	6.50	75	☐☐☐☐☐
456	A140	3c violet, Type I ('16)	190.00	75.00	☐☐☐☐☐
457	A140	4c brown ('16)	18.00	15.00	☐☐☐☐☐
458	A140	5c blue ('16)	22.50	15.00	☐☐☐☐☐
1914, June 30, Imperf.					
459	A140	2c carmine, Type I..............	375.00	*600.00*	☐☐☐☐☐
1915					
460	A148	$1 violet black	600.00	55.00	☐☐☐☐☐
461	A140	2c pale carmine red, Type I	75.00	*110.00*	☐☐☐☐☐
1916-17					
462	A140	1c green	5.00	15	☐☐☐☐☐
462a.		Booklet pane of 6.............	7.50	*1.00*	☐☐☐☐☐
463	A140	2c carmine, Type I..............	3.25	15	☐☐☐☐☐
463a.		Booklet pane of 6.............	70.00	*20.00*	☐☐☐☐☐
464	A140	3c violet, Type I................	52.50	8.00	☐☐☐☐☐
465	A140	4c orange brown	30.00	1.00	☐☐☐☐☐
466	A140	5c blue	52.50	1.00	☐☐☐☐☐
467	A140	5c carmine (error in plate of 2c, '17).	475.00	500.00	☐☐☐☐☐
468	A140	6c red orange	65.00	5.00	☐☐☐☐☐
469	A140	7c black	85.00	7.50	☐☐☐☐☐
470	A148	8c olive green..................	40.00	3.75	☐☐☐☐☐
471	A148	9c salmon red..................	41.00	9.50	☐☐☐☐☐
472	A148	10c orange yellow	77.50	75	☐☐☐☐☐
473	A148	11c dark green	22.50	11.00	☐☐☐☐☐
474	A148	12c claret brown	36.00	3.50	☐☐☐☐☐
475	A148	15c gray	120.00	7.00	☐☐☐☐☐
476	A148	20c light ultramarine............	175.00	7.50	☐☐☐☐☐
476A	A148	30c orange red	*3,000.*	–	☐☐☐☐☐
477	A148	50c light violet ('17).............	1,000.	40.00	☐☐☐☐☐
478	A148	$1 violet black	675.00	11.00	☐☐☐☐☐

TYPE Ia

TWO CENTS.

Type Ia. Design characteristics similar to type I except that all lines of design are stronger.

The toga button, toga rope and rope shading lines are heavy. The latter characteristics are those of type II, which, however, occur only on impressions from rotary plates.

Used only on flat plates 10208 and 10209.

TYPE II

THREE CENTS.

Type II. The top line of the toga rope is strong and the rope shading lines are heavy and complete.

The line between the lips is heavy.

Used on both flat plate and rotary press printings.

TYPE IV

TWO CENTS.

Type IV. Top line of toga rope is broken. Shading lines in toga button are so arranged that the curving of the first and last form "ɑID".

Line of color in left "2" is very thin and usually broken.

Used on offset printings only.

Scott No.	Illus. No.	Description	Unused Value	Used Value	//////
1917, Mar. 22					
479	A127	$2 dark blue..................	325.00	30.00	☐☐☐☐☐
480	A128	$5 light green	250.00	32.50	☐☐☐☐☐
1916-17 Imperf.					
481	A140	1c green	65	45	☐☐☐☐☐
482	A140	2c carmine, Type I............	1.00	1.00	☐☐☐☐☐
482A	A140	2c deep rose, Type Ia..........		7,000.	☐☐☐☐☐
483	A140	3c violet, Type I ('17)	9.50	6.50	☐☐☐☐☐
484	A140	3c violet, Type II	7.00	3.00	☐☐☐☐☐
485	A140	5c carmine (error in plate of 2c) ('17)	*9,000.*		☐☐☐☐☐
1916-19 Coil Stamps, Perf. 10 horizontally					
486	A140	1c green ('18)	60	20	☐☐☐☐☐
487	A140	2c carmine, Type II.............	10.00	2.50	☐☐☐☐☐
488	A140	2c carmine, Type III ('19)	1.75	1.35	☐☐☐☐☐
489	A140	3c violet, Type I ('17)	3.75	1.00	☐☐☐☐☐
1916-22 Coil Stamps, Perf. 10 vertically					
490	A140	1c green	40	15	☐☐☐☐☐
491	A140	2c carmine, Type II.............	1,450.	450.00	☐☐☐☐☐
492	A140	2c carmine, Type III	5.75	15	☐☐☐☐☐
493	A140	3c violet, Type I ('17)	13.50	1.75	☐☐☐☐☐
494	A140	3c violet, Type II ('18)..........	7.50	90	☐☐☐☐☐
495	A140	4c orange brown ('17)	8.00	3.00	☐☐☐☐☐
496	A140	5c blue ('19)	2.75	90	☐☐☐☐☐
497	A148	10c orange yellow ('22)	16.00	7.00	☐☐☐☐☐
1917-19					
498	A140	1c green	30	15	☐☐☐☐☐
498a.		Vertical pair, imperf. horizontally	175.00		☐☐☐☐☐
498b.		Horizontal pair, imperf. between .	75.00		☐☐☐☐☐
498c.		Vertical pair, imperf. between....	*450.00*	−	☐☐☐☐☐
498d.		Double impression.............	150.00	−	☐☐☐☐☐
498e.		Booklet pane of 6.............	3.50	35	☐☐☐☐☐
498f.		Booklet pane of 30.............	600.00		☐☐☐☐☐
499	A140	2c rose, Type I	35	15	☐☐☐☐☐
499a.		Vertical pair, imperf. horizontally	150.00		☐☐☐☐☐
499b.		Horizontal pair, imperf. vertically	200.00	*100.00*	☐☐☐☐☐
499c.		Vertical pair, imperf. between....	*500.00*	*225.00*	☐☐☐☐☐
499e.		Booklet pane of 6.............	3.50	50	☐☐☐☐☐
499f.		Booklet pane of 30.............	*10,000*		☐☐☐☐☐
499g.		Double impression.............	125.00	−	☐☐☐☐☐
500	A140	2c deep rose, Type Ia...........	200.00	110.00	☐☐☐☐☐
501	A140	3c light violet, Type I	8.00	15	☐☐☐☐☐
501b.		Booklet pane of 6.............	65.00	*15.00*	☐☐☐☐☐
501c.		Vertical pair, imperf. horizontally	300.00		☐☐☐☐☐
501d.		Double impression.............	200.00		☐☐☐☐☐

TYPE V

TWO CENTS.
   Type V. Top line of toga is complete.
Five vertical shading lines in toga
button.
   Line of color in left "2" is very thin
and usually broken.
   Shading dots on the nose and lip are as
indicated on the diagram.
   Used on offset printings only.

TYPE Va

TWO CENTS.
   Type Va. Characteristics same as type
V, except in shading dots of nose. Third
row from bottom has 4 dots instead of 6.
Overall height of type Va is 1/3 mm. less
than type V.
   Used on offset printings only.

TYPE VI

TWO CENTS.
   Type VI. General characteristics same
as type V, except that line of color in left
"2" is very heavy.
   Used on offset printings only.

HOW TO USE THIS BOOK

   The number in the first column is its Scott number or identifying number.
The letter and number that come next (A41) indicate the design and refer to
the illustration so designated. Following that is the denomination of the stamp
and its color. Finally, the value, unused and used is shown.

Scott No.	Illus. No.	Description	Unused Value	Used Value	//////
502	A140	3c dark violet, Type II............	11.00	15	☐☐☐☐☐
502b.		Booklet pane of 6.............	50.00	*10.00*	☐☐☐☐☐
502c.		Vertical pair, imperf. horizontally	250.00	125.00	☐☐☐☐☐
502d.		Double impression.............	200.00		☐☐☐☐☐
503	A140	4c brown	7.50	15	☐☐☐☐☐
503b.		Double impression.............	—		☐☐☐☐☐
504	A140	5c blue	6.50	15	☐☐☐☐☐
504a.		Horizontal pair, imperf. between .	*2,500.*	—	☐☐☐☐☐
505	A140	5c rose (error in plate of 2c)	350.00	400.00	☐☐☐☐☐
506	A140	6c red orange	9.50	20	☐☐☐☐☐
507	A140	7c black	20.00	85	☐☐☐☐☐
508	A148	8c olive bister.................	8.50	40	☐☐☐☐☐
508b.		Vertical pair, imperf. between....	—	—	☐☐☐☐☐
509	A148	9c salmon red..................	11.00	1.40	☐☐☐☐☐
510	A148	10c orange yellow	12.50	15	☐☐☐☐☐
511	A148	11c light green	6.75	2.00	☐☐☐☐☐
512	A148	12c claret brown	6.50	30	☐☐☐☐☐
512a.		12c brown carmine	7.00	35	☐☐☐☐☐
513	A148	13c apple green ('19)	8.00	4.75	☐☐☐☐☐
514	A148	15c gray	30.00	80	☐☐☐☐☐
515	A148	20c light ultramarine.............	37.50	16	☐☐☐☐☐
515b.		Vertical pair, imperf. between....	*325.00*		☐☐☐☐☐
515c.		Double impression.............	*400.00*		☐☐☐☐☐
516	A148	30c orange red	30.00	55	☐☐☐☐☐
517	A148	50c red violet	60.00	40	☐☐☐☐☐
517b.		Vertical pair, imperf. between....	*1,750.*	750.00	☐☐☐☐☐
518	A148	$1 violet brown	45.00	1.10	☐☐☐☐☐
518b.		$1 deep brown	*750.00*	*350.00*	☐☐☐☐☐

1917, Oct. 10
| 519 | A139 | 2c carmine .... | 200.00 | *400.00* | ☐☐☐☐☐ |

1918, Aug. 19
| 523 | A149 | $2 orange red & black........... | 675.00 | 250.00 | ☐☐☐☐☐ |
| 524 | A149 | $5 deep green & black........... | 275.00 | 20.00 | ☐☐☐☐☐ |

1918-20
525	A140	1c gray green	1.35	35	☐☐☐☐☐
525a.		1c dark green	1.50	75	☐☐☐☐☐
525c.		Horizontal pair, imperf. between .	60.00		☐☐☐☐☐
525d.		Double impression.............	15.00	15.00	☐☐☐☐☐
526	A140	2c carmine, Type IV ('20)	19.00	2.75	☐☐☐☐☐
527	A140	2c carmine, Type V	10.00	60	☐☐☐☐☐
527a.		Double impression.............	55.00	10.00	☐☐☐☐☐
527b.		Vertical pair, imperf. horizontally	*600.00*		☐☐☐☐☐
527c.		Horizontal pair, imperf. vertically	1,000.	—	☐☐☐☐☐
528	A140	2c carmine, Type Va	5.25	15	☐☐☐☐☐
528c.		Double impression.............	25.00		☐☐☐☐☐

TYPE VII

TWO CENTS.

Type VII. Line of color in left "2" is invariably continuous, clearly defined, and heavier than in type V or Va, but not as heavy as in type VI.

Additional vertical row of dots has been added to the upper lip.

Numerous additional dots have been added to hair on top of head.

Used on offset printings only.

TYPE III

TYPE IV

THREE CENTS.

Type IV. Shading lines of toga rope are complete.

Second and fourth shading lines in toga button are broken in the middle and the third line is continuous with a dot in the center.

"P" and "O" of "POSTAGE" are joined.

Frame line at bottom of vignette is broken.

Used on offset printings only.

THREE CENTS.

Type III. The top line of the toga rope is strong but the fifth shading line is missing as in type I.

Center shading line of the toga button consists of two dashes with a central dot.

The "P" and "O" of "POSTAGE" are separated by a line of color.

The frame line at the bottom of the vignette is complete.

Used on offset printings only.

Scott No.	Illus. No.	Description	Unused Value	Used Value	//////
528g.		Vertical pair, imperf. between....	*1,000.*		☐☐☐☐☐
528A	A140	2c carmine, Type VI	32.50	1.00	☐☐☐☐☐
528d.		Double impression.	150.00	—	☐☐☐☐☐
528f.		Vertical pair, imperf. horizontally	—		☐☐☐☐☐
528h.		Vertical pair, imperf. between....	*1,000.*		☐☐☐☐☐
528B	A140	2c carmine, Type VII	12.50	15	☐☐☐☐☐
528e.		Double impression.	55.00		☐☐☐☐☐
529	A140	3c violet, Type III	2.00	15	☐☐☐☐☐
529a.		Double impression.	30.00	—	☐☐☐☐☐
529b.		Printed on both sides.	*350.00*		☐☐☐☐☐
530	A140	3c purple, Type IV..............	75	15	☐☐☐☐☐
530a.		Double impression.	17.50	6.00	☐☐☐☐☐
530b.		Printed on both sides.	250.00		☐☐☐☐☐

1918-20 Imperf.

Scott No.	Illus. No.	Description	Unused Value	Used Value	//////
531	A140	1c green ('19)	6.00	7.00	☐☐☐☐☐
532	A140	2c carmine rose, Type IV ('20)	30.00	22.50	☐☐☐☐☐
533	A140	2c carmine, Type V	150.00	55.00	☐☐☐☐☐
534	A140	2c carmine, Type Va	8.50	6.00	☐☐☐☐☐
534A	A140	2c carmine, Type VI	27.50	17.50	☐☐☐☐☐
534B	A140	2c carmine, Type VII	1,250.	425.00	☐☐☐☐☐
535	A140	3c violet, Type IV	6.00	4.50	☐☐☐☐☐
535a.		Double impression.	100.00	—	☐☐☐☐☐

1919

Scott No.	Illus. No.	Description	Unused Value	Used Value	//////
536	A140	1c gray green	9.00	11.00	☐☐☐☐☐
536a.		Horizontal pair, imperf. vertically	*500.00*		☐☐☐☐☐
537	A150	3c violet	6.50	2.75	☐☐☐☐☐
537a.		3c deep red violet.	250.00	30.00	☐☐☐☐☐
537b.		3c light reddish violet	6.50	2.75	☐☐☐☐☐
536c.		3c red violet	30.00	7.50	☐☐☐☐☐
538	A140	1c green	6.50	6.00	☐☐☐☐☐
538a.		Vertical pair, imperf. horizontally	50.00	*100.00*	☐☐☐☐☐
539	A140	2c carmine rose, Type II	2,750.	750.00	☐☐☐☐☐
540	A140	2c carmine rose, Type III	7.00	6.00	☐☐☐☐☐
540a.		Vertical pair, imperf. horizontally	50.00	*100.00*	☐☐☐☐☐
540b.		Horizontal pair, imperf. vertically	*550.00*		☐☐☐☐☐
541	A140	3c violet, Type II	22.50	20.00	☐☐☐☐☐

1920, May 26

Scott No.	Illus. No.	Description	Unused Value	Used Value	//////
542	A140	1c green	6.50	65	☐☐☐☐☐

1921

Scott No.	Illus. No.	Description	Unused Value	Used Value	//////
543	A140	1c green	35	15	☐☐☐☐☐
543a.		Horizontal pair, imperf. between .	*550.00*		☐☐☐☐☐

1923

Scott No.	Illus. No.	Description	Unused Value	Used Value	//////
544	A140	1c green	*8,500.*	*2,500.*	☐☐☐☐☐

A149

A150

A151

A152

A153

A154

A155

A156

A157

A158

A159

A160

A161

A162

A163

A164

A165

A166

A167

A168

A169

38

Scott No.	Illus. No.	Description	Unused Value	Used Value	//////
1921					
545	A140	1c green	95.00	110.00	☐☐☐☐☐
546	A140	2c carmine rose, Type III	60.00	*110.00*	☐☐☐☐☐
1920					
547	A149	$2 carmine & black.............	225.00	25.00	☐☐☐☐☐
548	A151	1c green	3.25	1.65	☐☐☐☐☐
549	A152	2c carmine rose	5.25	1.25	☐☐☐☐☐
550	A153	5c deep blue...................	32.50	10.00	☐☐☐☐☐
1922-25					
551	A154	1/2c olive brown ('25)	15	15	☐☐☐☐☐
552	A155	1c deep green ('23).............	1.10	15	☐☐☐☐☐
552a.		Booket pane of 6	4.50	*50*	☐☐☐☐☐
553	A156	1 1/2c yellow brown ('25)	1.90	15	☐☐☐☐☐
554	A157	2c carmine ('23)	1.00	15	☐☐☐☐☐
554a.		Horizontal pair, imperf. vertically	175.00		☐☐☐☐☐
554b.		Vertical pair, imperf. horizontally	*500.00*		☐☐☐☐☐
554c.		Booklet pane of 6..............	6.00	*1.00*	☐☐☐☐☐
555	A158	3c violet ('23)...................	12.50	85	☐☐☐☐☐
556	A159	4c yellow brown ('23)	12.50	20	☐☐☐☐☐
556a.		Vertical pair, imperf. horizontally	—		☐☐☐☐☐
557	A160	5c dark blue	12.50	15	☐☐☐☐☐
557a.		Imperf., pair...................	*800.00*		☐☐☐☐☐
557b.		Horizontal pair, imperf. vertically	—		☐☐☐☐☐
558	A161	6c red orange	24.00	75	☐☐☐☐☐
559	A162	7c black ('23)	5.75	45	☐☐☐☐☐
560	A163	8c olive green ('23).............	35.00	35	☐☐☐☐☐
561	A164	9c rose ('23)	10.00	90	☐☐☐☐☐
562	A165	10c orange ('23)	14.00	15	☐☐☐☐☐
562a.		Vertical pair, imperf. horizontally	*750.00*		☐☐☐☐☐
562b.		Imperf., pair...................	*1,000.*		☐☐☐☐☐
563	A166	11c light blue	1.10	25	☐☐☐☐☐
563d.		Imperf., pair...................		—	☐☐☐☐☐
564	A167	12c brown violet ('23)	4.50	15	☐☐☐☐☐
564a.		Horizontal pair, imperf. vertically	*1,000.*		☐☐☐☐☐
564b.		Imperf., pair...................	—		☐☐☐☐☐
565	A168	14c blue ('23)	3.25	65	☐☐☐☐☐
566	A169	15c gray	17.50	15	☐☐☐☐☐
567	A170	20c carmine rose ('23)...........	17.50	15	☐☐☐☐☐
567a.		Horizontal pair, imperf. vertically	*750.00*		☐☐☐☐☐
568	A171	25c yellow green	15.00	38	☐☐☐☐☐
568b.		Vertical pair, imperf. horizontally	*850.00*		☐☐☐☐☐
569	A172	30c olive brown ('23).............	27.50	30	☐☐☐☐☐
570	A173	50c lilac	50.00	15	☐☐☐☐☐
571	A174	$1 violet black ('23).............	37.50	35	☐☐☐☐☐
572	A175	$2 deep blue ('23)	85.00	8.00	☐☐☐☐☐
573	A176	$5 carmine & blue ('23)..........	200.00	12.50	☐☐☐☐☐

A170   A171   A172

A173   A174   A175

A176   A177

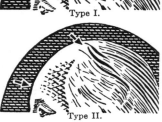

Type I.

Type I.   Type II.

Type II.

Type I—No heavy hair lines at top center of head. Outline of left acanthus scroll generally faint at top and toward base at left side.

Type II—The heavy hair lines at top center of head; two being outstanding in the white area. Outline of left acanthus scroll very strong and clearly defined at top (under left edge of lettered panel) and at lower curve (above and to left of numeral oval). Type II is found only on Nos. 599A and 634A.

A178   A179   A180

Scott No.	Illus. No.	Description	Unused Value	Used Value	//////

1923-25 Imperf.

Scott No.	Illus. No.	Description	Unused Value	Used Value	
575	A155	1c green	6.00	2.75	□□□□□
576	A156	1 1/2c yellow brown ('25)	1.25	1.00	□□□□□
577	A157	2c carmine	1.40	1.25	□□□□□

1923-25

Scott No.	Illus. No.	Description	Unused Value	Used Value	
578	A155	1c green	60.00	65.00	□□□□□
579	A157	2c carmine	50.00	60.00	□□□□□

1923-26

Scott No.	Illus. No.	Description	Unused Value	Used Value	
581	A155	1c green	6.00	55	□□□□□
582	A156	1 1/2c brown ('25)	3.00	45	□□□□□
583	A157	2c carmine ('24)	1.40	15	□□□□□
583a.		Booklet pane of 6	75.00	*25.00*	□□□□□
584	A158	3c violet ('25)	17.50	1.75	□□□□□
585	A159	4c yellow brown ('25)	11.00	30	□□□□□
586	A160	5c blue ('25)	11.50	18	□□□□□
586a.		Horizontal pair, imperf. between	—		□□□□□
587	A161	6c red orange ('25)	4.50	25	□□□□□
588	A162	7c black ('26)	7.00	4.25	□□□□□
589	A163	8c olive green ('26)	17.50	2.75	□□□□□
590	A164	9c rose ('26)	3.25	1.90	□□□□□
591	A165	10c orange ('25)	45.00	15	□□□□□
594	A155	1c green	10,000.	3,500.	□□□□□
595	A157	2c carmine	190.00	225.00	□□□□□
596	A155	1c green	15,000.		□□□□□

1923-29

Scott No.	Illus. No.	Description	Unused Value	Used Value	
597	A155	1c green	20	15	□□□□□
598	A156	1 1/2c brown ('25)	40	15	□□□□□
599	A157	2c carmine, Type I ('23)	25	15	□□□□□
599A	A157	2c carmine, Type II ('29)	100.00	8.50	□□□□□
600	A158	3c violet ('24)	4.25	15	□□□□□
601	A159	4c yellow brown	2.50	30	□□□□□
602	A160	5c dark blue ('24)	1.10	15	□□□□□
603	A165	10c orange ('24)	2.25	15	□□□□□
604	A155	1c yellow green	18	15	□□□□□
605	A156	1 1/2c yellow brown ('25)	18	15	□□□□□
606	A157	2c carmine	18	15	□□□□□

1923

Scott No.	Illus. No.	Description	Unused Value	Used Value	
610	A177	2c black	45	15	□□□□□
610a.		Horizontal pair, imperf. vertically	*800.00*		□□□□□
611	A177	2c black	6.50	4.25	□□□□□
612	A177	2c black	12.00	1.50	□□□□□
613	A177	2c black		*15,000.*	□□□□□

41

A181

A182

A183

A184

A185

A186

A187

A188

A190

A189

A191

A192

A193

Scott No.	Illus. No.	Description	Unused Value	Used Value	//////
1924, May 1					
614	A178	1c dark green	2.50	3.00 □□□□□
615	A179	2c carmine rose	5.25	1.90 □□□□□
616	A180	5c dark blue	25.00	11.00 □□□□□
1925					
617	A181	1c deep green	2.50	2.25 □□□□□
618	A182	2c carmine rose	5.00	3.75 □□□□□
619	A183	5c dark blue	24.00	12.50 □□□□□
620	A184	2c carmine & black	3.00	2.75 □□□□□
621	A185	5c dark blue & black	13.00	10.50 □□□□□
1925-26					
622	A186	13c green ('26)	11.00	40 □□□□□
623	A187	17c black	13.00	20 □□□□□
1926					
627	A188	2c carmine rose	2.25	35 □□□□□
628	A189	5c gray lilac	5.00	2.50 □□□□□
629	A190	2c carmine rose	1.50	1.25 □□□□□
629a.		Vertical pair, imperf. between. . . .	*1,250.*	□□□□□
630	A190	2c carmine rose, sheet of 25	300.00	300.00 □□□□□
Imperf.					
631	A156	1 1/2c yellow brown	1.75	1.40 □□□□□
1926-34					
632	A155	1c green ('27)	15	15 □□□□□
632a.		Booklet pane of 6.	4.50	25 □□□□□
632b.		Vertical pair, imperf. between. . . .	*200.00*	*125.00* □□□□□
633	A156	1 1/2c yellow brown ('27)	1.25	15 □□□□□
634	A157	2c carmine, Type I.	15	15 □□□□□
634b.		2c carmine lake	3.00	1.00 □□□□□
634c.		Horizontal pair, imperf. between .	*2,000.*	□□□□□
634d.		Booklet pane of 6.	1.75	*15* □□□□□
634A	A157	2c carmine, Type II ('28).	285.00	10.00 □□□□□
635	A158	3c violet ('27)	35	15 □□□□□
635a.		3c bright violet ('34).	25	15 □□□□□
636	A159	4c yellow brown ('27)	1.75	15 □□□□□
637	A160	5c dark blue ('27)	1.65	15 □□□□□
638	A161	6c red orange ('27).	1.75	15 □□□□□
639	A162	7c black ('27)	1.75	15 □□□□□
639a.		Vertical pair, imperf. between. . . .	125.00	80.00 □□□□□
640	A163	8c olive green ('27).	1.75	15 □□□□□
641	A164	9c orange red ('31).	1.75	15 □□□□□
642	A165	10c orange ('27)	2.75	15 □□□□□

A194

A195

A196

A197

A198

A199

A200

A201

A202

A203

A204

A205

HOW TO USE THIS BOOK

The number in the first column is its Scott number or identifying number. The letter and number that come next (A41) indicate the design and refer to the illustration so designated. Following that is the denomination of the stamp and its color. Finally, the value, unused and used is shown.

Scott No.	Illus. No.	Description	Unused Value	Used Value	//////
1927					
643	A191	2c carmine rose	1.25	75 □□□□□
644	A192	2c carmine rose	3.00	1.90 □□□□□
1928					
645	A193	2c carmine rose	90	35 □□□□□
646	A157	2c carmine	80	80 □□□□□
647	A157	2c carmine	3.00	3.25 □□□□□
648	A160	5c dark blue	10.00	10.00 □□□□□
649	A194	2c carmine rose	90	75 □□□□□
650	A195	5c blue	4.50	3.00 □□□□□
1929					
651	A196	2c carmine & black	45	35 □□□□□
653	A154	1/2c olive brown	15	15 □□□□□
654	A197	2c carmine rose	50	50 □□□□□
655	A197	2c carmine rose	45	15 □□□□□

1929 Coil Stamp, Perf. 10 vertically

Scott No.	Illus. No.	Description	Unused Value	Used Value	//////
656	A197	2c carmine rose	9.50	1.25 □□□□□

Scott No.	Illus. No.	Description	Unused Value	Used Value	//////
1929					
657	A198	2c carmine rose	60	50 □□□□□
658	A155	1c green	1.40	1.25 □□□□□
658a.		Vertical pair, one without overprint *300.00*		□□□□□
659	A156	1 1/2c brown	1.90	1.75 □□□□□
659a.		Vertical pair, one without overprint *325.00*		□□□□□
660	A157	2c carmine	2.50	70 □□□□□
661	A158	3c violet	11.00	9.00 □□□□□
661a.		Vertical pair, one without overprint *400.00*		□□□□□
662	A159	4c yellow brown.	11.00	5.50 □□□□□
662a.		Vertical pair, one without overprint *400.00*		□□□□□
663	A160	5c deep blue.....................	8.00	6.00 □□□□□
664	A161	6c red orange	17.50	11.50 □□□□□
665	A162	7c black	16.00	17.00 □□□□□
665a.		Vertical pair, one without overprint *400.00*		□□□□□
666	A163	8c olive green..................	55.00	45.00 □□□□□
667	A164	9c light rose	8.00	7.00 □□□□□
668	A165	10c orange yellow	14.00	7.50 □□□□□
669	A155	1c green	2.00	1.40 □□□□□
669a.		Vertical pair, one without overprint *275.00*		□□□□□
670	A156	1 1/2c brown	1.65	1.50 □□□□□

A206

A207

A208

A209

A210

A211

A212

A213

A214

A215

A216

A217

A218

A219

A220

A221

A222

A223

A224

A225

A226

A227

A228

Scott No.	Illus. No.	Description	Unused Value	Used Value	//////
671	A157	2c carmine	1.65	70	☐☐☐☐☐
672	A158	3c violet	7.00	6.50	☐☐☐☐☐
672a.		Vertical pair, one without			
		overprint	400.00		☐☐☐☐☐
673	A159	4c yellow brown.............	12.50	9.00	☐☐☐☐☐
674	A160	5c deep blue..................	10.00	9.00	☐☐☐☐☐
675	A161	6c red orange	24.00	14.00	☐☐☐☐☐
676	A162	7c black	13.00	11.00	☐☐☐☐☐
677	A163	8c olive green...............	17.00	15.00	☐☐☐☐☐
678	A164	9c light rose	22.50	17.00	☐☐☐☐☐
678a.		Vertical pair, one without			
		overprint	600.00		☐☐☐☐☐
679	A165	10c orange yellow	70.00	14.00	☐☐☐☐☐
680	A199	2c carmine rose	60	65	☐☐☐☐☐
681	A200	2c carmine rose	45	50	☐☐☐☐☐

1930

682	A201	2c carmine rose	50	38	☐☐☐☐☐
683	A202	2c carmine rose	85	85	☐☐☐☐☐
684	A203	1 1/2c brown	18	15	☐☐☐☐☐
685	A204	4c brown	65	15	☐☐☐☐☐

Coil Stamps, Perf. 10 vertically

686	A203	1 1/2c brown	1.25	15	☐☐☐☐☐
687	A204	4c brown	2.25	38	☐☐☐☐☐

1930

688	A205	2c carmine rose	65	65	☐☐☐☐☐
689	A206	2c carmine rose	38	40	☐☐☐☐☐
689a.		Imperf., pair................	2,250.		☐☐☐☐☐

1931

690	A207	2c carmine rose	16	15	☐☐☐☐☐
692	A166	11c light blue	1.65	15	☐☐☐☐☐
693	A167	12c brown violet	3.50	15	☐☐☐☐☐
694	A186	13c yellow green	1.40	15	☐☐☐☐☐
695	A168	14c dark blue..................	2.50	22	☐☐☐☐☐
696	A169	15c gray	6.25	15	☐☐☐☐☐
697	A187	17c black	3.50	15	☐☐☐☐☐
698	A170	20c carmine rose	7.50	15	☐☐☐☐☐
699	A171	25c blue green	6.75	15	☐☐☐☐☐
700	A172	30c brown	10.50	15	☐☐☐☐☐
701	A173	50c lilac	30.00	15	☐☐☐☐☐
702	A208	2c black & red	15	15	☐☐☐☐☐
703	A209	2c carmine rose & black	24	20	☐☐☐☐☐
703a.		2c lake & black...............	3.50	50	☐☐☐☐☐
703b.		2c dark lake & black	300.00		☐☐☐☐☐
703c.		Horizontal pair, imperf. vertically	3,250.		☐☐☐☐☐

A229

A230

A231

A232

A233

A234

A235

A236

A237

A238

Scott No.	Illus. No.	Description	Unused Value	Used Value	//////
1932					
704	A210	1/2c olive brown	15	15	□□□□□
705	A211	1c green	15	15	□□□□□
706	A212	1 1/2c brown	32	15	□□□□□
707	A213	2c carmine rose	15	15	□□□□□
708	A214	3c deep violet.	40	15	□□□□□
709	A215	4c light brown	22	15	□□□□□
710	A216	5c blue	1.40	15	□□□□□
711	A217	6c red orange	2.75	15	□□□□□
712	A218	7c black	22	15	□□□□□
713	A219	8c olive bister.	2.25	50	□□□□□
714	A220	9c pale red	2.00	15	□□□□□
715	A221	10c orange yellow	8.50	15	□□□□□
716	A222	2c carmine rose	35	16	□□□□□
717	A223	2c carmine rose	15	15	□□□□□
718	A224	3c violet	1.10	15	□□□□□
719	A225	5c blue	1.90	20	□□□□□
720	A226	3c deep violet.	15	15	□□□□□
720b.		Booklet pane of 6.	22.50	5.00	□□□□□
720c.		Vertical pair, imperf. between. . . .	250.00		□□□□□
1932 Coil Stamps, Perf. 10 vertically					
721	A226	3c deep violet.	2.25	15	□□□□□
Perf. 10 horizontally					
722	A226	3c deep violet.	1.00	30	□□□□□
Perf. 10 vertically					
723	A161	6c deep orange	7.50	25	□□□□□
1932					
724	A227	3c violet	22	15	□□□□□
724a.		Vertical pair, imperf. horizontally	—		□□□□□
725	A228	3c violet	28	24	□□□□□
1933					
726	A229	3c violet	20	18	□□□□□
727	A230	3c violet	15	15	□□□□□
728	A231	1c yellow green	15	15	□□□□□
729	A232	3c violet	15	15	□□□□□
Imperf.					
730		Sheet of 25	24.00	24.00	□□□□□
730a.	A231	1c deep yellow green	65	35	□□□□□
731		sheet of 25	22.50	22.50	□□□□□
731a.	A232	3c deep violet.	50	35	□□□□□
1933					
732	A233	3c violet	15	15	□□□□□

A240

A239

A241

A242

A243

A244

A245

A246

A247

A249

A248

A250

A252

A253

50

Scott No.	Illus. No.	Description	Unused Value	Used Value	//////
733	A234	3c dark blue	40	48	☐☐☐☐☐
734	A235	5c blue	40	22	☐☐☐☐☐
734a.		Horizontal pair, imperf. vertically	*2,000.*		☐☐☐☐☐

1934 Imperf.

735		Sheet of six	15.00	12.50	☐☐☐☐☐
735a.	A235	3c dark blue	2.00	2.00	☐☐☐☐☐

1934

736	A236	3c carmine rose	15	15	☐☐☐☐☐
737	A237	3c deep violet.	15	15	☐☐☐☐☐
738	A237	3c deep violet.	15	15	☐☐☐☐☐
739	A238	3c deep violet.	15	15	☐☐☐☐☐
739a.		Vertical pair, imperf. horizontally	250.00		☐☐☐☐☐
739b.		Horizontal pair, imperf. vertically	325.00		☐☐☐☐☐
740	A239	1c green	15	15	☐☐☐☐☐
740a.		Vertical pair, imperf. horizontally, with gum	450.00		☐☐☐☐☐
741	A240	2c red	15	15	☐☐☐☐☐
741a.		Vertical pair, imperf. horizontally, with gum	300.00		☐☐☐☐☐
741b.		Horizontal pair, imperf. vertically, with gum	300.00		☐☐☐☐☐
742	A241	3c deep violet.	15	15	☐☐☐☐☐
742a.		Vertical pair, imperf. horizontally, with gum	350.00		☐☐☐☐☐
743	A242	4c brown	35	32	☐☐☐☐☐
743a.		Vertical pair, imperf. horizontally, with gum	500.00		☐☐☐☐☐
744	A243	5c blue	60	55	☐☐☐☐☐
744a.		Horizontal pair, imperf. vertically, with gum	400.00		☐☐☐☐☐
745	A244	6c dark blue	1.00	75	☐☐☐☐☐
746	A245	7c black	55	65	☐☐☐☐☐
746a.		Horizontal pair, imperf. vertically, with gum	450.00		☐☐☐☐☐
747	A246	8c sage green	1.40	1.65	☐☐☐☐☐
748	A247	9c red orange	1.50	55	☐☐☐☐☐
749	A248	10c gray black	2.75	90	☐☐☐☐☐

Imperf.

750		Sheet of six	25.00	22.50	☐☐☐☐☐
750a.	A241	3c deep violet.	3.00	2.75	☐☐☐☐☐
751		Sheet of six	10.00	10.00	☐☐☐☐☐
751a.	A239	1c green	1.25	1.50	☐☐☐☐☐

Nos. 752-771 are found in the Special Printings section.

A251

A255

A254

A256

A257

A258

A259

A260

A261

A262

A263

A264

Scott No.	Illus. No.	Description	Unused Value	Used Value	//////

Catalogue values for unused stamps in this section, from this point to
the end of the section, are for Never Hinged items.

1935

772	A249	3c violet	15	15 ☐☐☐☐☐
773	A250	3c purple	15	15 ☐☐☐☐☐
774	A251	3c purple	15	15 ☐☐☐☐☐
775	A252	3c purple	15	15 ☐☐☐☐☐

1936

776	A253	3c purple	15	15 ☐☐☐☐☐
777	A254	3c purple	15	15 ☐☐☐☐☐

Imperf.

778		Sheet of 4	1.75	1.75 ☐☐☐☐☐
778a.	A249	3c violet	40	30 ☐☐☐☐☐
778b.	A250	3c violet	40	30 ☐☐☐☐☐
778c.	A252	3c violet	40	30 ☐☐☐☐☐
778d.	A253	3c violet	40	30 ☐☐☐☐☐

1936

782	A255	3c purple	15	15 ☐☐☐☐☐
783	A256	3c purple	15	15 ☐☐☐☐☐
784	A257	3c dark violet.	15	15 ☐☐☐☐☐

1936-37

785	A258	1c green	15	15 ☐☐☐☐☐
786	A259	2c carmine ('37).	15	15 ☐☐☐☐☐
787	A260	3c purple ('37)	15	15 ☐☐☐☐☐
788	A261	4c gray ('37)	30	15 ☐☐☐☐☐
789	A262	5c ultramarine ('37).	60	15 ☐☐☐☐☐
790	A263	1c green	15	15 ☐☐☐☐☐
791	A264	2c carmine ('37).	15	15 ☐☐☐☐☐
792	A265	3c purple ('37)	15	15 ☐☐☐☐☐
793	A266	4c gray ('37)	30	15 ☐☐☐☐☐
794	A267	5c ultramarine ('37).	60	15 ☐☐☐☐☐

1937

795	A268	3c red violet.	15	15 ☐☐☐☐☐
796	A269	5c gray blue	20	18 ☐☐☐☐☐

Imperf.

797	A269a	10c blue green	60	40 ☐☐☐☐☐

1937

798	A270	3c bright red violet	15	15 ☐☐☐☐☐
799	A271	3c violet	15	15 ☐☐☐☐☐
800	A272	3c violet	15	15 ☐☐☐☐☐

A265

A266

A267

A268

A269

A269a

A270

A272

A273

A274

A275

A271

A277

A276

A278

Scott No.	Illus. No.	Description	Unused Value	Used Value	//////
801	A273	3c bright violet..................	15	15	☐☐☐☐☐
802	A274	3c light violet...................	15	15	☐☐☐☐☐

1938-54

Scott No.	Illus. No.	Description	Unused Value	Used Value	//////
803	A275	½c deep orange	15	15	☐☐☐☐☐
804	A276	1c green	15	15	☐☐☐☐☐
804b.		Booklet pane of 6.............	1.50	20	☐☐☐☐☐
805	A277	1½c bister brown...............	15	15	☐☐☐☐☐
805b.		Horizontal pair, imperf. between .	175.00	25.00	☐☐☐☐☐
806	A278	2c rose carmine	15	15	☐☐☐☐☐
806b.		Booklet pane of 6.............	3.25	50	☐☐☐☐☐
807	A279	3c deep violet.................	15	15	☐☐☐☐☐
807a.		Booklet pane of 6.............	6.50	50	☐☐☐☐☐
807b.		Horizontal pair, imperf. between .	650.00	–	☐☐☐☐☐
807c.		Imperf., pair...................	2,500.		☐☐☐☐☐
808	A280	4c red violet...................	80	15	☐☐☐☐☐
809	A281	4 ½c dark gray..................	15	15	☐☐☐☐☐
810	A282	5c bright blue..................	22	15	☐☐☐☐☐
811	A283	6c red orange	25	15	☐☐☐☐☐
812	A284	7c sepia.......................	28	15	☐☐☐☐☐
813	A285	8c olive green..................	30	15	☐☐☐☐☐
814	A286	9c rose pink	38	15	☐☐☐☐☐
815	A287	10c brown red	28	15	☐☐☐☐☐
816	A288	11c ultramarine................	65	15	☐☐☐☐☐
817	A289	12c bright violet...............	1.10	15	☐☐☐☐☐
818	A290	13c blue green	1.50	15	☐☐☐☐☐
819	A291	14c blue	90	15	☐☐☐☐☐
820	A292	15c blue gray	50	15	☐☐☐☐☐
821	A293	16c black	90	25	☐☐☐☐☐
822	A294	17c rose red	85	15	☐☐☐☐☐
823	A295	18c brown carmine	1.50	15	☐☐☐☐☐
824	A296	19c bright violet...............	1.25	35	☐☐☐☐☐
825	A297	20c bright blue green	70	15	☐☐☐☐☐
826	A298	21c dull blue...................	1.50	15	☐☐☐☐☐
827	A299	22c vermilion..................	1.25	40	☐☐☐☐☐
828	A300	24c gray black	3.50	18	☐☐☐☐☐
829	A301	25c deep red lilac...............	80	15	☐☐☐☐☐
830	A302	30c deep ultramarine............	4.25	15	☐☐☐☐☐
831	A303	50c light red violet.............	7.00	15	☐☐☐☐☐
832	A304	$1 purple & black	8.00	15	☐☐☐☐☐
832a.		Vertical pair, imperf. horizontally	1,000.		☐☐☐☐☐
832b.		Wmkd. USIR ('51).............	300.00	70.00	☐☐☐☐☐
832c.		$1 red violet & black ('54).......	6.75	15	☐☐☐☐☐
832d.		As c, vert. pair, imperf. horizontally	1,000.		☐☐☐☐☐
832e.		Vertical pair, imperf. between....	2,500.		☐☐☐☐☐
832f.		As c, vert. pair, imperf. between ..	6,000.		☐☐☐☐☐
833	A305	$2 yellow green & black	21.00	3.75	☐☐☐☐☐

Thomas Jefferson
A279

James Madison
A280

White House
A281

James Monroe
A282

John Q. Adams
A283

Andrew Jackson
A284

Martin
Van Buren
A285

William H.
Harrison
A286

John Tyler
A287

James K. Polk
A288

Zachary Taylor
A289

Millard Fillmore
A290

Franklin Pierce
A291

James Buchanan
A292

Abraham Lincoln
A293

Andrew Johnson
A294

Ulysses S.
Grant
A295

Rutherford B.
Hayes
A296

James A. Garfield
A297

Chester A. Arthur
A298

Grover
Cleveland
A299

Benjamin
Harrison
A300

William
McKinley
A301

Theodore
Roosevelt
A302

William
Howard Taft
A303

Woodrow
Wilson
A304

Warren G.
Harding
A305

Calvin
Coolidge
A306

A308

A307

A309

A311

A310

A312

A314

A313

A315

A316

A317

Washington
Irving
A318

James Fenimore
Cooper
A319

Ralph Waldo
Emerson
A320

Louisa May
Alcott
A321

Samuel L. Clemens (Mark Twain)
A322

Henry W.
Longfellow
A323

John Greenleaf
Whittier
A324

James Russell
Lowell
A325

Walt
Whitman
A326

James Whitcomb Riley
A327

Horace Mann
A328

Mark Hopkins
A329

Charles W.
Eliot
A330

Frances E.
Willard
A331

Booker T. Washington
A332

Scott No.	Illus. No.	Description	Unused Value	Used Value	//////
834	A306	$5 carmine & black.............	95.00	3.00	☐☐☐☐☐
834a.		$5 red brown & black	*1,000.*	*500.00*	☐☐☐☐☐

1938

835	A307	3c deep violet...................	18	15	☐☐☐☐☐
836	A308	3c red violet....................	15	15	☐☐☐☐☐
837	A309	3c bright violet.................	15	15	☐☐☐☐☐
838	A310	3c violet	15	15	☐☐☐☐☐

1939 Coil Stamps, Perf. 10 Vertically

839	A276	1c green	20	15	☐☐☐☐☐
840	A277	1½c bister brown...............	24	15	☐☐☐☐☐
841	A278	2c rose carmine	24	15	☐☐☐☐☐
842	A279	3c deepviolet	42	15	☐☐☐☐☐
843	A280	4c red violet....................	6.75	35	☐☐☐☐☐
844	A281	4½c dark gray...................	42	35	☐☐☐☐☐
845	A282	5c bright blue..................	4.50	30	☐☐☐☐☐
846	A283	6c red orange	1.10	15	☐☐☐☐☐
847	A287	10c brown red	10.00	40	☐☐☐☐☐

Perf. 10 Horizontally

848	A276	1c green	55	15	☐☐☐☐☐
849	A277	1½c bister brown...............	1.10	30	☐☐☐☐☐
850	A278	2c rose carmine	2.00	40	☐☐☐☐☐
851	A279	3c deep violet..................	1.90	35	☐☐☐☐☐

1939

852	A311	3c bright purple	15	15	☐☐☐☐☐
853	A312	3c deep purple	15	15	☐☐☐☐☐
854	A313	3c bright red violet	30	15	☐☐☐☐☐
855	A314	3c violet	80	15	☐☐☐☐☐
856	A315	3c deep red violet	18	15	☐☐☐☐☐
857	A316	3c violet	15	15	☐☐☐☐☐
858	A317	3c rose violet	15	15	☐☐☐☐☐

1940

859	A318	1c bright blue green..............	15	15	☐☐☐☐☐
860	A319	2c rose carmine	15	15	☐☐☐☐☐
861	A320	3c bright red violet	15	15	☐☐☐☐☐
862	A321	5c ultramarine	28	20	☐☐☐☐☐
863	A322	10c dark brown	1.60	1.35	☐☐☐☐☐
864	A323	1c bright blue green..............	15	15	☐☐☐☐☐
865	A324	2c rose carmine	15	15	☐☐☐☐☐
866	A325	3c bright red violet	15	15	☐☐☐☐☐
867	A326	5c ultramarine	32	18	☐☐☐☐☐
868	A327	10c dark brown	1.75	1.40	☐☐☐☐☐
869	A328	1c bright blue green..............	15	15	☐☐☐☐☐
870	A329	2c rose carmine	15	15	☐☐☐☐☐

John James
Audubon

A333

Dr. Crawford
W. Long

A334

Luther Burbank

A335

Dr. Walter Reed

A336

Jane Addams

A337

Stephen Collins
Foster

A338

John Philip
Sousa

A339

Victor
Herbert

A340

Edward
MacDowell

A341

Ethelbert Nevin

A342

Gilbert Charles
Stuart

A343

James A. McNeill
Whistler

A344

Augustus
Saint-Gaudens

A345

Daniel Chester
French

A346

Frederic Remington— A347

60

Eli Whitney
A348

Samuel F. B. Morse
A349

Cyrus Hall
McCormick
A350

Elias Howe
A351

A353

A352

A355

A356

A354

A361

A358

A357

A359

A362

A360

A363

A364

A366

A367

A365

A368

A369

A370

A371

A372

A373

A374

A375

A377

A376

A378

A379

A380

A381

A382

A383

Scott No.	Illus. No.	Description	Unused Value	Used Value	//////
871	A330	3c bright red violet	15	15	☐☐☐☐☐
872	A331	5c ultramarine	38	25	☐☐☐☐☐
873	A332	10c dark brown	1.25	1.25	☐☐☐☐☐
874	A333	1c bright blue green	15	15	☐☐☐☐☐
875	A334	2c rose carmine	15	15	☐☐☐☐☐
876	A335	3c bright red violet	15	15	☐☐☐☐☐
877	A336	5c ultramarine	25	15	☐☐☐☐☐
878	A337	10c dark brown	1.05	95	☐☐☐☐☐
879	A338	1c bright blue green	15	15	☐☐☐☐☐
880	A339	2c rose carmine	15	15	☐☐☐☐☐
881	A340	3c bright red violet	15	15	☐☐☐☐☐
882	A341	5c ultramarine	40	22	☐☐☐☐☐
883	A342	10c dark brown	3.50	1.35	☐☐☐☐☐
884	A343	1c bright blue green	15	15	☐☐☐☐☐
885	A344	2c rose carmine	15	15	☐☐☐☐☐
886	A345	3c bright red violet	15	15	☐☐☐☐☐
887	A346	5c ultramarine	48	22	☐☐☐☐☐
888	A347	10c dark brown	1.75	1.40	☐☐☐☐☐
889	A348	1c bright blue green	15	15	☐☐☐☐☐
890	A349	2c rose carmine	15	15	☐☐☐☐☐
891	A350	3c bright red violet	25	15	☐☐☐☐☐
892	A351	5c ultramarine	1.00	32	☐☐☐☐☐
893	A352	10c dark brown	10.50	2.25	☐☐☐☐☐
894	A353	3c henna brown	25	15	☐☐☐☐☐
895	A354	3c light violet....................	20	15	☐☐☐☐☐
896	A355	3c bright violet.	15	15	☐☐☐☐☐
897	A356	3c brown violet	15	15	☐☐☐☐☐
898	A357	3c violet	15	15	☐☐☐☐☐
899	A358	1c bright blue green	15	15	☐☐☐☐☐
899a.		Vertical pair, imperf. between....	*500.00*	—	☐☐☐☐☐
899b.		Horizontal pair, imperf. between .	40.00	—	☐☐☐☐☐
900	A359	2c rose carmine	15	15	☐☐☐☐☐
900a.		Horizontal pair, imperf. between .	40.00	—	☐☐☐☐☐
901	A360	3c bright violet.	15	15	☐☐☐☐☐
901a.		Horizontal pair, imperf. between .	30.00	—	☐☐☐☐☐
902	A361	3c deep violet.	16	15	☐☐☐☐☐

1941, Mar. 4

903	A362	3c light violet...................	15	15	☐☐☐☐☐

1942

904	A363	3c violet	15	15	☐☐☐☐☐
905	A364	3c violet	15	15	☐☐☐☐☐
905b.		3c purple......................	20.00	8.00	☐☐☐☐☐
906	A365	5c bright blue...................	18	16	☐☐☐☐☐

A384

A385

A386

A387

A388

A389

A390

A391

A392

A393

A394

A399

A395

A396

A397

A398

A401

A400

A402

64

Scott No.	Illus. No.	Description	Unused Value	Used Value	//////
1943					
907	A366	2c rose carmine	15	15 ☐☐☐☐☐
908	A367	1c bright blue green	15	15 ☐☐☐☐☐
1943-44					
909	A368	5c Poland	18	15 ☐☐☐☐☐
910	A368	5c Czechoslovakia	18	15 ☐☐☐☐☐
911	A368	5c Norway	15	15 ☐☐☐☐☐
912	A368	5c Luxembourg	15	15 ☐☐☐☐☐
913	A368	5c Netherlands................	15	15 ☐☐☐☐☐
914	A368	5c Belgium	15	15 ☐☐☐☐☐
915	A368	5c France	15	15 ☐☐☐☐☐
916	A368	5c Greece	38	25 ☐☐☐☐☐
917	A368	5c Yugoslavia.................	28	15 ☐☐☐☐☐
918	A368	5c Albania	18	15 ☐☐☐☐☐
919	A368	5c Austria....................	18	15 ☐☐☐☐☐
920	A368	5c Denmark...................	18	15 ☐☐☐☐☐
921	A368	5c Korea ('44)	15	15 ☐☐☐☐☐
1944					
922	A369	3c violet	18	15 ☐☐☐☐☐
923	A370	3c violet	15	15 ☐☐☐☐☐
924	A371	3c bright red violet	15	15 ☐☐☐☐☐
925	A372	3c deep violet.................	15	15 ☐☐☐☐☐
926	A373	3c deep violet.................	15	15 ☐☐☐☐☐
1945					
927	A374	3c bright red violet	15	15 ☐☐☐☐☐
928	A375	5c ultramarine	15	15 ☐☐☐☐☐
929	A376	3c yellow green	15	15 ☐☐☐☐☐
1945-46					
930	A377	1c blue green	15	15 ☐☐☐☐☐
931	A378	2c carmine rose	15	15 ☐☐☐☐☐
932	A379	3c purple	15	15 ☐☐☐☐☐
933	A380	5c bright blue ('46)............	15	15 ☐☐☐☐☐
1945					
934	A381	3c olive......................	15	15 ☐☐☐☐☐
935	A382	3c blue	15	15 ☐☐☐☐☐
936	A383	3c bright blue green	15	15 ☐☐☐☐☐
937	A384	3c purple	15	15 ☐☐☐☐☐
938	A385	3c dark blue	15	15 ☐☐☐☐☐
1946					
939	A386	3c blue green	15	15 ☐☐☐☐☐
940	A387	3c dark violet.................	15	15 ☐☐☐☐☐
941	A388	3c dark violet.................	15	15 ☐☐☐☐☐

A403

A404

A405

A406

A407

A408

A409

A410

A411

A412

A413

A414

A416

A415

A417

A416

A418

A419

A420

A421

66

Scott No.	Illus. No.	Description	Unused Value	Used Value	//////
942	A389	3c deep blue....................	15	15 ☐☐☐☐☐
943	A390	3c violet brown	15	15 ☐☐☐☐☐
944	A391	3c brown violet	15	15 ☐☐☐☐☐

1947

945	A392	3c bright red violet	15	15 ☐☐☐☐☐
946	A393	3c purple	15	15 ☐☐☐☐☐
947	A394	3c deep blue...................	15	15 ☐☐☐☐☐

Imperf.

948	A395	Sheet of two....................	55	45 ☐☐☐☐☐
948a.		A1 5c blue	25	20 ☐☐☐☐☐
948b.		A2 10c brown orange..........	30	25 ☐☐☐☐☐

1947

949	A396	3c brown violet	15	15 ☐☐☐☐☐
950	A397	3c dark violet..................	15	15 ☐☐☐☐☐
951	A398	3c blue green	15	15 ☐☐☐☐☐
952	A399	3c bright green	15	15 ☐☐☐☐☐

1948

953	A400	3c bright red violet	15	15 ☐☐☐☐☐
954	A401	3c dark violet..................	15	15 ☐☐☐☐☐
955	A402	3c brown violet	15	15 ☐☐☐☐☐
956	A403	3c gray black	15	15 ☐☐☐☐☐
957	A404	3c dark violet..................	15	15 ☐☐☐☐☐
958	A405	5c deep blue...................	15	15 ☐☐☐☐☐
959	A406	3c dark violet..................	15	15 ☐☐☐☐☐
960	A407	3c bright red violet	15	15 ☐☐☐☐☐
961	A408	3c blue	15	15 ☐☐☐☐☐
962	A409	3c rose pink	15	15 ☐☐☐☐☐
963	A410	3c deep blue...................	15	15 ☐☐☐☐☐
964	A411	3c brown red	15	15 ☐☐☐☐☐
965	A412	3c bright red violet	15	15 ☐☐☐☐☐
966	A413	3c blue	15	15 ☐☐☐☐☐
966a.		Vertical pair, imperf between	*550.00*	☐☐☐☐☐
967	A414	3c rose pink	15	15 ☐☐☐☐☐
968	A415	3c sepia.......................	15	15 ☐☐☐☐☐
969	A416	3c orange yellow	15	15 ☐☐☐☐☐
970	A417	3c violet	15	15 ☐☐☐☐☐
971	A418	3c bright rose carmine...........	15	15 ☐☐☐☐☐
972	A419	3c dark brown	15	15 ☐☐☐☐☐
973	A420	3c violet brown	15	15 ☐☐☐☐☐
974	A421	3c blue green	15	15 ☐☐☐☐☐
975	A422	3c bright red violet	15	15 ☐☐☐☐☐
976	A423	3c henna brown	15	15 ☐☐☐☐☐
977	A424	3c rose pink	15	15 ☐☐☐☐☐
978	A425	3c bright blue..................	15	15 ☐☐☐☐☐

A422

A423

A424

A425

A426

A427

A428

A429

A430

A432

A433

A431

A434

A435

A436

Scott No.	Illus. No.	Description	Unused Value	Used Value	//////
979	A426	3c carmine	15	15 ☐☐☐☐☐
980	A427	3c bright red violet	15	15 ☐☐☐☐☐

1949

981	A428	3c blue green	15	15 ☐☐☐☐☐
982	A429	3c ultramarine	15	15 ☐☐☐☐☐
983	A430	3c green	15	15 ☐☐☐☐☐
984	A431	3c aquamarine	15	15 ☐☐☐☐☐
985	A432	3c bright rose carmine	15	15 ☐☐☐☐☐
986	A433	3c bright red violet	15	15 ☐☐☐☐☐

1950

987	A434	3c yellow green	15	15 ☐☐☐☐☐
988	A435	3c bright red violet	15	15 ☐☐☐☐☐
989	A436	3c bright blue	15	15 ☐☐☐☐☐
990	A437	3c deep green	15	15 ☐☐☐☐☐
991	A438	3c light violet	15	15 ☐☐☐☐☐
992	A439	3c bright red violet	15	15 ☐☐☐☐☐
993	A440	3c violet brown	15	15 ☐☐☐☐☐
994	A441	3c violet	15	15 ☐☐☐☐☐
995	A442	3c sepia	15	15 ☐☐☐☐☐
996	A443	3c bright blue	15	15 ☐☐☐☐☐
997	A444	3c yellow orange	15	15 ☐☐☐☐☐

1951

998	A445	3c gray	15	15 ☐☐☐☐☐
999	A446	3c light olive green	15	15 ☐☐☐☐☐
1000	A447	3c blue	15	15 ☐☐☐☐☐
1001	A448	3c blue violet	15	15 ☐☐☐☐☐
1002	A449	3c violet brown	15	15 ☐☐☐☐☐
1003	A450	3c violet	15	15 ☐☐☐☐☐

1952

1004	A451	3c carmine rose	15	15 ☐☐☐☐☐
1005	A452	3c blue green	15	15 ☐☐☐☐☐
1006	A453	3c bright blue	15	15 ☐☐☐☐☐
1007	A454	3c deep blue	15	15 ☐☐☐☐☐
1008	A455	3c deep violet	15	15 ☐☐☐☐☐
1009	A456	3c blue green	15	15 ☐☐☐☐☐
1010	A457	3c bright blue	15	15 ☐☐☐☐☐
1011	A458	3c blue green	15	15 ☐☐☐☐☐
1012	A459	3c violet blue	15	15 ☐☐☐☐☐
1013	A460	3c deep blue	15	15 ☐☐☐☐☐
1014	A461	3c violet	15	15 ☐☐☐☐☐
1015	A462	3c violet	15	15 ☐☐☐☐☐
1016	A463	3c deep blue & carmine	15	15 ☐☐☐☐☐

A437

A438

A439

A440

A441

A442

A443

A444

A445

A446

A447

A448

A449

A450

A451

A452

A453

70

Scott No.	Illus. No.	Description	Unused Value	Used Value	//////
1953					
1017	A464	3c bright blue...................	15	15 □□□□□
1018	A465	3c chocolate....................	15	15 □□□□□
1019	A466	3c green	15	15 □□□□□
1020	A467	3c violet brown	15	15 □□□□□
1021	A468	5c green	15	15 □□□□□
1022	A469	3c rose violet	15	15 □□□□□
1023	A470	3c yellowgreen..................	15	15 □□□□□
1024	A471	3c deep blue....................	15	15 □□□□□
1025	A472	3c violet.......................	15	15 □□□□□
1026	A473	3c blue violet..................	15	15 □□□□□
1027	A474	3c bright red violet	15	15 □□□□□
1028	A475	3c copper brown	15	15 □□□□□
1954					
1029	A476	3c blue	15	15 □□□□□
1954-68					
1030	A477	½c red orange ('55)	15	15 □□□□□
1031	A478	1c dark green	15	15 □□□□□
1031A	A478a	1¼c turquoise ('60)	15	15 □□□□□
1032	A479	1½c brown carmine ('56).........	15	15 □□□□□
1033	A480	2c carmine rose	15	15 □□□□□
1034	A481	2½c gray blue ('59).............	15	15 □□□□□
1035	A482	3c deep violet..................	15	15 □□□□□
1035a.		Booklet pane of 6..............	3.00	*50* □□□□□
1035b.		Tagged ('66)	25	20 □□□□□
1035c.		Vertical pair, imperf...........	*1,500.*	□□□□□
1035d.		Horizontal pair, imperf. between .	800.00	□□□□□
1036	A483	4c red violet	15	15 □□□□□
1036a.		Booklet pane of 6 ('58).........	2.25	*50* □□□□□
1036b.		Tagged ('63)	48	16 □□□□□
1037	A484	4½c blue green ('59).............	15	15 □□□□□
1038	A485	5c deep blue...................	15	15 □□□□□
1039	A486	6c carmine ('55)	25	15 □□□□□
1040	A487	7c rose carmine ('56)...........	20	15 □□□□□
1041	A488	8c dark violet blue & carmine	24	15 □□□□□
1041a.		Double impression of carmine ...	*650.00*	□□□□□
1042	A489	8c dark violet blue & carmine rose ('58)	25	15 □□□□□
1042A	A489a	8c brown ('61)	22	15 □□□□□
1043	A490	9c rose lilac ('56)	28	15 □□□□□
1044	A491	10c rose lake ('56)	22	15 □□□□□
1044b.		Tagged ('66)	1.20	1.00 □□□□□
1044A	A491a	11c carmine & dark violet blue ('61)	30	15 □□□□□
1044c.		Tagged ('67)	2.00	1.60 □□□□□
1045	A492	12c red ('59)...................	32	15 □□□□□
1045a.		Tagged ('68)	45	15 □□□□□

A454

A455

A456

A457

A458

A459

A460

A461

A462

A463

A464

A465

A466

A467

A468

A469

A470

A471

A472

A473

A474

A475

A476

A477

A478

A478a

A479

A480

A481

A482

A483

A484

A485

A486

A487

A488

A489

A489a

A490

A491

73

A491a

A492

A493

A494

A495

A496

A497

A498

A499

A500

A507

A509

A508

A510

A511

A512

A513

A514

Scott No.	Illus. No.	Description	Unused Value	Used Value	//////
1046	A493	15c rose lake ('58)	90	15	☐☐☐☐☐
1046a.		Tagged ('66)	1.10	22	☐☐☐☐☐
1047	A494	20c ultramarine ('56)...........	50	15	☐☐☐☐☐
1048	A495	25c green ('58)	1.50	15	☐☐☐☐☐
1049	A496	30c black ('55)	1.00	15	☐☐☐☐☐
1050	A497	40c brown red ('55)	2.00	15	☐☐☐☐☐
1051	A498	50c bright purple ('55)...........	1.75	15	☐☐☐☐☐
1052	A499	$1 purple ('55)	5.50	15	☐☐☐☐☐
1053	A500	$5 black ('56)	75.00	6.75	☐☐☐☐☐

1954-73 Coil Stamps, Perf. 10

Scott No.	Illus. No.	Description	Unused Value	Used Value	//////
1054	A478	1c dark green	18	15	☐☐☐☐☐
1054b.		Imperf., pair.................	*2,000.*	—	☐☐☐☐☐
1054A	A478a	1¼c turquoise ('60)	15	15	☐☐☐☐☐
1055	A480	2c rose carmine	15	15	☐☐☐☐☐
1055a.		Tagged ('68)	15	15	☐☐☐☐☐
1055b.		Imperf., pair (Bureau precanceled)		*500.00*	☐☐☐☐☐
1055c.		As **a**, imperf. pair............	*600.00*		☐☐☐☐☐
1056	A481	2½c gray blue ('59)............	30	25	☐☐☐☐☐
1057	A482	3c deep violet.................	15	15	☐☐☐☐☐
1057a.		Imperf., pair.................	*1,000.*	—	☐☐☐☐☐
1057b.		Tagged ('66)	50	25	☐☐☐☐☐
1058	A483	4c red violet ('58).............	15	15	☐☐☐☐☐
1058a.		Imperf., pair.................	90.00	70.00	☐☐☐☐☐
1059	A484	4½c blue green ('59)...........	1.50	1.20	☐☐☐☐☐
1059A	A495	25c green ('65)	50	30	☐☐☐☐☐
1059b.		Tagged ('73)	55	20	☐☐☐☐☐
1059c.		Imperf., pair.................	*45.00*		☐☐☐☐☐

1954

Scott No.	Illus. No.	Description	Unused Value	Used Value	//////
1060	A507	3c violet	15	15	☐☐☐☐☐
1061	A508	3c brown orange	15	15	☐☐☐☐☐
1062	A509	3c violet brown	15	15	☐☐☐☐☐
1063	A510	3c violet brown	15	15	☐☐☐☐☐

1955

Scott No.	Illus. No.	Description	Unused Value	Used Value	//////
1064	A511	3c violet brown	15	15	☐☐☐☐☐
1065	A512	3c green	15	15	☐☐☐☐☐
1066	A513	8c deep blue..................	16	15	☐☐☐☐☐
1067	A514	3c purple	15	15	☐☐☐☐☐
1068	A515	3c green	15	15	☐☐☐☐☐
1069	A516	3c blue	15	15	☐☐☐☐☐
1070	A517	3c deep blue..................	15	15	☐☐☐☐☐
1071	A518	3c light brown	15	15	☐☐☐☐☐
1072	A519	3c rose carmine	15	15	☐☐☐☐☐

1956

Scott No.	Illus. No.	Description	Unused Value	Used Value	//////
1073	A520	3c bright carmine..............	15	15	☐☐☐☐☐
1074	A521	3c deep blue..................	15	15	☐☐☐☐☐

A516

A515

A517

A518

A519

A520

A521

Souvenir Sheet.

A523

A522

A524

A525

A526

A527

A528

76

Scott No.	Illus. No.	Description	Unused Value	Used Value	//////
1075	A522	Sheet of two....................	2.25	2.00	☐☐☐☐☐
1075a.		A482 3c deep violet............	90	80	☐☐☐☐☐
1075b.		A488 8c dark violet blue			
		& carmine	1.25	1.00	☐☐☐☐☐
1076	A523	3c deep violet...............	15	15	☐☐☐☐☐
1077	A524	3c rose lake.................	15	15	☐☐☐☐☐
1078	A525	3c brown	15	15	☐☐☐☐☐
1079	A526	3c blue green	15	15	☐☐☐☐☐
1080	A527	3c dark blue green	15	15	☐☐☐☐☐
1081	A528	3c black brown...............	15	15	☐☐☐☐☐
1082	A529	3c deep blue.................	15	15	☐☐☐☐☐
1083	A530	3c black, orange..............	15	15	☐☐☐☐☐
1084	A531	3c violet	15	15	☐☐☐☐☐
1085	A532	3c dark blue	15	15	☐☐☐☐☐

1957

Scott No.	Illus. No.	Description	Unused Value	Used Value	//////
1086	A533	3c rose red	15	15	☐☐☐☐☐
1087	A534	3c red lilac	15	15	☐☐☐☐☐
1088	A535	3c dark blue	15	15	☐☐☐☐☐
1089	A536	3c red lilac	15	15	☐☐☐☐☐
1090	A537	3c bright ultramarine.........	15	15	☐☐☐☐☐
1091	A538	3c blue green	15	15	☐☐☐☐☐
1092	A539	3c dark blue	15	15	☐☐☐☐☐
1093	A540	3c rose lake..................	15	15	☐☐☐☐☐
1094	A541	4c dark blue & deep carmine	15	15	☐☐☐☐☐
1095	A542	3c deep violet................	15	15	☐☐☐☐☐
1096	A543	8c carmine, ultramarine & ocher	16	15	☐☐☐☐☐
1097	A544	3c rose lake..................	15	15	☐☐☐☐☐
1098	A545	3c blue, ocher & green........	15	15	☐☐☐☐☐
1099	A546	3c black	15	15	☐☐☐☐☐

1958

Scott No.	Illus. No.	Description	Unused Value	Used Value	//////
1100	A547	3c green	15	15	☐☐☐☐☐
1104	A551	3c deep claret................	15	15	☐☐☐☐☐
1105	A552	3c purple	15	15	☐☐☐☐☐
1106	A553	3c green	15	15	☐☐☐☐☐
1107	A554	3c black & red orange	15	15	☐☐☐☐☐
1108	A555	3c light green	15	15	☐☐☐☐☐
1109	A556	3c bright grnsh blue..........	15	15	☐☐☐☐☐
1110	A557	4c olive bister...............	15	15	☐☐☐☐☐
1111	A557	8c carmine, ultramarine & ocher ...	16	15	☐☐☐☐☐
1112	A558	4c reddish purple.............	15	15	☐☐☐☐☐

1958-59

Scott No.	Illus. No.	Description	Unused Value	Used Value	//////
1113	A559	1c green ('59)	15	15	☐☐☐☐☐
1114	A560	3c purple ('59)	15	15	☐☐☐☐☐
1115	A561	4c sepia.....................	15	15	☐☐☐☐☐
1116	A562	4c dark blue ('59)............	15	15	☐☐☐☐☐

A529

A530

A531

A532

A534

A535

A537

A538

A533

A536

A539

A540

A541

A542

A543

A544

A545

A546

A547

A551

A552

A553

A554

A555

A556

A557

A558

A561

A561

A559

A560

A562

A564

A563

79

A565

A566

A568

A567

A569

A570

A572

A571

A573

A574

A578

A575

A577

A576

A580

A579

A581

Scott No.	Illus. No.	Description	Unused Value	Used Value	//////
1958					
1117	A563	4c green	15	15 ☐☐☐☐☐
1118	A563	8c carmine, ultramarine & ocher ...	16	15 ☐☐☐☐☐
1119	A564	4c black	15	15 ☐☐☐☐☐
1120	A565	4ccrimson rose...................	15	15 ☐☐☐☐☐
1121	A566	4c dark carmine rose.............	15	15 ☐☐☐☐☐
1122	A567	4c green, yellow& brown..........	15	15 ☐☐☐☐☐
1123	A568	4c blue	15	15 ☐☐☐☐☐
1959					
1124	A569	4c blue green	15	15 ☐☐☐☐☐
1125	A570	4c blue	15	15 ☐☐☐☐☐
1125a.		Horizontal pair, imperf. between .	*1,250.*	☐☐☐☐☐
1126	A570	8c carmine, ultramarine & ocher ...	16	15 ☐☐☐☐☐
1127	A571	4c blue	15	15 ☐☐☐☐☐
1128	A572	4c bright greenish blue	15	15 ☐☐☐☐☐
1129	A573	8c rose lake.....................	16	15 ☐☐☐☐☐
1130	A574	4c black	15	15 ☐☐☐☐☐
1131	A575	4c red & dark blue...............	15	15 ☐☐☐☐☐
1132	A576	4c ocher, dark blue & deep carmine .	15	15 ☐☐☐☐☐
1133	A577	4c blue, green & ocher.............	15	15 ☐☐☐☐☐
1134	A578	4c brown	15	15 ☐☐☐☐☐
1135	A579	4c green	15	15 ☐☐☐☐☐
1136	A580	4c gray	15	15 ☐☐☐☐☐
1137	A580	8c carmine, ultramarine & ocher ...	16	15 ☐☐☐☐☐
1138	A581	4c rose lake.....................	15	15 ☐☐☐☐☐
1138a.		Vertical pair, imperf. between....	*500.00*	☐☐☐☐☐
1138b.		Vertical pair, imperf. horizontally	*400.00*	☐☐☐☐☐
1960-61					
1139	A582	4c dark violet blue & carmine	15	15 ☐☐☐☐☐
1140	A583	4c olive bister & green............	15	15 ☐☐☐☐☐
1141	A584	4c gray & vermilion..............	15	15 ☐☐☐☐☐
1142	A585	4c carmine & dark blue...........	15	15 ☐☐☐☐☐
1143	A586	4c magenta & green..............	15	15 ☐☐☐☐☐
1144	A587	4c green & brown ('61)	15	15 ☐☐☐☐☐
1960					
1145	A588	4c red, dark blue & dark bister.....	15	15 ☐☐☐☐☐
1146	A589	4c dull blue.....................	15	15 ☐☐☐☐☐
1147	A590	4c blue	15	15 ☐☐☐☐☐
1147a.		Vertical pair, imperf. between....	*2,250.*	☐☐☐☐☐
1148	A590	8c carmine, ultramarine & ocher ...	16	15 ☐☐☐☐☐
1148a.		Horizontal pair, imperf. between .	—	☐☐☐☐☐
1149	A591	4c gray black	15	15 ☐☐☐☐☐
1150	A592	4c dark blue, brown orange & green.	15	15 ☐☐☐☐☐
1151	A593	4c blue	15	15 ☐☐☐☐☐
1151a.		Vertical pair, imperf. between....	*150.00*	☐☐☐☐☐

A582

A583

A584

A589

A585

A586

A587

A588

A590

A591

A592

A593

A594

A595

A596

A597

82

Scott No.	Illus. No.	Description	Unused Value	Used Value	//////
1152	A594	4c deep violet....................	15	15 ☐☐☐☐☐
1153	A595	4c dark blue & red..............	15	15 ☐☐☐☐☐
1154	A596	4c sepia........................	15	15 ☐☐☐☐☐
1155	A597	4c dark blue	15	15 ☐☐☐☐☐
1156	A598	4c green	15	15 ☐☐☐☐☐
1157	A599	4c green & rose red	15	15 ☐☐☐☐☐
1158	A600	4c blue & pink	15	15 ☐☐☐☐☐
1159	A601	4c blue	15	15 ☐☐☐☐☐
1160	A601	8c carmine, ultramarine & ocher ...	16	15 ☐☐☐☐☐
1161	A602	4c dull violet	15	15 ☐☐☐☐☐
1162	A603	4c dark blue....................	15	15 ☐☐☐☐☐
1163	A604	4c indigo, slate & rose red........	15	15 ☐☐☐☐☐
1164	A605	4c dark blue & carmine...........	15	15 ☐☐☐☐☐
1165	A606	4c blue	15	15 ☐☐☐☐☐
1166	A606	8c carmine, ultramarine & ocher ...	16	15 ☐☐☐☐☐
1167	A607	4c dark blue & bright red	15	15 ☐☐☐☐☐
1168	A608	4c green	15	15 ☐☐☐☐☐
1169	A608	8c carmine, ultramarine & ocher ...	16	15 ☐☐☐☐☐
1170	A609	4c dull violet	15	15 ☐☐☐☐☐
1171	A610	4c deep claret	15	15 ☐☐☐☐☐
1172	A611	4c dull violet	15	15 ☐☐☐☐☐
1173	A612	4c deep violet...................	18	15 ☐☐☐☐☐

1961

1174	A613	4c red orange	15	15 ☐☐☐☐☐
1175	A613	8c carmine, ultramarine & ocher ...	16	15 ☐☐☐☐☐
1176	A614	4c blue, slate & brown orange......	15	15 ☐☐☐☐☐
1177	A615	4c dull violet	15	15 ☐☐☐☐☐

1961-65

1178	A616	4c light green	16	15 ☐☐☐☐☐
1179	A617	4c black, *peach blossom* ('62)	15	15 ☐☐☐☐☐
1180	A618	5c gray & blue ('63)	15	15 ☐☐☐☐☐
1181	A619	5c dark red & black ('64)..........	15	15 ☐☐☐☐☐
1182	A620	5c Prussian blue & black ('65)	18	15 ☐☐☐☐☐
1182a.		Horizontal pair, imperf. vertically	*4,500.*	☐☐☐☐☐

1961

1183	A621	4c brown, dark red & green, *yellow* .	15	15 ☐☐☐☐☐
1184	A622	4c blue green	15	15 ☐☐☐☐☐
1185	A623	4c blue	15	15 ☐☐☐☐☐
1186	A624	4c ultramarine, *grayish*	15	15 ☐☐☐☐☐
1187	A625	4c multicolored	15	15 ☐☐☐☐☐
1188	A626	4c blue	15	15 ☐☐☐☐☐
1189	A627	4c brown	15	15 ☐☐☐☐☐
1190	A628	4c blue, green, orange & black	15	15 ☐☐☐☐☐

A598

A599

A600

A604

A608

A603

A601

A613

A605

A606

A602

A609

A610

A611

A612

A607

A614

A616

A615

A617

A618

A619

A621

A622

A620

A623

A624

A625

A626

A627

A628

A629

A631

A630

A633

A632

A634

A636

A637

A638

A635

A640

A639

A642

A645

A646

A650

A663

A644

A643

A641

A662

A664

A665

Scott No.	Illus. No.	Description	Unused Value	Used Value	//////
1962					
1191	A629	4c light blue, maroon & bister	15	15 ☐☐☐☐☐
1192	A630	4c carmine, violet blue & green	15	15 ☐☐☐☐☐
1193	A631	4c dark blue & yellow	15	15 ☐☐☐☐☐
1194	A632	4c blue & bister	15	15 ☐☐☐☐☐
1195	A633	4c black, *buff*	15	15 ☐☐☐☐☐
1196	A634	4c red & dark blue...............	15	15 ☐☐☐☐☐
1197	A635	4c blue, dark slate green & red	15	15 ☐☐☐☐☐
1198	A636	4c slate	15	15 ☐☐☐☐☐
1199	A637	4c rose red	15	15 ☐☐☐☐☐
1200	A638	4c violet	15	15 ☐☐☐☐☐
1201	A639	4c black, *yellow bister*	15	15 ☐☐☐☐☐
1202	A640	4c dark blue & red brown	15	15 ☐☐☐☐☐
1203	A641	4c black, brown & yellow	15	15 ☐☐☐☐☐
1204	A641	4c black, brown & yellow (yellow inverted)	15	15 ☐☐☐☐☐
1205	A642	4c green & red	15	15 ☐☐☐☐☐
1206	A643	4c blue green & black	15	15 ☐☐☐☐☐
1207	A644	4c *Breezing Up*.................	15	15 ☐☐☐☐☐
1207a.		Horizontal pair, imperf. between .	—	☐☐☐☐☐
1963-66					
1208	A645	5c blue & red	15	15 ☐☐☐☐☐
1208a.		Tagged ('66)	16	15 ☐☐☐☐☐
1208b.		Horizontal pair, imperf. between .	*1,250.*	☐☐☐☐☐
1962-66					
1209	A646	1c green ('63)	15	15 ☐☐☐☐☐
1209a.		Tagged ('66)	15	15 ☐☐☐☐☐
1213	A650	5c dark blue gray	15	15 ☐☐☐☐☐
1213a.		Booklet pane 5 + label..........	2.25	*1.50* ☐☐☐☐☐
1213b.		Tagged ('63)	50	22 ☐☐☐☐☐
1213c.		As **a**, tagged ('63)	3.00	*1.50* ☐☐☐☐☐
Coil Stamps, Perf. 10 vertically					
1225	A646	1c green ('63)	15	15 ☐☐☐☐☐
1225a.		Tagged ('66)	15	15 ☐☐☐☐☐
1229	A650	5c dark blue gray	1.00	15 ☐☐☐☐☐
1229a.		Tagged ('63)	1.25	15 ☐☐☐☐☐
1229b.		Imperf., pair..................	*375.00*	☐☐☐☐☐
1963					
1230	A662	5c dark carmine & brown	15	15 ☐☐☐☐☐
1231	A663	5c green, buff & red.............	15	15 ☐☐☐☐☐
1232	A664	5c green, red & black............	15	15 ☐☐☐☐☐
1233	A665	5c dark blue, black & red	15	15 ☐☐☐☐☐
1234	A666	5c ultramarine & green	15	15 ☐☐☐☐☐
1235	A667	5c blue green	15	15 ☐☐☐☐☐

A666

A667

A668

A669

A671

A675

A670

A676

A680

A672

A678

A679

A673

A677

A674

A681

A682

Scott No.	Illus. No.	Description	Unused Value	Used Value	//////
1236	A668	5c bright purple	15	15 □□□□□
1237	A669	5c Prussian blue & black.	15	15 □□□□□
1238	A670	5c gray, dark blue & red	15	15 □□□□□
1239	A671	5c bluish black & red.	15	15 □□□□□
1240	A672	5c dark blue, bluish black & red. . . .	15	15 □□□□□
1240a.		Tagged	65	25 □□□□□
1241	A673	5c dark blue & multi	15	15 □□□□□

1964

Scott No.	Illus. No.	Description	Unused Value	Used Value	//////
1242	A674	5c black	15	15 □□□□□
1243	A675	5c indigo, red brown & olive	15	15 □□□□□
1244	A676	5c blue green	15	15 □□□□□
1245	A677	5c brown, green, yellow green & olive.	15	15 □□□□□
1246	A678	5c blue gray	15	15 □□□□□
1247	A679	5c bright ultramarine.	15	15 □□□□□
1248	A680	5c red, yellow & blue.	15	15 □□□□□
1249	A681	5c dark blue & red.	15	15 □□□□□
1250	A682	5c black brown, *tan*.	15	15 □□□□□
1251	A683	5c green	15	15 □□□□□
1252	A684	5c red, black & blue.	15	15 □□□□□
1252a.		Blue omitted.	*1,250.*	□□□□□
1253	A685	5c Farm scene sampler	15	15 □□□□□
1254	A686	5c green, carmine & black.	30	15 □□□□□
1254a.		Tagged	75	25 □□□□□
1255	A687	5c carmine, green & black.	30	15 □□□□□
1255a.		Tagged	75	25 □□□□□
1256	A688	5c carmine, green & black.	30	15 □□□□□
1256a.		Tagged	75	25 □□□□□
1257	A689	5c black, green & carmine.	30	15 □□□□□
1257a.		Tagged	75	25 □□□□□
1257b.		Block of 4, #1254-1257	1.25	1.00 □□□□□
1257c.		Block of 4, #1254a-1257a	4.25	2.00 □□□□□
1258	A690	5c blue green	15	15 □□□□□
1259	A691	5c ultramarine, black & dull red. . . .	15	15 □□□□□
1260	A692	5c red lilac	15	15 □□□□□

1965

Scott No.	Illus. No.	Description	Unused Value	Used Value	//////
1261	A693	5c deep carmine, violet blue & gray .	15	15 □□□□□
1262	A694	5c maroon & black	15	15 □□□□□
1263	A695	5c black, purple & red orange.	15	15 □□□□□
1264	A696	5c black	15	15 □□□□□
1265	A697	5c black, yellow ocher & red lilac. . .	15	15 □□□□□
1266	A698	5c dull blue & black.	15	15 □□□□□
1267	A699	5c red, black & dark blue	15	15 □□□□□
1268	A700	5c maroon, *tan*.	15	15 □□□□□
1269	A701	5c rose red	15	15 □□□□□
1270	A702	5c black & blue	15	15 □□□□□

A684

A683

A685

A686

A687

A688

A689

A690

A691

A692

A696

A694

A695

A693

A697

A698

Scott No.	Illus. No.	Description	Unused Value	Used Value	//////
1271	A703	5c red, yellow & black............	15	15	☐☐☐☐☐
1271a.		Yellow omitted	700.00		☐☐☐☐☐
1272	A704	5c emerald, black & red	15	15	☐☐☐☐☐
1273	A705	5c black, brown & olive	15	15	☐☐☐☐☐
1274	A706	11c black, carmine & bister	32	16	☐☐☐☐☐
1275	A707	5c pale blue, black, carmine & violet blue	15	15	☐☐☐☐☐
1276	A708	5c carmine, dark olive green & bister	15	15	☐☐☐☐☐
1276a.		Tagged	75	15	☐☐☐☐☐

1965-78

Scott No.	Illus. No.	Description	Unused Value	Used Value	//////
1278	A710	1c green, tagged	15	15	☐☐☐☐☐
1278a.		Booklet pane of 8............	1.00	25	☐☐☐☐☐
1278b.		Booklet pane of 4 + 2 labels	75	20	☐☐☐☐☐
1278c.		Untagged (Bureau precanceled) ..		15	☐☐☐☐☐
1279	A711	1¼c light green..................	15	15	☐☐☐☐☐
1280	A712	2c dark blue gray, tagged.........	15	15	☐☐☐☐☐
1280a.		Booklet pane of 5 + label........	1.20	40	☐☐☐☐☐
1280b.		Untagged (Bureau precanceled) ..		15	☐☐☐☐☐
1280c.		Booklet pane of 6............	1.00	35	☐☐☐☐☐
1281	A713	3c violet, tagged................	15	15	☐☐☐☐☐
1281a.		Untagged (Bureau precanceled) ..		15	☐☐☐☐☐
1282	A714	4c black	15	15	☐☐☐☐☐
1282a.		Tagged	15	15	☐☐☐☐☐
1283	A715	5c blue	15	15	☐☐☐☐☐
1283a.		Tagged	15	15	☐☐☐☐☐
1283B	A715a	5c blue, tagged.................	15	15	☐☐☐☐☐
1283d.		Untagged (Bureau precanceled) ..		15	☐☐☐☐☐
1284	A716	6c gray brown	15	15	☐☐☐☐☐
1284a.		Tagged	15	15	☐☐☐☐☐
1284b.		Booklet pane of 8.............	1.50	50	☐☐☐☐☐
1284c.		Booklet pane of 5 + label........	1.25	50	☐☐☐☐☐
1285	A717	8c violet	20	15	☐☐☐☐☐
1285a.		Tagged	16	15	☐☐☐☐☐
1286	A718	10c lilac, tagged	20	15	☐☐☐☐☐
1286b.		Untagged (Bureau precanceled) ..		20	☐☐☐☐☐
1286A	A718a	12c black, tagged	28	15	☐☐☐☐☐
1286c.		Untagged (Bureau precanceled) ..		25	☐☐☐☐☐
1287	A719	13c brown, tagged	24	15	☐☐☐☐☐
1287a.		Untagged (Bureau precanceled) ..		25	☐☐☐☐☐
1288	A720	15c rose claret, tagged	30	15	☐☐☐☐☐
1288a.		Untagged (Bureau precanceled) ..		30	☐☐☐☐☐
1288d.		Type II	30	15	☐☐☐☐☐
1288B	A720	15c dark rose claret (from booklet pane)	30	15	☐☐☐☐☐
1288c.		Booklet pane of 8.............	2.40	1.25	☐☐☐☐☐
1288e.		As c vert. imperf. between.......	—		☐☐☐☐☐

A700

A706

A701

A703

A702

A705

A704

A708

A707

A699

A710

A711

A712

A713

A714

A715

A715a
Redrawn

A716

A717

92

Scott No.	Illus. No.	Description	Unused Value	Used Value	//////
1289	A721	20c deep olive	42	15	☐☐☐☐☐
1289a.		Tagged	40	15	☐☐☐☐☐
1290	A722	25c rose lake..............	55	15	☐☐☐☐☐
1290a.		Tagged	50	15	☐☐☐☐☐
1290b.		25c maroon	—		☐☐☐☐☐
1291	A723	30c red lilac	65	15	☐☐☐☐☐
1291a.		Tagged	60	15	☐☐☐☐☐
1292	A724	40c blue black	85	15	☐☐☐☐☐
1292a.		Tagged	80	15	☐☐☐☐☐
1293	A725	50c rose magenta.............	1.00	15	☐☐☐☐☐
1293a.		Tagged	1.00	15	☐☐☐☐☐
1294	A726	$1 dull purple..............	2.50	15	☐☐☐☐☐
1294a.		Tagged	2.00	15	☐☐☐☐☐
1295	A727	$5 gray black	12.50	2.00	☐☐☐☐☐
1295a.		Tagged	9.00	2.00	☐☐☐☐☐

1966-81 Coil stamps, Perf. 10 horizontally

1297	A713	3c violet	15	15	☐☐☐☐☐
1297a.		Imperf., pair................	*30.00*		☐☐☐☐☐
1297b.		Untagged (Bureau precanceled) ..		15	☐☐☐☐☐
1297c.		As **b**, imperf. pair.............	10.00		☐☐☐☐☐
1298	A716	6c gray brown	15	15	☐☐☐☐☐
1298a.		Imperf., pair.................	*2,250.*		☐☐☐☐☐

Perf. 10 Vertically

1299	A710	1c green	15	15	☐☐☐☐☐
1299a.		Untagged (Bureau precanceled) ..		15	☐☐☐☐☐
1299b.		Imperf., pair.................	40.00	—	☐☐☐☐☐
1303	A714	4c black	15	15	☐☐☐☐☐
1303a.		Untagged (Bureau precanceled) ..		15	☐☐☐☐☐
1303b.		Imperf., pair.................	*500.00*		☐☐☐☐☐
1304	A715	5c blue	15	15	☐☐☐☐☐
1304a.		Untagged (Bureau precanceled) ..		15	☐☐☐☐☐
1304b.		Imperf., pair.................	*200.00*		☐☐☐☐☐
1304e.		As **a**, imperf. pair.............	300.00		☐☐☐☐☐
1304C	A715a	5c blue	15	15	☐☐☐☐☐
1304d.		Imperf., pair.................	—		☐☐☐☐☐
1305	A727a	6c gray brown	15	15	☐☐☐☐☐
1305a.		Imperf., pair.................	*75.00*		☐☐☐☐☐
1305b.		Untagged (Bureau precanceled) ..		20	☐☐☐☐☐
1305E	A720	15c rose claret	25	15	☐☐☐☐☐
1305f.		Untagged (Bureau precanceled) ..		30	☐☐☐☐☐
1305g.		Imperf., pair.................	*30.00*		☐☐☐☐☐
1305h.		Pair, imperf. between..........	*200.00*		☐☐☐☐☐
1305i.		Type II	35	15	☐☐☐☐☐
1305j.		Imperf., pair, type II	*100.00*		☐☐☐☐☐
1305C	A726	$1 dull purple..............	1.50	20	☐☐☐☐☐
1305d.		Imperf., pair.................	*2,000.*		☐☐☐☐☐

A718

A718a

A719

A720

A721

A723

A722

A724

A725

A726

A727

A727a

A730

A732

A731

A728

A729

A734

A733

A735

94

A737

A736

A739

A738

A741

A743

A745

A747

A744

A742

A746

A749

A748

A751

A750

A752

A753 **A754**

A755

A757

Finland
Independence 1917-67

United States 5c

A756

A758

A759

A760

SUPPORT OUR YOUTH

A764

ILLINOIS 1818 1968

6¢ U.S. POSTAGE

A761

AIRLIFT

FOR OUR SERVICEMEN

A763

HEMISFAIR '68

A762

6¢ LAW AND ORDER

UNITED STATES POSTAGE

A765

AN APPEAL TO HEAVEN

WASHINGTON'S CRUISERS FLAG 1775

A769

REGISTER & VOTE

A766

Scott No.	Illus. No.	Description	Unused Value	Used Value	//////
1966					
1306	A728	5c black, crimson & dark blue	15	15	☐☐☐☐☐
1307	A729	5c orange brown & black	15	15	☐☐☐☐☐
1308	A730	5c yellow, ocher & violet blue.	15	15	☐☐☐☐☐
1309	A731	5c Clown	15	15	☐☐☐☐☐
1310	A732	5c Stamped cover	15	15	☐☐☐☐☐
1311	A733	5c souvenir sheet.	15	15	☐☐☐☐☐
1312	A734	5c carmine, dark & light blue	15	15	☐☐☐☐☐
1313	A735	5c red	15	15	☐☐☐☐☐
1314	A736	5c yellow, black & green	15	15	☐☐☐☐☐
1314a.		Tagged	30	15	☐☐☐☐☐
1315	A737	5c black, bister, red & ultramarine. .	15	15	☐☐☐☐☐
1315a.		Tagged	30	15	☐☐☐☐☐
1315b.		Black & bister (engraved) omitted	—		☐☐☐☐☐
1316	A738	5c black, pink & blue.	15	15	☐☐☐☐☐
1316a.		Tagged	30	15	☐☐☐☐☐
1317	A739	5c green, red & black.	15	15	☐☐☐☐☐
1317a.		Tagged	30	15	☐☐☐☐☐
1318	A740	5c emerald, pink & black	15	15	☐☐☐☐☐
1318a.		Tagged	30	15	☐☐☐☐☐
1319	A741	5c vermilion, yellow, blue & green. .	15	15	☐☐☐☐☐
1319a.		Tagged	30	15	☐☐☐☐☐
1320	A742	5c red, dark blue, light blue & black.	15	15	☐☐☐☐☐
1320a.		Tagged	30	15	☐☐☐☐☐
1320b.		Red, dark blue & black omitted . .	*3,500.*		☐☐☐☐☐
1320c.		Dark blue (engraved) omitted. . . .	*4,000.*		☐☐☐☐☐
1321	A743	5c Madonna and Child	15	15	☐☐☐☐☐
1321a.		Tagged	30	15	☐☐☐☐☐
1322	A744	5c *The Boating Party.*	15	15	☐☐☐☐☐
1322a.		Tagged	25	15	☐☐☐☐☐
1967					
1323	A745	5c Grange poster	15	15	☐☐☐☐☐
1324	A746	5c Canadian Landscape.	15	15	☐☐☐☐☐
1325	A747	5c Stern of early canal boat	15	15	☐☐☐☐☐
1326	A748	5c blue, red & black	15	15	☐☐☐☐☐
1327	A749	5c red, black & green.	15	15	☐☐☐☐☐
1328	A750	5c dark red brown, lemon & yellow .	15	15	☐☐☐☐☐
1329	A751	5c red, blue, black & carmine	15	15	☐☐☐☐☐
1330	A752	5c green, black & yellow	15	15	☐☐☐☐☐
1330a.		Vertical pair, imperf. between. . . .	—		☐☐☐☐☐
1330b.		Green (engraved) omitted.	—		☐☐☐☐☐
1330c.		Black & green (engraved) omitted	—		☐☐☐☐☐
1330d.		Yellow & green (litho.) omitted . .	—		☐☐☐☐☐
1331	A753	5c Space-walking astronaut.	65	15	☐☐☐☐☐
1331a.		Pair, #1331-1332	1.40	1.25	☐☐☐☐☐
1332	A754	5c Gemini 4 capsule, Earth.	65	15	☐☐☐☐☐

6¢ U.S. POSTAGE LIBERTY
FORT MOULTRIE FLAG 1776
A767

6¢ U.S. POSTAGE
U.S. FLAG 1795-1818 (FT. McHENRY FLAG)
A768

6¢ U.S. POSTAGE
76
BENNINGTON FLAG 1777
A770

6¢ U.S. POSTAGE
HOPE
RHODE ISLAND FLAG 1776
A771

6¢ U.S. POSTAGE
FIRST STARS AND STRIPES 1777
A772

6¢ U.S. POSTAGE
BUNKER HILL FLAG 1775
A773

6¢ U.S. POSTAGE
GRAND UNION FLAG 1776
A774

6¢ U.S. POSTAGE
PHILADELPHIA LIGHT HORSE FLAG 1775
A775

6¢ U.S. POSTAGE
DONT TREAD ON ME
FIRST NAVY JACK 1775
A776

WALT DISNEY UNITED STATES 6¢
A777

Marquette 6¢ UNITED STATES
A778

leif erikson U.S. postage 6¢
A781

UNITED STATES 6¢ POSTAGE DANIEL BOONE 1777
A779

CHRISTMAS 6¢ UNITED STATES
A785

UNITED STATES 6¢ John Trumbull AMERICAN ARTIST BATTLE OF BUNKER'S HILL
A783

UNITED STATES POSTAGE 6¢ ARKANSAS RIVER NAVIGATION
A780

CHEROKEE STRIP UNITED STATES POSTAGE 6¢
A782

Chief Joseph · National Portrait Gallery United States Postage 6¢
A786

6¢ WATERFOWL CONSERVATION UNITED STATES
A784

98

Scott No.	Illus. No.	Description	Unused Value	Used Value	//////
1333	A755	5c dark blue, light blue & black	15	15	☐☐☐☐☐
1334	A756	5c blue	15	15	☐☐☐☐☐
1335	A757	5c gold & multicolored	15	15	☐☐☐☐☐
1336	A758	5c Madonna & Child.............	15	15	☐☐☐☐☐
1337	A759	5c bright greenish blue, green & red brown	15	15	☐☐☐☐☐

1968-69
1338	A760	6c dark blue, red & green	15	15	☐☐☐☐☐
1338k.		Vertical pair, imperf. between....	400.00		☐☐☐☐☐

Coil Stamps, Perf. 10 vertically
1338A	A760	6c dark blue, red & green ('69)	15	15	☐☐☐☐☐
1338b.		Imperf., pair.................	500.00		☐☐☐☐☐

1970-71
1338D	A760	6c dark blue, red & green ('70)	15	15	☐☐☐☐☐
1338e.		Horizontal pair, imperf. between .	150.00		☐☐☐☐☐
1338F	A760	8c Flag & White House ('71).......	16	15	☐☐☐☐☐
1338i.		Vertical pair, imperf. between....	65.00		☐☐☐☐☐
1338j.		Horizontal pair, imperf. between .	50.00		☐☐☐☐☐

1971 Coil Stamp, Perf. 10 vertically
1338G	A760	8c Flag & White House............	18	15	☐☐☐☐☐
1338h.		Imperf., pair..................	55.00		☐☐☐☐☐

1968
1339	A761	6c Illinois statehood	15	15	☐☐☐☐☐
1340	A762	6c blue, rose red & white..........	15	15	☐☐☐☐☐
1340a.		White omitted	1,250.		☐☐☐☐☐
1341	A763	$1 sepia, dark blue, ocher & brown red	2.50	1.25	☐☐☐☐☐
1342	A764	6c ultramarine & orange red.......	15	15	☐☐☐☐☐
1343	A765	6c chalky blue, black & red........	15	15	☐☐☐☐☐
1344	A766	6c black, yellow & orange	15	15	☐☐☐☐☐
1345	A767	6c dark blue	50	25	☐☐☐☐☐
1346	A768	6c dark blue & red..............	35	25	☐☐☐☐☐
1347	A769	6c dark blue & olive green	30	25	☐☐☐☐☐
1348	A770	6c dark blue & red..............	30	25	☐☐☐☐☐
1349	A771	6c dark blue, yellow & red	30	25	☐☐☐☐☐
1350	A772	6c dark blue & red..............	30	25	☐☐☐☐☐
1351	A773	6c dark blue, olive green & red.....	30	25	☐☐☐☐☐
1352	A774	6c dark blue & red..............	30	25	☐☐☐☐☐
1353	A775	6c dark blue, yellow & red	30	25	☐☐☐☐☐
1354	A776	6c dark blue, red & yellow	30	25	☐☐☐☐☐
1354a.		Strip of 10, Nos. 1345-1354	3.25	3.00	☐☐☐☐☐
1355	A777	6c Walt Disney, children..........	16	15	☐☐☐☐☐
1355a.		Ocher (Walt Disney, 6c, etc.) omitted	850.00	–	☐☐☐☐☐

PLANT for more BEAUTIFUL CITIES

A787

PLANT for more BEAUTIFUL PARKS

A788

PLANT for more BEAUTIFUL HIGHWAYS

A789

PLANT for more BEAUTIFUL STREETS

A790

CALIFORNIA 1769 1969
United States 6 cents

A795

The American Legion
50 years
Veterans as Citizens
U.S. POSTAGE 6 CENTS

A791

Grandma Moses
6c U.S. Postage

A792

In the beginning God...
APOLLO 8
SIX CENTS · UNITED STATES

A793

FIRST EXPEDITION
6c U.S. POSTAGE

A796

Father of the Blues
6c UNITED STATES

A794

ALABAMA 1819 1969
UNITED STATES

A797

Pseudotsuga menziesii
XIth INTERNATIONAL
6¢ UNITED STATES
BOTANICAL

A798

6¢ UNITED STATES
Cypripedium reginae

A799

Pinus
6¢ UNITED STATES

A800

6¢ UNITED STATES
Franklinia alatamaha

A801

Scott No.	Illus. No.	Description	Unused Value	Used Value	//////
1355b.		Vertical pair, imperf. horizontally	725.00		☐☐☐☐☐
1355c.		Imperf., pair....................	800.00		☐☐☐☐☐
1355d.		Black omitted.................	1,750.		☐☐☐☐☐
1355e.		Horizontal pair, imperf. between .	3,250.		☐☐☐☐☐
1355f.		Blue omitted..................	2,000.		☐☐☐☐☐
1356	A778	6c black, apple green & orange brown	15	15	☐☐☐☐☐
1357	A779	6c yellow, deep yellow, maroon & black	15	15	☐☐☐☐☐
1358	A780	6c bright blue, dark blue & black ...	15	15	☐☐☐☐☐
1359	A781	6c light gray brown & black brown .	15	15	☐☐☐☐☐
1360	A782	6c brown	15	15	☐☐☐☐☐
1361	A783	6c Detail from *The Battle of Bunker Hill*	15	15	☐☐☐☐☐
1362	A784	6c black & multicolored	15	15	☐☐☐☐☐
1362a.		Vertical pair, imperf. between....	600.00		☐☐☐☐☐
1362b.		Red & dark blue omitted	1,700.		☐☐☐☐☐
1363	A785	6c Gabriel......................	15	15	☐☐☐☐☐
1363a.		Untagged	15	15	☐☐☐☐☐
1363b.		Imperf., pair, tagged............	275.00		☐☐☐☐☐
1363c.		Light yellow omitted	150.00		☐☐☐☐☐
1363d.		Imperf., pair, untagged	400.00		☐☐☐☐☐
1364	A786	6c black & multicolored	16	15	☐☐☐☐☐

1969

Scott No.	Illus. No.	Description	Unused Value	Used Value	//////
1365	A787	6c Capitol, azaleas, tulips	40	15	☐☐☐☐☐
1366	A788	6c Washington Monument, etc.	40	15	☐☐☐☐☐
1367	A789	6c Poppies & lupines along road ...	40	15	☐☐☐☐☐
1368	A790	6c Blooming crabapples along street	40	15	☐☐☐☐☐
1368a.		Block of 4, #1365-1368	1.70	1.25	☐☐☐☐☐
1369	A791	6c red, blue & black.............	15	15	☐☐☐☐☐
1370	A792	6c Grandma Moses	15	15	☐☐☐☐☐
1370a.		Horizontal pair, imperf. between .	275.00		☐☐☐☐☐
1370b.		Black and Prussian blue omitted .	950.00		☐☐☐☐☐
1371	A793	6c black, blue & ocher...........	15	15	☐☐☐☐☐
1371a.		Red, dark blue & black omitted ..	—		☐☐☐☐☐
1372	A794	6c W.C. Handy	15	15	☐☐☐☐☐
1373	A795	6c California settlement	15	15	☐☐☐☐☐
1374	A796	6c John Wesley Powell	15	15	☐☐☐☐☐
1375	A797	6c Alabama statehood............	15	15	☐☐☐☐☐
1376	A798	6c Douglas fir.................	75	15	☐☐☐☐☐
1377	A799	6c Lady's slipper	75	15	☐☐☐☐☐
1378	A800	6c Ocotillo	75	15	☐☐☐☐☐
1379	A801	6c Franklinia	75	15	☐☐☐☐☐
1379a.		Block of 4, #1376-1379	3.00	3.00	☐☐☐☐☐
1380	A802	6c green	15	15	☐☐☐☐☐
1381	A803	6c yellow, red, black & green	45	15	☐☐☐☐☐

A802

A803

A807

A806

A808

A805

A804

A809

A810

A811

A812

A813

A814

Scott No.	Illus. No.	Description	Unused Value	Used Value	//////
1381a.		Black (1869-1969, United States, 6c, Professional Baseball) omitted	*1,350.*		☐☐☐☐☐
1382	A804	6c red & green	15	15	☐☐☐☐☐
1383	A805	6c blue, black & red	15	15	☐☐☐☐☐
1384	A806	6c dark green & multicolored	15	15	☐☐☐☐☐
1384b.		Imperf., pair	*1,250.*		☐☐☐☐☐
1384c.		Light green omitted	*30.00*		☐☐☐☐☐
1384d.		Light green, red & yellow omitted	*1,200.*	—	☐☐☐☐☐
1384e.		Yellow omitted	—		☐☐☐☐☐
1385	A807	6c Hope for crippled children	15	15	☐☐☐☐☐
1386	A808	6c William M. Harnett	15	15	☐☐☐☐☐

1970

Scott No.	Illus. No.	Description	Unused Value	Used Value	//////
1387	A809	6c American bald eagle	15	15	☐☐☐☐☐
1388	A810	6c African elephant herd	15	15	☐☐☐☐☐
1389	A811	6c Haida ceremonial canoe	15	15	☐☐☐☐☐
1390	A812	6c Dinosaurs	15	15	☐☐☐☐☐
1390a.		Block of 4, #1387-1390	50	50	☐☐☐☐☐
1391	A813	6c black & multicolored	15	15	☐☐☐☐☐
1392	A814	6c black, light brown	15	15	☐☐☐☐☐

1970-74

Scott No.	Illus. No.	Description	Unused Value	Used Value	//////
1393	A815	6c dark blue gray	15	15	☐☐☐☐☐
1393a.		Booklet pane of 8	1.10	*50*	☐☐☐☐☐
1393b.		Booklet pane of 5 + label	1.10	*50*	☐☐☐☐☐
1393c.		Untagged (Bureau precanceled)	15		☐☐☐☐☐
1393D	A816	7c bright blue ('72)	15	15	☐☐☐☐☐
1393e.		Untagged (Bureau precanceled)	15		☐☐☐☐☐
1394	A815a	8c black, red & blue gray ('71)	16	15	☐☐☐☐☐
1395	A815	8c deep claret ('71)	16	15	☐☐☐☐☐
1395a.		Booklet pane of 8	1.80	*1.25*	☐☐☐☐☐
1395b.		Booklet pane of 6	1.25	*75*	☐☐☐☐☐
1395c.		Booklet pane of 4 + 2 labels ('72)	1.40	*50*	☐☐☐☐☐
1395d.		Booklet pane of 7 + label ('72)	1.60	*1.00*	☐☐☐☐☐
1396	A817	8c USPS emblem ('71)	15	15	☐☐☐☐☐
1397	A817a	14c gray brown ('72)	25	15	☐☐☐☐☐
1397a.		Untagged (Bureau precanceled)		25	☐☐☐☐☐
1398	A818	16c brown ('71)	30	15	☐☐☐☐☐
1398a.		Untagged (Bureau precanceled)		35	☐☐☐☐☐
1399	A818a	18c violet ('74)	32	15	☐☐☐☐☐
1400	A818b	21c green ('73)	35	15	☐☐☐☐☐

1970-71 Coil Stamps, Perf. 10 vertically

Scott No.	Illus. No.	Description	Unused Value	Used Value	//////
1401	A815	6c dark blue gray	15	15	☐☐☐☐☐
1401a.		Untagged (Bureau precanceled)		15	☐☐☐☐☐
1401b.		Imperf., pair	*1,200.*		☐☐☐☐☐
1402	A815	8c deep claret	15	15	☐☐☐☐☐
1402a.		Imperf., pair	*45.00*		☐☐☐☐☐

EISENHOWER·USA
Dot between "R"
and "U"

A815

EISENHOWER USA
No dot between
"R" and "U"

A815a

A816

A817

LaGuardia 14¢

A817a

Ernie Pyle
Journalist 16¢

A818

18¢

A818a

GIANNINI
AMADEO P.
USA 21¢

A818b

WOMAN SUFFRAGE
1920-1970
50™ ANNIVERSARY 6¢

A820

EDGAR LEE
MASTERS
AMERICAN POET

UNITED STATES 6¢

A819

SOUTH CAROLINA
1670
1970
6¢

A821

Stone Mountain Memorial

UNITED STATES 6 CENTS

A822

GREAT NORTHWEST
1820 FORT SNELLING 1970
US 6¢

A823

SAVE OUR SOIL

UNITED STATES · SIX CENTS

A824

SAVE OUR CITIES

UNITED STATES · SIX CENTS

A825

SAVE OUR WATER

UNITED STATES · SIX CENTS

A826

SAVE OUR AIR

UNITED STATES · SIX CENTS

A827

A828

A829

A830

A831

A832

A835

A836

A833

A834

A837

A838

A839

A840

A841

A842

A843

A844

A845

A846

A847

A848

A849

A850

A851

A852

A853

Scott No.	Illus. No.	Description	Unused Value	Used Value	//////
1402b.		Untagged (Bureau precanceled) ..		15	☐☐☐☐☐
1402c.		Pair, imperf. between...........	−		☐☐☐☐☐

1970

Scott No.	Illus. No.	Description	Unused Value	Used Value	//////
1405	A819	6c black & olive bister...........	15	15	☐☐☐☐☐
1406	A820	6c blue	15	15	☐☐☐☐☐
1407	A821	6c bister, black & red...........	15	15	☐☐☐☐☐
1408	A822	6c gray	15	15	☐☐☐☐☐
1409	A823	6c yellow & multicolored	15	15	☐☐☐☐☐
1410	A824	6c Globe & wheat	22	15	☐☐☐☐☐
1411	A825	6c Globe & city	22	15	☐☐☐☐☐
1412	A826	6c Globe & bluegill	22	15	☐☐☐☐☐
1413	A827	6c Globe & seabill.............	22	15	☐☐☐☐☐
1413a.		Block of 4, #1410-1413	1.00	1.00	☐☐☐☐☐

1970

Scott No.	Illus. No.	Description	Unused Value	Used Value	//////
1414	A828	6c *Nativity*	15	15	☐☐☐☐☐
1414a.		Precanceled	15	15	☐☐☐☐☐
1414b.		Black omitted.................	650.00		☐☐☐☐☐
1414c.		As **a,** blue omitted	2,000.		☐☐☐☐☐
1415	A829	6c Tin & locomotive	40	15	☐☐☐☐☐
1415a.		Precanceled	90	15	☐☐☐☐☐
1415b.		Black omitted.................	−		☐☐☐☐☐
1416	A830	6c Toy horse on wheels...........	40	15	☐☐☐☐☐
1416a.		Precanceled	90	15	☐☐☐☐☐
1416b.		Black omitted.................	−		☐☐☐☐☐
1416c.		Imperf., pair (#1416, 1418)		−	☐☐☐☐☐
1417	A831	6c Mechanical tricycle............	40	15	☐☐☐☐☐
1417a.		Precanceled	90	15	☐☐☐☐☐
1417b.		Black omitted.................	−		☐☐☐☐☐
1418	A832	6c Doll carriage	40	15	☐☐☐☐☐
1418a.		Precanceled	90	15	☐☐☐☐☐
1418b.		Block of 4, #1415-1418	1.90	1.75	☐☐☐☐☐
1418c.		As **b,** precanceled..............	3.75	3.50	☐☐☐☐☐
1418d.		Black omitted.................	−		☐☐☐☐☐
1419	A833	6c black, vermilion & ultramarine ..	15	15	☐☐☐☐☐
1420	A834	6c black, orange, yellow, brown, magenta & blue..............	15	15,	☐☐☐☐☐
1420a.		Orange & yellow omitted	1,400.		☐☐☐☐☐
1421	A835	6c Disabled veterans	15	15	☐☐☐☐☐
1421a.		Pair, #1421-1422	25	25	☐☐☐☐☐
1422	A836	6c dark blue, black & red	15	15	☐☐☐☐☐

1971

Scott No.	Illus. No.	Description	Unused Value	Used Value	//////
1423	A837	6c Ewe & lamb..................	15	15	☐☐☐☐☐
1424	A838	6c black, red & dark blue	15	15	☐☐☐☐☐
1425	A839	6c light blue, scarlet & indigo	15	15	☐☐☐☐☐
1426	A840	8c Missouri sesquicentennial	15	15	☐☐☐☐☐

A854

A855

A856

A857

A862

A863

A864

A865

A858

A860

A859

A867

A861

A866

A868

108

Scott No.	Illus. No.	Description	Unused Value	Used Value	//////
1427	A841	8c Trout......................	16	15	☐☐☐☐☐
1428	A842	8c Alligator....................	16	15	☐☐☐☐☐
1429	A843	8c Polar bear,cubs.............	16	15	☐☐☐☐☐
1430	A844	8c California condor	16	15	☐☐☐☐☐
1430a.		Block of 4, #1427-1430	65	65	☐☐☐☐☐
1430b.		As **a**, light green & dark green omitted from #1427-1428	*3,500.*		☐☐☐☐☐
1430c.		As **a**, red omitted from #1427, 1429-1430	—		☐☐☐☐☐
1431	A845	8c red & dark blue..............	15	15	☐☐☐☐☐
1432	A846	8c red, blue, gray & black	16	15	☐☐☐☐☐
1432a.		Gray & black omitted	*650.00*		☐☐☐☐☐
1432b.		Gray (U.S. Postage 8c) omitted...	*1,100.*		☐☐☐☐☐
1433	A847	8c John Sloan..................	15	15	☐☐☐☐☐
1434	A848	8c black, blue, yellow & red	15	15	☐☐☐☐☐
1434a.		Pair, #1434-1435	30	25	☐☐☐☐☐
1434b.		As **a**, blue & red (litho.) omitted..	*1,250.*		☐☐☐☐☐
1435	A849	8c black, yellow & red	15	15	☐☐☐☐☐
1436	A850	8c multicolored, *greenish—*	15	1⁵	☐☐☐☐☐
1436a.		Black & olive (engraved) omitted .	*1,100.*		☐☐☐☐☐
1436b.		Pale rose omitted..............	—		☐☐☐☐☐
1437	A851	8c San Juan	15	15	☐☐☐☐☐
1438	A852	8c blue, deep blue & black	15	15	☐☐☐☐☐
1439	A853	8c CARE	15	15	☐☐☐☐☐
1439a.		Black omitted..................	—		☐☐☐☐☐
1440	A854	8c black brown & ocher	16	15	☐☐☐☐☐
1441	A855	8c black brown & ocher	16	15	☐☐☐☐☐
1442	A856	8c black brown & ocher	16	15	☐☐☐☐☐
1443	A857	8c black brown & ocher	16	15	☐☐☐☐☐
1443a.		Block of 4, #1440-1443	65	65	☐☐☐☐☐
1443b.		As **a**, black brown omitted	*3,000.*		☐☐☐☐☐
1443c.		As **a**, ocher omitted	—		☐☐☐☐☐
1444	A858	8c gold & multicolored	15	15	☐☐☐☐☐
1444a.		Gold omitted	*575.00*		☐☐☐☐☐
1445	A859	8c *Partridge in a Pear Tree*........	15	15	☐☐☐☐☐
1972					
1446	A860	8c black, brown & light blue.......	15	15	☐☐☐☐☐
1447	A861	8c dark blue, light blue & red	15	15	☐☐☐☐☐
1448	A862	2c black & multicolored	15	15	☐☐☐☐☐
1449	A863	2c black & multicolored	15	15	☐☐☐☐☐
1450	A864	2c black & multicolored	15	15	☐☐☐☐☐
1451	A865	2c black & multicolored	15	15	☐☐☐☐☐
1451a.		Block of 4, #1448-1451	20	20	☐☐☐☐☐
1451b.		As **a**, black (litho.) omitted	*2,000.*		☐☐☐☐☐
1452	A866	6c black & multicolored	15	15	☐☐☐☐☐
1453	A867	8c black, blue, brown & multicolored	15	15	☐☐☐☐☐

Family Planning

UNITED STATES 8¢

A869

COLONIAL AMERICAN CRAFTSMEN

BICENTENNIAL ERA

UNITED STATES POSTAGE 8 CENTS

A870

COLONIAL AMERICAN CRAFTSMEN

BICENTENNIAL ERA

UNITED STATES POSTAGE 8 CENTS

A871

COLONIAL AMERICAN CRAFTSMEN

BICENTENNIAL ERA

UNITED STATES POSTAGE 8 CENTS

A872

COLONIAL AMERICAN CRAFTSMEN

BICENTENNIAL ERA

UNITED STATES POSTAGE 8 CENTS

A873

XX OLYMPIC SUMMER GAMES MUNICH 1972

A874

XI OLYMPIC WINTER GAMES SAPPORO 1972

A875

XX OLYMPIC SUMMER GAMES MUNICH 1972

A876

P.T.A. 1897 1972 8¢
Parent Teacher Association U.S.

A877

FUR SEAL

UNITED STATES

8¢

·WILDLIFE CONSERVATION·

A878

UNITED STATES

CARDINAL

8¢

·WILDLIFE CONSERVATION·

A879

·WILDLIFE CONSERVATION·

BROWN PELICAN

8¢

UNITED STATES

A880

·WILDLIFE CONSERVATION·

UNITED STATES

8¢

BIGHORN SHEEP

A881

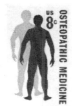

A883

A882

A884

A885

A887

A886

A888

A889

A890

A891

A892

A893

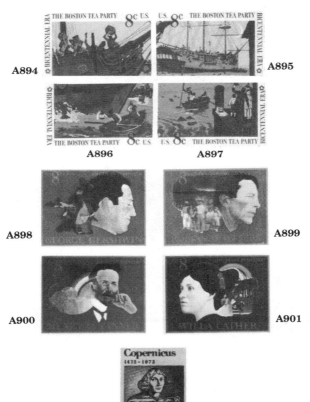

A894 A895 A896 A897 A898 A899 A900 A901 A902

A902

HOW TO USE THIS BOOK

The number in the first column is its Scott number or identifying number. The letter and number that come next (A41) indicate the design and refer to the illustration so designated. Following that is the denomination of the stamp and its color. Finally, the value, unused and used is shown.

Scott No.	Illus. No.	Description	Unused Value	Used Value	//////
1454	A868	15c black & multicolored	30	18	☐☐☐☐☐
1455	A869	8c black & multicolored	15	15	☐☐☐☐☐
1455a.		Yellow omitted	—		☐☐☐☐☐
1456	A870	8c deep brown	16	15	☐☐☐☐☐
1457	A871	8c deep brown	16	15	☐☐☐☐☐
1458	A872	8c deep brown	16	15	☐☐☐☐☐
1459	A873	8c deep brown	16	15	☐☐☐☐☐
1459a.		Block of 4, #1456-1459	65	65	☐☐☐☐☐
1460	A874	6c Bicycling	15	15	☐☐☐☐☐
1461	A875	8c Bobsledding.................	15	15	☐☐☐☐☐
1462	A876	15c Running....................	28	18	☐☐☐☐☐
1463	A877	8c yellow & black	15	15	☐☐☐☐☐
1464	A878	8c Fur seals	16	15	☐☐☐☐☐
1465	A879	8c Cardinal....................	16	15	☐☐☐☐☐
1466	A880	8c Brown pelican	16	15	☐☐☐☐☐
1467	A881	8c Bighorn sheep	16	15	☐☐☐☐☐
1467a.		Block of 4, #1464-1467	65	65	☐☐☐☐☐
1467b.		As **a**, brown omitted	3,750.		☐☐☐☐☐
1467c.		As **a**, green & blue omitted	—		☐☐☐☐☐
1468	A882	8c Rural post office store	15	15	☐☐☐☐☐
1469	A883	8c yellow, orange & dark brown....	15	15	☐☐☐☐☐
1470	A884	8c black & multicolored	15	15	☐☐☐☐☐
1470a.		Horizontal pair, imperf. between .	2,500.		☐☐☐☐☐
1470b.		Red & black (engraved) omitted..	1,500.		☐☐☐☐☐
1470c.		Yellow & tan (litho.) omitted	1,500.		☐☐☐☐☐
1471	A885	8c Angel......................	15	15	☐☐☐☐☐
1471a.		Pink omitted	400.00		☐☐☐☐☐
1471b.		Black omitted.................	4,000.		☐☐☐☐☐
1472	A886	8c Santa Claus	15	15	☐☐☐☐☐
1473	A887	8c black & multicolored	15	15	☐☐☐☐☐
1473a.		Blue & orange omitted	1,150.		☐☐☐☐☐
1473b.		Blue omitted..................	2,000.		☐☐☐☐☐
1473c.		Orange omitted...............	2,000.		☐☐☐☐☐
1474	A888	8c dark blue green, black & brown..	15	15	☐☐☐☐☐
1474a.		Black (litho.) omitted...........	1,250.		☐☐☐☐☐

1973

Scott No.	Illus. No.	Description	Unused Value	Used Value	//////
1475	A889	8c red, emerald & violet blue	15	15	☐☐☐☐☐
1476	A890	8c ultramarine, greenish black & red	15	15	☐☐☐☐☐
1477	A891	8c black, vermilion & ultramarine ..	15	15	☐☐☐☐☐
1478	A892	8c Postrider	15	15	☐☐☐☐☐
1479	A893	8c Drummer	15	15	☐☐☐☐☐
1480	A894	8c black & multicolored	15	15	☐☐☐☐☐
1481	A895	8c black & multicolored	15	15	☐☐☐☐☐
1482	A896	8c black & multicolored	15	15	☐☐☐☐☐
1483	A897	8c black & multicolored	15	15	☐☐☐☐☐
1483a.		Block of 4, #1480-1483	60	45	☐☐☐☐☐

U.S. POSTAL SERVICE 8c

A903

U.S. POSTAL SERVICE 8c

A904

U.S. POSTAL SERVICE 8c

A905

U.S. POSTAL SERVICE 8c

A906

U.S. POSTAL SERVICE 8c

A907

U.S. POSTAL SERVICE 8c

A908

U.S. POSTAL SERVICE 8c

A909

U.S. POSTAL SERVICE 8c

A910

U.S. POSTAL SERVICE 8c

A911

U.S. POSTAL SERVICE 8c

A912

Harry S. Truman
U.S. Postage 8 cents

A913

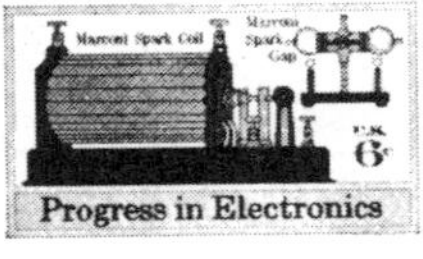
Marconi Spark Coil
Marconi Spark Gap
U.S. 6c
Progress in Electronics

A914

U.S. 8c
Progress in Electronics

A915

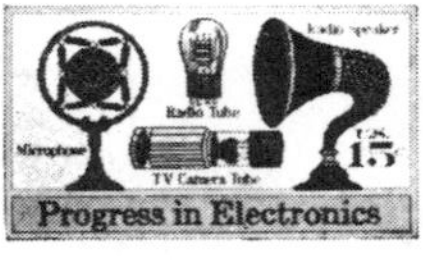
Radio Speaker
Radio Tube
Microphone
TV Camera Tube
U.S. 15c
Progress in Electronics

A916

Scott No.	Illus. No.	Description	Unused Value	Used Value	//////
1483b.		As **a**, black (engraved) omitted	*2,000.*		☐☐☐☐☐
1483c.		As **a**, black (litho.) omitted	*1,500.*		☐☐☐☐☐
1484	A898	8c deep green & multicolored	15	15	☐☐☐☐☐
1484a.		Vertical pair, imperf. horizontally	275.00		☐☐☐☐☐
1485	A899	8c Prussian blue & multicolored	15	15	☐☐☐☐☐
1485a.		Vertical pair, imperf. horizontally	325.00		☐☐☐☐☐
1486	A900	8c yellow brown & multicolored	15	15	☐☐☐☐☐
1487	A901	8c deep brown & multicolored	15	15	☐☐☐☐☐
1487a.		Vertical pair, imperf. horizontally	350.00		☐☐☐☐☐
1488	A902	8c black & orange	15	15	☐☐☐☐☐
1488a.		Orange omitted	*1,100.*		☐☐☐☐☐
1488b.		Black (engraved) omitted	*2,000.*		☐☐☐☐☐
1489	A903	8c Stamp counter	15	15	☐☐☐☐☐
1490	A904	8c Mail collecltion	15	15	☐☐☐☐☐
1491	A905	8c Letters, conveyor belt	15	15	☐☐☐☐☐
1492	A906	8c Parcel post sorting	15	15	☐☐☐☐☐
1493	A907	8c Mail canceling	15	15	☐☐☐☐☐
1494	A908	8c Manual letter routing	15	15	☐☐☐☐☐
1495	A909	8c Electronic letter routing	15	15	☐☐☐☐☐
1496	A910	8c Loading mail on truck	15	15	☐☐☐☐☐
1497	A911	8c Mailman	15	15	☐☐☐☐☐
1498	A912	8c Rural mail delivery	15	15	☐☐☐☐☐
1498a.		Strip of 10, Nos. 1489-1498	1.50	1.00	☐☐☐☐☐
1499	A913	8c carmine rose, black & blue	15	15	☐☐☐☐☐
1500	A914	6c lilac & multicolored	15	· 15	☐☐☐☐☐
1501	A915	8c tan & multicolored	15	15	☐☐☐☐☐
1501a.		Black (inscriptions & **U.S. 8c**) omitted	*850.00*		☐☐☐☐☐
1501b.		Tan (background) & lilac omitted.	*1,500.*		☐☐☐☐☐
1502	A916	15c gray green & multicolored	28	15	☐☐☐☐☐
1502a.		Black (inscriptions & **U.S. 15c**) omitted	*1,600.*		☐☐☐☐☐
1503	A917	8c black & multicolored	15	15	☐☐☐☐☐
1503a.		Horizontal pair, imperf. vertically	375.00		☐☐☐☐☐

1973-74
Scott No.	Illus. No.	Description	Unused Value	Used Value	//////
1504	A918	8c Angus & longhorn cattle	15	15	☐☐☐☐☐
1504a.		Green & red brown omitted	*1,000.*		☐☐☐☐☐
1504b.		Vertical pair, imperf. between		—	☐☐☐☐☐
1505	A919	10c Chautauqya tent, bugggies	18	15	☐☐☐☐☐
1506	A920	10c Wheat fields, tent	18	15	☐☐☐☐☐
1506a.		Black & blue (engraved) omitted	*850.00*		☐☐☐☐☐

1973
Scott No.	Illus. No.	Description	Unused Value	Used Value	//////
1507	A921	8c tan & multicolored	15	15	☐☐☐☐☐
1508	A922	8c green & multicolored	15	15	☐☐☐☐☐
1508a.		Vertical pair, imperf. between	*675.00*		☐☐☐☐☐

A917

A918

A919

A920

A921

A922

A923

A924

A925

A926

A928

A929

A930

A931

A932

A933

A934

A935

A936

A937

A938

A939

A940

117

A941

A942

A943

A944

A946

A947

A948

A949

A945

A951

A950

Scott No.	Illus. No.	Description	Unused Value	Used Value	//////
1973-74					
1509	A923	10c red & blue	18	15	☐☐☐☐☐
1509a.		Horizontal pair, imperf. between .	60.00	–	☐☐☐☐☐
1509b.		Blue omitted.	200.00		☐☐☐☐☐
1509c.		Vertical pair, imperf.	1,000.		☐☐☐☐☐
1510	A924	10c blue	18	15	☐☐☐☐☐
1510a.		Untagged (Bureau precanceled) . .		18	☐☐☐☐☐
1510b.		Booklet pane of 5 + label.	1.50	30	☐☐☐☐☐
1510c.		Booklet pane of 8.	1.65	30	☐☐☐☐☐
1510d.		Booklet pane of 6 ('74).	4.25	30	☐☐☐☐☐
1510e.		Vertical pair, imperf. horizontally	250.00		☐☐☐☐☐
1510f.		Vertical pair, imperf. between. . . .	–		☐☐☐☐☐
1511	A925	10c Mail Transport	18	15	☐☐☐☐☐
1511a.		Yellow omitted	50.00		☐☐☐☐☐

Coil stamps, Perf. 10 vertically

Scott No.	Illus. No.	Description	Unused Value	Used Value	//////
1518	A926	6.3c brick red	15	15	☐☐☐☐☐
1518a.		Untagged (Bureau precanceled) . .		15	☐☐☐☐☐
1518b.		Imperf., pair	300.00		☐☐☐☐☐
1518c.		As a., imperf. pair		150.00	☐☐☐☐☐
1519	A923	10c red & blue	18	15	☐☐☐☐☐
1519a.		Imperf., pair	40.00		☐☐☐☐☐
1520	A924	10c blue	18	15	☐☐☐☐☐
1520a.		Untagged (Bureau precanceled) . .		25	☐☐☐☐☐
1520b.		Imperf., pair	47.50		☐☐☐☐☐
1974					
1525	A928	10c red & dark blue.	18	15	☐☐☐☐☐
1526	A929	10c black	18	15	☐☐☐☐☐
1527	A930	10c EXPO '74	18	15	☐☐☐☐☐
1528	A931	10c yellow & multicolored	18	15	☐☐☐☐☐
1528a.		Blue (**Horse Racing**) omitted.	1,300.		☐☐☐☐☐
1528b.		Red (**U.S. postage 10 cents**)			
		omitted	–		☐☐☐☐☐
1529	A932	10c Skylab	18	15	☐☐☐☐☐
1529a.		Vertical pair, imperf. between. . . .	–		☐☐☐☐☐
1530	A933	10c Michelangelo.	20	15	☐☐☐☐☐
1531	A934	10c *Five Feminine Virtues.*	20	15	☐☐☐☐☐
1532	A935	10c Old-time letter rack	20	15	☐☐☐☐☐
1533	A936	10c *Mlle. La Vergne*	20	15	☐☐☐☐☐
1534	A937	10c *Lady Writing Letter*	20	15	☐☐☐☐☐
1535	A938	10c *Inkwell and Quill*	20	15	☐☐☐☐☐
1536	A939	10c *Mrs. John Douglas*	20	15	☐☐☐☐☐
1537	A940	10c *Don Antonio Noreiga*	20	15	☐☐☐☐☐
1537a.		Block or strip of 8, #1530-1537. . .	1.60	1.50	☐☐☐☐☐
1537b.		As a (block), imperf. vertically . . .	7,500.		☐☐☐☐☐
1538	A941	10c light blue & multicolored	18	15	☐☐☐☐☐
1538a.		Light blue & yellow omitted	–		☐☐☐☐☐

Retarded Children
Can Be Helped

A952

A953

A954

A955

Benjamin West

American artist
10 cents U.S. postage

A956

MOVIE MAKER   US 10 c
D.W. GRIFFITH

A958

Paul Laurence
Dunbar

American poet

10 cents U.S. postage

A957

PIONEER ★ JUPITER

US
10c

A959

MARINER 10 ★ VENUS/MERCURY

US 10c

A960

Contributors
To The
Cause...

Sybil Ludington   Youthful Heroine

A962

Contributors
To The
Cause...

Salem Poor   Gallant Soldier

A963

Contributors
To The
Cause...

Haym Salomon   Financial Hero

A964

Contributors
To The
Cause...

Peter Francisco   Fighter Extraordinary

A965

120

Scott No.	Illus. No.	Description	Unused Value	Used Value	//////
1539	A942	10c light blue & multicolored......	18	15	□□□□□
1539a.		Light blue omitted.............	—		□□□□□
1539b.		Black & purple omitted.........	—		□□□□□
1540	A943	10c light blue & multicolored......	18	15	□□□□□
1540a.		Light blue & yellow omitted.....	—		□□□□□
1541	A944	10c light blue & multicolored......	18	15	□□□□□
1541a.		Block or strip of 4, #1538-1541...	75	75	□□□□□
1541b.		As a, light blue & yellow omitted .	2,400.		□□□□□
1541c.		Light blue omitted.............	—		□□□□□
1541d.		Black & red omitted	—		□□□□□
1542	A945	10c green & multicolored	18	15	□□□□□
1542a.		Dull black (litho.) omitted.......	1,250.		□□□□□
1542b.		Green (engraved & litho.), black (engraved & litho.), blue omitted	2,500.		□□□□□
1542c.		Green (engraved) omitted	—		□□□□□
1542d.		Green (engraved), black (litho.) omitted	—		□□□□□
1543	A946	10c dark blue & red.............	18	15	□□□□□
1544	A947	10c gray, dark blue & red	18	15	□□□□□
1545	A948	10c gray, dark blue & red	18	15	□□□□□
1546	A949	10c red & dark blue.............	18	15	□□□□□
1546a.		Block of 4, #1543-1546	75	75	□□□□□
1547	A950	10c Energy conservation	18	15	□□□□□
1547a.		Blue & orange omitted	1,100.		□□□□□
1547b.		Orange & green omitted	1,100.		□□□□□
1547c.		Green omitted	950.00		□□□□□
1548	A951	10c dark blue, black, orange & yellow	18	15	□□□□□
1549	A952	10c brown red & dark brown	18	15	□□□□□
1550	A953	10c Angel	18	15	□□□□□
1551	A954	10c *The Road — Winter*..........	18	15	□□□□□
1552	A955	10c Dove weather vane...........	18	15	□□□□□

1975

Scott No.	Illus. No.	Description	Unused Value	Used Value	//////
1553	A956	10c Benjamin West	18	15	□□□□□
1554	A957	10c Paul Laurence Dunbar	18	15	□□□□□
1554a.		Imperf., pair..................	1,100.		□□□□□
1555	A958	10c D.W. Griffith	18	15	□□□□□
1555a.		Brown (engraved) omitted.......	900.00		□□□□□
1556	A959	10c violet blue, yellow & red	18	15	□□□□□
1556a.		Red (litho.) omitted............	1,500.		□□□□□
1556b.		Blue (engraved) omitted	1,250.		□□□□□
1556c.		Imperf., pair..................	—		□□□□□
1557	A960	10c black, red, ultramarine & bister.	18	15	□□□□□
1557a.		Red omitted...................	800.00		□□□□□
1557b.		Ultramarine & bister omitted....	2,000.		□□□□□
1558	A961	10c Collective bargaining	18	15	□□□□□

A961

US Bicentennial IOcents

A966

US Bicentennial IOc

A967

A968

A969

A970

A971

A972

A973

122

A974

A979

A975

A976

A977

A978

A980

A981

A982

A983

A984

A985

A987

A988

A994

A995

A996

A997

A998

A999

A1001

A1002

A1003

A1004

A1005

A1006

A1007

A1008

A1009

A1010

124

Scott No.	Illus. No.	Description	Unused Value	Used Value	//////
1559	A962	8c Sybil Ludington	16	15	□□□□□
1559a.		Back inscription omitted.	350.00		□□□□□
1560	A963	10c Salem Poor	18	15	□□□□□
1560a.		Back inscription omitted.	300.00		□□□□□
1561	A964	10c Haym Solomon.	18	15	□□□□□
1561a.		Back inscription omitted.	350.00		□□□□□
1561b.		Red omitted	250.00		□□□□□
1562	A965	18c Peter Francisco	35	20	□□□□□
1563	A966	10c Lexington-Concord battle	18	15	□□□□□
1563a.		Vertical pair, imperf. horizontally	500.00		□□□□□
1564	A967	10c Battle of Bunker Hill	18	15	□□□□□
1565	A968	10c Soldier with flintlock musket. . .	18	15	□□□□□
1566	A969	10c Sailor with grappling hook.	18	15	□□□□□
1567	A970	10c Marine with musket.	18	15	□□□□□
1568	A971	10c Militiaman with musket.	18	15	□□□□□
1568a.		Block of 4, #1565-1568	75	75	□□□□□
1569	A972	10c Apollo & Soyuz crafts.	18	15	□□□□□
1569a.		Pair, #1569-1570	36	25	□□□□□
1568b.		As **a**, vert. pair, imperf.			
		horizontally.	1,200.		□□□□□
1570	A973	10c Apollo & Soyuz crafts.	18	15	□□□□□
1571	A974	10c blue, orange & dark blue	18	15	□□□□□
1572	A975	10c Stagecoach, trailer truck	18	15	□□□□□
1573	A976	10c Locomotives	18	15	□□□□□
1574	A977	10c Mail plane, jet	18	15	□□□□□
1575	A978	10c Satellite	18	15	□□□□□
1575a.		Block of 4, #1572-1575	75	75	□□□□□
1575b.		As **a**, red (**10c**) omitted	—		□□□□□
1576	A979	10c green, Prussian blue			
		& rose brown.	18	15	□□□□□
1577	A980	10c Penny, silver dollar.	18	15	□□□□□
1577a.		Pair, #1577-1578	36	20	□□□□□
1577b.		As **a**, brown & blue (litho.)			
		omitted	1,250.		□□□□□
1578	A981	10c Liberty quarter, gold piece	18	15	□□□□□
1579	A982	(10c) Madonna.	18	15	□□□□□
1579a.		Imperf., pair	125.00		□□□□□
1580	A983	(10c) *Christmas Card*.	18	15	□□□□□
1580a.		Imperf., pair.	125.00		□□□□□
1580b.		Perf. 10½x11	60	15	□□□□□

1975-81

1581	A984	1c dark blue, *greenish* ('77)	15	15	□□□□□
1581a.		Untagged (Bureau precanceled) . .		15	□□□□□
1582	A985	2c red brown, *greenish* ('77)	15	15	□□□□□
1582a.		Untagged (Bureau precanceled) . .		15	□□□□□
1582b.		Cream paper ('81)	15	15	□□□□□
1584	A987	3c olive, *greenish* ('77).	15	15	□□□□□

125

A1011

A1012

A1013

A1014

United States 13c
A1015

A1016

A1019

A1020

A1021

A1022

HOW TO USE THIS BOOK

The number in the first column is its Scott number or identifying number. The letter and number that come next (A41) indicate the design and refer to the illustration so designated. Following that is the denomination of the stamp and its color. Finally, the value, unused and used is shown.

Scott No.	Illus. No.	Description	Unused Value	Used Value	//////
1584a.		Untagged (Bureau precanceled) ..		15	□□□□□
1585	A988	4c rose magenta, *cream* ('77)......	15	15	□□□□□
1585a.		Untagged (Bureau precanceled) ..		15	□□□□□
1590	A994	9c slate green ('77)...............	50	20	□□□□□
1590a.		Perf. 10......................	18.50	10.00	□□□□□
1591	A994	9c slate green, *gray*.............	16	15	□□□□□
1591a.		Untagged (Bureau precanceled) ..		18	□□□□□
1592	A995	10c violet, *gray* ('77)...........	18	15	□□□□□
1592a.		Untagged (Bureau precanceled) ..		25	□□□□□
1593	A996	11c orange, *gray*...............	20	15	□□□□□
1594	A997	12c brown red, *beige* ('81)........	22	15	□□□□□
1595	A998	13c brown	26	15	□□□□□
1595a.		Booklet pane of 6.............	1.90	50	□□□□□
1595b.		Booklet pane of 7 + label.......	2.00	50	□□□□□
1595c.		Booklet pane of 8.............	2.25	50	□□□□□
1595d.		Booklet pane of 5 + label ('76) ...	1.30	50	□□□□□
1595e.		Vertical pair, imperf between	—		□□□□□
1596	A999	13c Eagle & Shield..............	26	15	□□□□□
1596a.		Imperf., pair..................	45.00	—	□□□□□
1596b.		Yellow omitted	225.00		□□□□□
1597	A1001	15c gray, dark blue & red ('78)....	28	15	□□□□□
1597a.		Vertical pair, imperf...........	17.50		□□□□□
1597b.		Gray omitted	—		□□□□□
1598	A1001	15c gray, dark blue & red ('78)....	30	15	□□□□□
1598a.		Booklet pane of 8.............	3.50	60	□□□□□
1599	A1002	16c blue ('78).................	34	15	□□□□□
1603	A1003	24c red, *blue*.................	45	15	□□□□□
1604	A1004	28c brown, *blue* ('78)..........	55	15	□□□□□
1605	A1005	29c blue, *blue* ('78)..........	55	15	□□□□□
1606	A1006	30c green, *blue* ('79)	55	15	□□□□□
1608	A1007	50c tan, black & orange ('79)	95	15	□□□□□
1608a.		Black omitted.................	450.00		□□□□□
1608b.		Vertical pair, imperf. horizontally	—		□□□□□
1610	A1008	$1 tan, brown, orange & yellow ('79)	1.75	20	□□□□□
1610a.		Brown (engraved) omitted.......	425.00		□□□□□
1610b.		Tan, orange & yellow omitted ...	400.00		□□□□□
1610c.		Brown inverted	—		□□□□□
1611	A1009	$2 tan, dark green, orange & yellow ('78)	3.75	45	□□□□□
1612	A1010	$5 tan, red brown, yellow & orange ('79)	9.00	1.50	□□□□□

Coil Stamps, Perf. 10 vertically

Scott No.	Illus. No.	Description	Unused Value	Used Value	//////
1613	A1011	3.1c brown, *yellow* ('79)...........	15	15	□□□□□
1613a.		Untagged (Bureau precanceled) ..		40	□□□□□
1613b.		Imperf., pair..................	1,100.		□□□□□
1614	A1012	7.7c brown, *bright yellow* ('76)	18	15	□□□□□
1614a.		Untagged (Bureau precanceled) ..		35	□□□□□

State Flags A1023-A1072

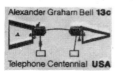

A1073

Commercial Aviation

A1074

CHEMISTRY

A1075

Scott No.	Illus. No.	Description	Unused Value	Used Value	—//—//—
1614b.		As **a**, imperf., pair	*1,400.*		☐☐☐☐☐
1615	A1013	7.9c carmine, *yellow* ('76)	15	15	☐☐☐☐☐
1615a.		Untagged (Bureau precanceled) ..		16	☐☐☐☐☐
1615b.		Imperf., pair..................	*800.00*		☐☐☐☐☐
1615C	A1014	8.4c dark blue, *yellow* ('78)	22	15	☐☐☐☐☐
1615d.		Untagged (Bureau precanceled) ..		16	☐☐☐☐☐
1615e.		As **d**, pair, imperf. between		60.00	☐☐☐☐☐
1615f.		As **d**, imperf., pair		15.00	☐☐☐☐☐
1616	A994	9c slate green, *gray*.	20	15	☐☐☐☐☐
1616a.		Imperf., pair..................	*110.00*		☐☐☐☐☐
1616b.		Untagged (Bureau precanceled) ..		28	☐☐☐☐☐
1616c.		As **b**, imperf., pair		*190.00*	☐☐☐☐☐
1617	A995	10c violet, *gray* ('77)	24	15	☐☐☐☐☐
1617a.		Untagged (Bureau precanceled) ..		25	☐☐☐☐☐
1617b.		Imperf., pair..................	*60.00*		☐☐☐☐☐
1618	A998	13c brown	25	15	☐☐☐☐☐
1618a.		Untagged (Bureau precanceled) ..		38	☐☐☐☐☐
1618b.		Imperf., pair..................	25.00		☐☐☐☐☐
1618g.		Pair, imperf. between........	—		☐☐☐☐☐
1618C	A1001	15c gray, dark blue & red ('78)	40	15	☐☐☐☐☐
1618d.		Imperf., pair..................	20.00		☐☐☐☐☐
1618e.		Pair, imperf. between.	150.00		☐☐☐☐☐
1618f.		Gray omitted	40.00		☐☐☐☐☐
1619	A1002	16c blue ('78)	32	15	☐☐☐☐☐
1619a.		Huck press printing	50	15	☐☐☐☐☐

1975-77

Scott No.	Illus. No.	Description	Unused Value	Used Value	—//—//—
1622	A1015	13c dark blue & red............	24	15	☐☐☐☐☐
1622a.		Horizontal pair, imperf. between .	60.00		☐☐☐☐☐
1622b.		Vertical pair, imperf............	—		☐☐☐☐☐
1622c.		Perf. 11 ('81)	65	15	☐☐☐☐☐
1622d.		As **c**, vert. pair, imperf.	—		☐☐☐☐☐
1623	A1016	13c blue & red ('77).............	22	15	☐☐☐☐☐
1623a.		Booklet pane of 8 (1 #1590 and			
		7 #1623).................	2.00	60	☐☐☐☐☐
1623b.		Perf. 10.....................	1.00	1.00	☐☐☐☐☐
1623c.		Booklet pane of 8 (1 #1590a + and			
		7 #1623b)................	27.50	—	☐☐☐☐☐
1623d.		Se-tenant pair, #1590 & 1623	75	—	☐☐☐☐☐
1623e.		Se-tenant pair, #1590a & 1623b ..	20.00	—	☐☐☐☐☐

Coil Stamps, Perf. 10 vertically

Scott No.	Illus. No.	Description	Unused Value	Used Value	—//—//—
1625	A1015	13c dark blue & red............	30	15	☐☐☐☐☐
1625a.		Imperf., pair..................	22.50		☐☐☐☐☐

1976

Scott No.	Illus. No.	Description	Unused Value	Used Value	—//—//—
1629	A1019	13c Drummer Boy..............	25	15	☐☐☐☐☐
1630	A1020	13c Old Drummer..............	25	15	☐☐☐☐☐

Surrender of Cornwallis at Yorktown, by John Trumbull– **A1076**

Declaration of Independence, by John Trumbull– **A1077**

Scott No.	Illus. No.	Description	Unused Value	Used Value	//////
1631	A1021	13c Fifer........................	25	15	☐☐☐☐☐
1631a.		Strip of 3, #1629-1631..........	75	60	☐☐☐☐☐
1631b.		As a, imperf..................	*1,500.*		☐☐☐☐☐
1631c.		Vertical pair, imperf...........	*800.00*		☐☐☐☐☐
1632	A1022	13c dark blue, red & ultramarine ...	24	15	☐☐☐☐☐
1633	A1023	13c Delaware..................	24	20	☐☐☐☐☐
1634	A1024	13c Pennsylvania..............	24	20	☐☐☐☐☐
1635	A1025	13c New Jersey	24	20	☐☐☐☐☐
1636	A1026	13c Georgia	24	20	☐☐☐☐☐
1637	A1027	13c Connecticut...............	24	20	☐☐☐☐☐
1638	A1028	13c Massachusetts.............	24	20	☐☐☐☐☐
1639	A1029	13c Maryland..................	24	20	☐☐☐☐☐
1640	A1030	13c South Carolina	24	20	☐☐☐☐☐
1641	A1031	13c New Hampshire	24	20	☐☐☐☐☐
1642	A1032	13c Virginia	24	20	☐☐☐☐☐
1643	A1033	13c New York	24	20	☐☐☐☐☐
1644	A1034	13c North Carolina	24	20	☐☐☐☐☐
1645	A1035	13c Rhode Island..............	24	20	☐☐☐☐☐
1646	A1036	13c Vermont	24	20	☐☐☐☐☐
1647	A1037	13c Kentucky..................	24	20	☐☐☐☐☐
1648	A1038	13c Tennessee	24	20	☐☐☐☐☐
1649	A1039	13c Ohio......................	24	20	☐☐☐☐☐
1650	A1040	13c Louisiana.................	24	20	☐☐☐☐☐
1651	A1041	13c Indiana	24	20	☐☐☐☐☐
1652	A1042	13c Mississippi	24	20	☐☐☐☐☐
1653	A1043	13c Illinois....................	24	20	☐☐☐☐☐
1654	A1044	13c Alabama	24	20	☐☐☐☐☐
1655	A1045	13c Maine	24	20	☐☐☐☐☐
1656	A1046	13c Missouri	24	20	☐☐☐☐☐
1657	A1047	13c Arkansas..................	24	20	☐☐☐☐☐
1658	A1048	13c Michigan..................	24	20	☐☐☐☐☐
1659	A1049	13c Florida....................	24	20	☐☐☐☐☐
1660	A1050	13c Texas.....................	24	20	☐☐☐☐☐
1661	A1051	13c Iowa......................	24	20	☐☐☐☐☐
1662	A1052	13c Wisconsin	24	20	☐☐☐☐☐
1663	A1053	13c California	24	20	☐☐☐☐☐
1664	A1054	13c Minnesota.................	24	20	☐☐☐☐☐
1665	A1055	13c Oregon	24	20	☐☐☐☐☐
1666	A1056	13c Kansas....................	24	20	☐☐☐☐☐
1667	A1057	13c West Virginia	24	20	☐☐☐☐☐
1668	A1058	13c Nevada	24	20	☐☐☐☐☐
1669	A1059	13c Nebraska..................	24	20	☐☐☐☐☐
1670	A1060	13c Colorado..................	24	20	☐☐☐☐☐
1671	A1061	13c North Dakota	24	20	☐☐☐☐☐
1672	A1062	13c South Dakota	24	20	☐☐☐☐☐
1673	A1063	13c Montana	24	20	☐☐☐☐☐
1674	A1064	13c Washington................	24	20	☐☐☐☐☐
1675	A1065	13c Idaho.....................	24	20	☐☐☐☐☐

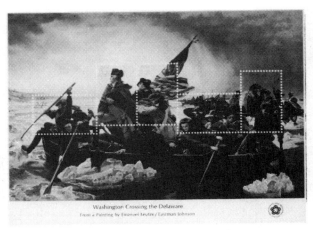

**Washington Crossing the Delaware, by
Emanuel Leutze/Eastman Johnson— A1078**

**Washington Reviewing Army at Valley Forge,
by William T. Trego— A1079**

A1080

JULY 4,1776• JULY 4,1776• JULY 4,1776• JULY 4,1776•
Declaration of Independence, by John Trumbull

A1081   A1082   A1083   A1084

A1085

A1086

A1089

A1087

A1088

A1090

A1091

A1092

A1093

A1094

Zia: Museum of New Mexico
Pueblo Art USA 13c

A1095

San Ildefonso: Denver Art Museum
Pueblo Art USA 13c

A1096

Hopi: Heard Museum, Phoenix
Pueblo Art USA 13c

A1097

Acoma: School of American Research
Pueblo Art USA 13c

A1098

COLORADO

A1099

13c
usa
THE CENTENNIAL STATE

A1100

Lafayette

US Bicentennial 13c

A1105

Swallowtail
USA 13c *Papilio oregonius*

A1101

Checkerspot
USA 13c *Euphydryas phaeton*

A1102

Dogface
USA 13c *Colias eurydice*

A1103

Orange-Tip
USA 13c *Anthocaris midea*

A1104

134

Scott No.	Illus. No.	Description	Unused Value	Used Value	//////
1676	A1066	13c Wyoming.	24	20	☐☐☐☐☐
1677	A1067	13c Utah.	24	20	☐☐☐☐☐
1678	A1068	13c Oklahoma	24	20	☐☐☐☐☐
1679	A1069	13c New Mexico	24	20	☐☐☐☐☐
1680	A1070	13c Arizona	24	20	☐☐☐☐☐
1681	A1071	13c Alaska	24	20	☐☐☐☐☐
1682	A1072	13c Hawaii.	24	20	☐☐☐☐☐
1682a.		Pane of 50.	12.00	—	☐☐☐☐☐
1683	A1073	13c black, purple & red, tan	24	15	☐☐☐☐☐
1684	A1074	13c blue & multicolored	24	15	☐☐☐☐☐
1685	A1075	13c Chemistry	24	15	☐☐☐☐☐
1686	A1076	Sheet of 5	3.25	—	☐☐☐☐☐
1686a.-e.		13c multicolored, any single	45	40	☐☐☐☐☐
1686f.		USA 13c omitted on **b, c & d**,			
		imperf., untagged	—	1,500.	☐☐☐☐☐
1686g.		USA 13c omitted on **a & e**	—	—	☐☐☐☐☐
1686h.		Imperf., untagged.		1,750.	☐☐☐☐☐
1686i.		USA 13c omitted on **b, c & d**	—		☐☐☐☐☐
1686j.		USA 13c double on **b**	—		☐☐☐☐☐
1686k.		USA 13c omitted on **c & d**	—		☐☐☐☐☐
1686l.		USA 13c omitted on **e**	—		☐☐☐☐☐
1686m.		USA 13c omitted, imperf.,			
		untagged	—	—	☐☐☐☐☐
1687	A1077	Sheet of 5	4.25	—	☐☐☐☐☐
1687a.-e.		18c multicolored, any single	55	55	☐☐☐☐☐
1687f.		Design & marginal inscriptions			
		omitted		2,250.	☐☐☐☐☐
1687g.		USA 18c omitted on **a & c**	—		☐☐☐☐☐
1687h.		USA 18c omitted on **b, d & e**	—		☐☐☐☐☐
1687i.		USA 18c omitted on **d**.	—		☐☐☐☐☐
1687j.		Black omitted in design.	800.00		☐☐☐☐☐
1687k.		USA 18c omitted, imperf.,			
		untagged		1,750.	☐☐☐☐☐
1687m.		USA 18c omitted on **b & e**	—		☐☐☐☐☐
1688	A1078	Sheet of 5	5.25	—	☐☐☐☐☐
1688a.-e.		24c multicolored, any single	70	70	☐☐☐☐☐
1688f.		USA 24c omitted, imperf.,			
		untagged		1,750.	☐☐☐☐☐
1688g.		USA 24c omitted on **d & e**	—	—	☐☐☐☐☐
1688h.		Design & marginal inscriptions			
		omitted		2,250.	☐☐☐☐☐
1688i.		USA 24c omitted on **a, b & c**	—	—	☐☐☐☐☐
1688j.		Imperf., untagged.	1,750.		☐☐☐☐☐
1688k.		USA 24c of **d & e** inverted	—		☐☐☐☐☐
1689	A1079	Sheet of 5	6.25	—	☐☐☐☐☐
1689a.-e.		31c multicolored, any single	85	85	☐☐☐☐☐
1689f.		USA 31c omitted, imperf.,			
		untagged	—		☐☐☐☐☐

the SEAMSTRESS
for INDEPENDENCE USA 13c

A1106

the BLACKSMITH
for INDEPENDENCE USA 13c

A1107

the WHEELWRIGHT
for INDEPENDENCE USA 13c

A1108

the LEATHERWORKER
for INDEPENDENCE USA 13c

A1109

United States & Canada
Peace Bridge 1927-77
USA 13c

A1110

ENERGY
CONSERVATION USA 13c

A1112

Herkimer at Oriskany 1777 by Yohn
US Bicentennial 13 cents

A1111

First Civil Settlement Alta California 1777 USA 13c

A1114

ENERGY
DEVELOPMENT USA 13c

A1113

Drafting the Articles of Confederation
York Town, Pennsylvania 1777 13c USA

A1115

13c USA

A1116

Surrender at Saratoga 1777 by Trumbull
US Bicentennial 13 cents

A1117

VALLEY FORGE
Christmas
USA 13c

A1118

Carl Sandburg
USA 13c

A1120

USA
Christmas 13c

A1119

136

Scott No.	Illus. No.	Description	Unused Value	Used Value	//////
1689g.		USA 31c omitted on **a** & **c**	—		☐☐☐☐☐
1689h.		USA 31c omitted on **b, d** & **e**	—	—	☐☐☐☐☐
1689i.		USA 31c omitted on **e**	—		☐☐☐☐☐
1689j.		Black omitted in design.	900.00		☐☐☐☐☐
1689k.		Imperf., untagged.		1,600.	☐☐☐☐☐
1689l.		USA 31c omitted on **b** & **d**	—		☐☐☐☐☐
1689m.		USA 31c omitted on **a c** & **e**	—		☐☐☐☐☐
1689n.		As **m**, imperf., untagged.	—		☐☐☐☐☐
1689p.		As **h**, imperf., untagged		1,750.	☐☐☐☐☐
1689q.		As **g**, imperf., untagged	1,750.		☐☐☐☐☐
1690	A1080	13c ultramarine & multicolored. . . .	20	15	☐☐☐☐☐
1690a.		Light blue omitted	525.00		☐☐☐☐☐
1691	A1081	13c Declaration of Independence . . .	22	15	☐☐☐☐☐
1692	A1082	13c Declaration of Independence . . .	22	15	☐☐☐☐☐
1693	A1083	13c Declaration of Independence . . .	22	15	☐☐☐☐☐
1694	A1084	13c Declaration of Independence . . .	22	15	☐☐☐☐☐
1694a.		Strip of 4, #1691-1694.	95	75	☐☐☐☐☐
1695	A1085	13c Diving	28	15	☐☐☐☐☐
1696	A1086	13c Skiing.	28	15	☐☐☐☐☐
1697	A1087	13c Running.	28	15	☐☐☐☐☐
1698	A1088	13c Skating.	28	15	☐☐☐☐☐
1698a.		Block of 4, #1695-1698	1.15	85	☐☐☐☐☐
1698b.		As **a**, imperf.	800.00		☐☐☐☐☐
1699	A1089	13c Clara Maass.	26	15	☐☐☐☐☐
1699a.		Horizontal pair, imperf. vertically	475.00		☐☐☐☐☐
1700	A1090	13c black & gray	24	15	☐☐☐☐☐
1701	A1091	13c Nativity.	24	15	☐☐☐☐☐
1701a.		Imperf., pair.	95.00		☐☐☐☐☐
1702	A1092	13c *Winter Pastime*.	24	15	☐☐☐☐☐
1702a.		Imperf., pair.	120.00		☐☐☐☐☐
1703	A1092	13c *Winter Pastime*.	24	15	☐☐☐☐☐
1703a.		Imperf., pair.	140.00		☐☐☐☐☐
1703b.		Vertical pair, imperf. between. . . .	—		☐☐☐☐☐
1977					
1704	A1093	13c Washington at Princeton	24	15	☐☐☐☐☐
1704a.		Horizontal pair, imperf. vertically	500.00		☐☐☐☐☐
1705	A1094	13c black & multicolored	24	15	☐☐☐☐☐
1706	A1095	13c Zia pot.	24	15	☐☐☐☐☐
1707	A1096	13c San Ildefonso pot	24	15	☐☐☐☐☐
1708	A1097	13c Hopi pot	24	15	☐☐☐☐☐
1709	A1098	13c Acoma pot.	24	15	☐☐☐☐☐
1709a.		Block or strip of 4	1.00	60	☐☐☐☐☐
1709b.		As **a**, imperf. vertically	2,500.		☐☐☐☐☐
1710	A1099	13c *Spirit of St. Louis*	24	15	☐☐☐☐☐
1710a.		Imperf., pair.	1,400.		☐☐☐☐☐
1711	A1100	13c Colorado statehood	24	15	☐☐☐☐☐
1711a.		Horizontal pair, imperf. between .	500.00		☐☐☐☐☐

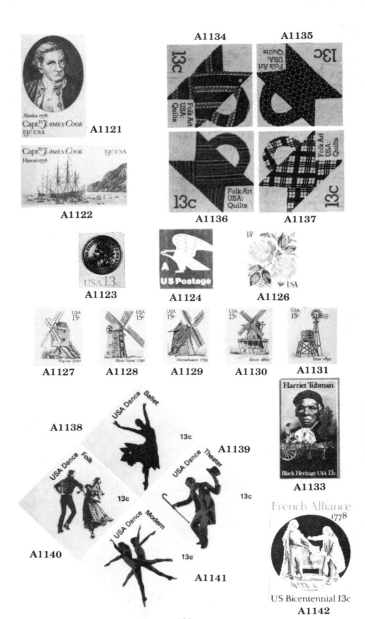

A1121

A1122

A1134

A1135

A1136

A1137

A1123

A1124

A1126

A1127

A1128

A1129

A1130

A1131

A1133

A1138

A1139

A1140

A1141

A1142

Scott No.	Illus. No.	Description	Unused Value	Used Value	//////
1711b.		Horizontal pair, imperf. vertically	—		□□□□□
1712	A1101	13c tan& multicolored	24	15	□□□□□
1713	A1102	13c tan & multicolored	24	15	□□□□□
1714	A1103	13c tan & multicolored	24	15	□□□□□
1715	A1104	13c tan & multicolored	24	15	□□□□□
1715a.		Block of 4, #1712-1715	1.00	60	□□□□□
1715b.		As **a,** imperf. horizontally	—		□□□□□
1716	A1105	13c blue, black & red............	24	15	□□□□□
1717	A1106	13c Seamstress...................	24	15	□□□□□
1718	A1107	13c Blacksmith	24	15	□□□□□
1719	A1108	13c Wheelwright	24	15	□□□□□
1720	A1109	13c Leatherworker..............	24	15	□□□□□
1720a.		Block of 4, #1717-1720	1.00	80	□□□□□
1721	A1110	13c blue	24	15	□□□□□
1722	A1111	13c *Herkimer at Oriskany.*........	24	15	□□□□□
1723	A1112	13c Energy conservation	24	15	□□□□□
1723a.		Pair, #1723-1724	48	40	□□□□□
1724	A1113	13c Energy development...........	24	15	□□□□□
1725	A1114	13c black & multicolored	24	15	□□□□□
1726	A1115	13c red & brown, *cream*	24	15	□□□□□
1727	A1116	13c Movie projector, phonograph ..	24	15	□□□□□
1728	A1117	13c *Surrender of Burgoyne*	24	15	□□□□□
1729	A1118	13c Washington at Valley Forge....	24	15	□□□□□
1729a.		Imperf., pair..................	*90.00*		□□□□□
1730	A1119	13c Rural mailbox...............	24	15	□□□□□
1730a.		Imperf., pair.................	*250.00*		□□□□□

1978

Scott No.	Illus. No.	Description	Unused Value	Used Value	//////
1731	A1120	13c black & brown...............	24	15	□□□□□
1732	A1121	13c dark blue	24	15	□□□□□
1732a.		Pair, #1732-1733	50	30	□□□□□
1732b.		As **a,** imperf. between	*4,500.*		□□□□□
1733	A1122	13c green	24	15	□□□□□
1733a.		Vertical pair, imperf. horizontally	—		□□□□□
1734	A1123	13c brown & blue green, *bister*	24	15	□□□□□
1734a.		Horizontal pair, imperf. vertically	*300.00*		□□□□□
1735	A1124	(15c) orange	24	15	□□□□□
1735a.		Imperf., vert. pair..............	*80.00*		□□□□□
1735b.		Vertical pair, imperf. horizontally	*300.00*		□□□□□
1736	A1124	(15c) orange	25	15	□□□□□
1736a.		Booklet pane of 8..............	2.40	60	□□□□□
1737	A1126	15c Roses	25	15	□□□□□
1737a.		Booklet pane of 8..............	2.50	60	□□□□□
1737b.		As **a,** imperf...................	—		□□□□□

1980, Feb. 7

Scott No.	Illus. No.	Description	Unused Value	Used Value	//////
1738	A1127	15c sepia, *yellow*	30	15	□□□□□
1739	A1128	15c sepia, *yellow*	30	15	□□□□□

A1143

A1146

A1144

A1149

A1150

A1145

A1151

A1152

A1147

A1153

A1154

A1155

A1156

140

Scott No.	Illus. No.	Description	Unused Value	Used Value	//////
1740	A1129	15c sepia, *yellow*	30	15 ☐☐☐☐☐	
1741	A1130	15c sepia, *yellow*	30	15 ☐☐☐☐☐	
1742	A1131	15c sepia, *yellow*	30	15 ☐☐☐☐☐	
1742a.		Booklet pane of 10.	3.60	60 ☐☐☐☐☐	

1978 Coil Stamp, Perf. 10 vertically

Scott No.	Illus. No.	Description	Unused Value	Used Value	//////
1743	A1124	(15c) orange	25	15 ☐☐☐☐☐	
1743a.		Imperf., pair.	*100.00*	☐☐☐☐☐	
1744	A1133	13c Harriet Tubman	24	15 ☐☐☐☐☐	
1745	A1134	13c Quilt	24	15 ☐☐☐☐☐	
1746	A1135	13c Quilt	24	15 ☐☐☐☐☐	
1747	A1136	13c Quilt	24	15 ☐☐☐☐☐	
1748	A1137	13c Quilt	24	15 ☐☐☐☐☐	
1748a.		Block of 4, #1745-1748	1.00	60 ☐☐☐☐☐	
1749	A1138	13c Ballet	24	15 ☐☐☐☐☐	
1750	A1139	13c Theater	24	15 ☐☐☐☐☐	
1751	A1140	13c Folk dance.	24	15 ☐☐☐☐☐	
1752	A1141	13c Modern dance.	24	15 ☐☐☐☐☐	
1752a.		Block of 4, #1749-1752	1.00	60 ☐☐☐☐☐	
1753	A1142	13c blue, black & red.	24	15 ☐☐☐☐☐	
1754	A1143	13c brown	24	15 ☐☐☐☐☐	
1755	A1144	13c Jimmie Rodgers	24	15 ☐☐☐☐☐	
1756	A1145	15c George M. Cohan	28	15 ☐☐☐☐☐	
1757	A1146	Block of 8.	1.65	1.65 ☐☐☐☐☐	
1757a.		13c Cardinal.	20	15 ☐☐☐☐☐	
1757b.		13c Mallard	20	15 ☐☐☐☐☐	
1757c.		13c Canada goose.	20	15 ☐☐☐☐☐	
1757d.		13c Blue jay	20	15 ☐☐☐☐☐	
1757e.		13c Moose.	20	15 ☐☐☐☐☐	
1757f.		13c Chipmunk	20	15 ☐☐☐☐☐	
1757g.		13c Red fox	20	15 ☐☐☐☐☐	
1757h.		13c Raccoon.	20	15 ☐☐☐☐☐	
1757i.		Yellow, green, red, brown, blue, black (litho.) omitted	*3,500.*	☐☐☐☐☐	
1758	A1147	15c Photographic equipment	26	15 ☐☐☐☐☐	
1759	A1148	15c Viking 1 lander	28	15 ☐☐☐☐☐	
1760	A1149	15c Great gray owl.	28	15 ☐☐☐☐☐	
1761	A1150	15c Saw-whet owl	28	15 ☐☐☐☐☐	
1762	A1151	15c Barred owl.	28	15 ☐☐☐☐☐	
1763	A1152	15c Great horned owl	28	15 ☐☐☐☐☐	
1763a.		Block of 4, #1760-1763	1.15	85 ☐☐☐☐☐	
1764	A1153	15c Giant sequoia	28	15 ☐☐☐☐☐	
1765	A1154	15c White pine.	28	15 ☐☐☐☐☐	
1766	A1155	15c White oak	28	15 ☐☐☐☐☐	
1767	A1156	15c Gray birch.	28	15 ☐☐☐☐☐	
1767a.		Block of 4, #1764-1767	1.15	85 ☐☐☐☐☐	
1767b.		As **a**, imperf. horizontally	*12,500.*	☐☐☐☐☐	

Viking missions to Mars

USA 15c

A1148

Christmas USA 15c

A1157

USA 15c

A1158

Robert F. Kennedy
USA 15c

A1159

USA 15c

International Year of the Child

A1161

Martin Luther King Jr.

Black Heritage USA 15c

A1160

John Steinbeck

USA 15c

A1162

Einstein
USA 15c

A1163

Pennsylvania Toleware
Folk Art USA 15c

A1164

Pennsylvania Toleware
Folk Art USA 15c

A1165

Pennsylvania Toleware
Folk Art USA 15c

A1166

Pennsylvania Toleware
Folk Art USA 15c

A1167

A1168

Jefferson 1743-1826 · Virginia Rotunda

Architecture USA 15c

A1169

Latrobe 1764-1820 · Baltimore Cathedral

Architecture USA 15c

A1170

Bulfinch 1763-1844 · Boston State House

Architecture USA 15c

A1171

Strickland 1788-1854 · Philadelphia Exchange

Architecture USA 15c

Endangered Flora

15c
USA

PERSISTENT TRILLIUM

A1172

Endangered Flora

15c
USA

HAWAIIAN WILD BROADBEAN

A1173

USA 15c

Seeing For Me

A1176

Endangered Flora

15c
USA

CONTRA COSTA WALLFLOWER

A1174

Endangered Flora

15c
USA

ANTIOCH DUNES EVENING PRIMROSE

A1175

Special
Olympics

Skill · Sharing · Joy
USA 15c

A1177

I have not yet
begun to fight

John Paul Jones
US Bicentennial 15c

A1178

A1179

A1180

A1181

A1182

A1183

A1184

A1185

A1186

A1187

A1188

A1191

A1189

Scott No.	Illus. No.	Description	Unused Value	Used Value	//////
1768	A1157	15c blue & multicolored	28	15	☐☐☐☐☐
1768a.		Imperf., pair...................	100.00		☐☐☐☐☐
1769	A1158	15c red & multicolored...........	28	15	☐☐☐☐☐
1769a.		Imperf., pair...................	100.00		☐☐☐☐☐
1769b.		Vertical pair, imperf. horizontally	1,750.		☐☐☐☐☐

1979

Scott No.	Illus. No.	Description	Unused Value	Used Value	//////
1770	A1159	15c blue	28	15	☐☐☐☐☐
1771	A1160	15c Dr. Martin Luther King	28	15	☐☐☐☐☐
1771a.		Imperf., pair...................	—		☐☐☐☐☐
1772	A1161	15c orange red	28	15	☐☐☐☐☐
1773	A1162	15c dark blue	28	15	☐☐☐☐☐
1774	A1163	15c chocolate	28	15	☐☐☐☐☐
1775	A1164	15c Coffeepot..................	28	15	☐☐☐☐☐
1776	A1165	15c Tea caddy	28	15	☐☐☐☐☐
1777	A1166	15c Sugar bowl.................	28	15	☐☐☐☐☐
1778	A1167	15c Coffeepot.................	28	15	☐☐☐☐☐
1778a.		Block of 4, #1775-1778	1.15	85	☐☐☐☐☐
1778b.		As a, imperf. horizontally	3,250.		☐☐☐☐☐
1779	A1168	15c black & brick red	28	15	☐☐☐☐☐
1780	A1169	15c black & brick red	28	15	☐☐☐☐☐
1781	A1170	15c black & brick red	28	15	☐☐☐☐☐
1782	A1171	15c black & brick red	28	15	☐☐☐☐☐
1782a.		Block of 4,#1779-1782..........	1.15	85	☐☐☐☐☐
1783	A1172	15c Persistent trillium	28	15	☐☐☐☐☐
1784	A1173	15c Hawaiian wild broadbean	28	15	☐☐☐☐☐
1785	A1174	15c Contra costa wallflower	28	15	☐☐☐☐☐
1786	A1175	15c Antioch Dunes evening primrose	28	15	☐☐☐☐☐
1786a.		Block of 4, #1783-1786	1.15	85	☐☐☐☐☐
1786b.		As a, imperf...................	750.00		☐☐☐☐☐
1787	A1176	15c Seeing eye dog..............	28	15	☐☐☐☐☐
1787a.		Imperf., pair...................	400.00		☐☐☐☐☐
1788	A1177	15c Special Olympics	28	15	☐☐☐☐☐
1789	A1178	15c John Paul Jones	28	15	☐☐☐☐☐
1789a.		Perf. 11......................	30	15	☐☐☐☐☐
1789b.		Perf. 12......................	2,000.	1,000.	☐☐☐☐☐
1789c.		Vertical pair, imperf. horizontally	240.00		☐☐☐☐☐
1789d.		As a, vertical pair, imperf horizontally.................	200.00		☐☐☐☐☐
1790	A1179	10c Javelin, decathelon	20	20	☐☐☐☐☐
1791	A1180	15c Running..................	28	15	☐☐☐☐☐
1792	A1181	15c Swimming.................	28	15	☐☐☐☐☐
1793	A1182	15c Rowing	28	15	☐☐☐☐☐
1794	A1183	15c Equestrian	28	15	☐☐☐☐☐
1794a.		Block of 4, #1791-1794	1.15	85	☐☐☐☐☐
1794b.		As a, imperf...................	1,850.		☐☐☐☐☐

A1190

A1192

A1193

A1194

A1195

A1196

A1197

A1199

A1209

A1208

A1210

A1211

A1212

A1213

146

Scott No.	Illus. No.	Description	Unused Value	Used Value	`//////`
1980					
1795	A1184	15c Speed skating	32	15 ☐☐☐☐☐
1795a.		Perf.11	1.05	– ☐☐☐☐☐
1796	A1185	15c Downhill skiing.	32	15 ☐☐☐☐☐
1796a.		Perf.11	1.05	– ☐☐☐☐☐
1797	A1186	15c Ski jump	32	15 ☐☐☐☐☐
1797a.		Perf.11	1.05	– ☐☐☐☐☐
1798	A1187	15c Hockey goalkeeper	32	15 ☐☐☐☐☐
1798a.		Perf.11	1.05	– ☐☐☐☐☐
1798b.		Block of 4, #1795-1798	1.30	1.00 ☐☐☐☐☐
1798c.		Block of 4, #1795a-1798a	4.25	– ☐☐☐☐☐
1979					
1799	A1188	15c *Virgin and Child*	28	15 ☐☐☐☐☐
1799a.		Imperf., pair	*125.00*	☐☐☐☐☐
1799b.		Vertical pair, imperf. horizontally	*850.00*	☐☐☐☐☐
1799c.		Vertical pair, imperf. between	–	☐☐☐☐☐
1800	A1189	15c Santa Claus, tree, ornament	28	15 ☐☐☐☐☐
1800a.		Green & yellow omitted	*750.00*	☐☐☐☐☐
1800b.		Green, yellow & tan omitted.	*800.00*	☐☐☐☐☐
1801	A1190	15c Will Rogers	28	15 ☐☐☐☐☐
1801a.		Imperf., pair	*275.00*	☐☐☐☐☐
1802	A1191	15c Viet Nam veterans	28	15 ☐☐☐☐☐
1803	A1192	15c W.C. Fields	28	15 ☐☐☐☐☐
1980					
1804	A1193	15c Benjamin Benneker	28	15 ☐☐☐☐☐
1804a.		Horizontal pair, imperf. vertically	–	☐☐☐☐☐
1805	A1194	15c Letters Preserve Memories.	28	15 ☐☐☐☐☐
1806	A1195	15c claret & multicolored	28	15 ☐☐☐☐☐
1807	A1196	15c Letters Lift Spirits.	28	15 ☐☐☐☐☐
1808	A1195	15c green & multicolored	28	15 ☐☐☐☐☐
1809	A1197	15c Letters Shape Opinions	28	15 ☐☐☐☐☐
1810	A1195	15c red & multicolored	28	15 ☐☐☐☐☐
1810a.		Strip of 6 #1805-1810	1.70	1.50 ☐☐☐☐☐
1980-81					
1811	A984	1c dark blue, *greenish*	15	15 ☐☐☐☐☐
1811a.		Imperf., pair	*225.00*	☐☐☐☐☐
1813	A1199	3.5c purple, *yellow*	15	15 ☐☐☐☐☐
1813a.		Untagged (Bureau precanceled,		
		lines only)		15 ☐☐☐☐☐
1813b.		Imperf., pair	*300.00*	☐☐☐☐☐
1816	A997	12c brown red, beige ('81)	24	15 ☐☐☐☐☐
1816a.		Untagged (Bureau precanceled) . .		25 ☐☐☐☐☐
1816b.		Imperf., pair	*225.00*	☐☐☐☐☐

A1214 — Coral Reefs USA 15c, Brain Coral, U.S. Virgin Islands

A1215 — Coral Reefs USA 15c, Elkhorn Coral, Florida

A1218 — Organized Labor Proud and Free USA 15c

A1219 — Edith Wharton, USA 15c

A1216 — Coral Reefs USA 15c, Chalice Coral, American Samoa

A1217 — Coral Reefs USA 15c, Finger Coral, Hawaii

A1220 — Learning never ends, USA 15c

A1221 — Heiltsuk, Bella Bella, Indian Art USA 15c

A1222 — Chilkat Tlingit, Indian Art USA 15c

A1223 — Tlingit, Indian Art USA 15c

A1224 — Bella Coola, Indian Art USA 15c

HOW TO USE THIS BOOK

The number in the first column is its Scott number or identifying number. The letter and number that come next (A41) indicate the design and refer to the illustration so designated. Following that is the denomination of the stamp and its color. Finally, the value, unused and used is shown.

Scott No.	Illus. No.	Description	Unused Value	Used Value	//////
1981					
1818	A1207	(18c) violet.....................	32	15 ☐☐☐☐☐	
1819	A1207	(18c) violet, from booklet pane.....	40	15 ☐☐☐☐☐	
1819a.		Booklet pane of 8..............	4.50	1.50 ☐☐☐☐☐	
		Coil stamps, Perf. 10 vertically			
1820	A1207	(18c) violet.....................	40	15 ☐☐☐☐☐	
1820a.		Imperf., pair...................	*110.00*	☐☐☐☐☐	
1980					
1821	A1208	15c Prussian blue.............	28	15 ☐☐☐☐☐	
1822	A1209	15c red brown & sepia............	28	15 ☐☐☐☐☐	
1823	A1210	15c black & red	28	15 ☐☐☐☐☐	
1823a.		Vertical pair, imperf. horizontally	*300.00*	☐☐☐☐☐	
1824	A1211	15c Helen Keller, Anne Sullivan ...	28	15 ☐☐☐☐☐	
1825	A1212	15c carmine & violet blue.........	28	15 ☐☐☐☐☐	
1825a.		Horizontal pair, imperf. vertically	*500.00*	☐☐☐☐☐	
1826	A1213	15c Gen. Bernardo de Galvez......	28	15 ☐☐☐☐☐	
1826a.		Red, brown & blue (engraved) omitted	*900.00*	☐☐☐☐☐	
1826b.		Red, brown, blue (engraved), blue & yellow (litho.) omitted	*1,400.*	☐☐☐☐☐	
1827	A1214	15c Berain coral, Beaugregory fish ..	30	15 ☐☐☐☐☐	
1828	A1215	15c Elkhorn coral, porkfish........	30	15 ☐☐☐☐☐	
1829	A1216	15c Chalice coral, Moorish idol fish.	30	15 ☐☐☐☐☐	
1830	A1217	15c Finger coral, sabertooth blenny fish......................	30	15 ☐☐☐☐☐	
1830a.		Block of 4 (#1827-1830)	1.20	85 ☐☐☐☐☐	
1830b.		As **a**, imperf...................	*1,600.*	☐☐☐☐☐	
1830c.		As **a**, imperf. between, vertically..	—	☐☐☐☐☐	
1830d.		As **a**, imperf. vertically	*3,000.*	☐☐☐☐☐	
1831	A1218	15c American bald eagle..........	28	15 ☐☐☐☐☐	
1831a.		Imperf., pair...................	*450.00*	☐☐☐☐☐	
1832	A1219	15c purple	28	15 ☐☐☐☐☐	
1833	A1220	15c American education	28	15 ☐☐☐☐☐	
1833a.		Horizontal pair, imperf. between .	*300.00*	☐☐☐☐☐	
1834	A1221	15c Heitsuk , Bella Bella tribe......	30	15 ☐☐☐☐☐	
1835	A1222	15c Chilkat, Tlingit tribe..........	30	15 ☐☐☐☐☐	
1836	A1223	15c Tlingit tribe................	30	15 ☐☐☐☐☐	
1837	A1224	15c Bella Coola tribe............	30	15 ☐☐☐☐☐	
1837a.		Block of 4, #1834-1837	1.20	85 ☐☐☐☐☐	
1838	A1225	15c black & brick red	30	15 ☐☐☐☐☐	
1839	A1226	15c black & brick red	30	15 ☐☐☐☐☐	
1840	A1227	15c black & brick red	30	15 ☐☐☐☐☐	
1841	A1228	15c black & brick red	30	15 ☐☐☐☐☐	
1841a.		Block of 4, #1838-1841	1.20	85 ☐☐☐☐☐	
1842	A1229	15c Madonna and Child	28	15 ☐☐☐☐☐	
1842a.		Imperf., pair...................	*100.00*	☐☐☐☐☐	

Renwick 1818-1895 Smithsonian Washington

A1225 Architecture USA 15c

Richardson 1838-1886 Trinity Church Boston

Architecture USA 15c **A1226**

Furness 1839-1912 Penn. Academy Philadelphia

A1227 Architecture USA 15c

A.J. Davis 1803-1892 Lyndhurst Tarrytown NY

Architecture USA 15c **A1228**

Christmas USA 15c

A1229

USA 15c
Season's Greetings

A1230

USA 15c
Everett Dirksen

A1261

Whitney Moore Young

Black Heritage USA 15c

A1262

A1263 Rose USA 18c

Camellia USA 18c **A1264**

A1265 Dahlia USA 18c

Lily USA 18c **A1266**

Scott No.	Illus. No.	Description	Unused Value	Used Value	//////
1843	A1230	15c Wreath, toys	28	15 ☐☐☐☐☐
1843a.		Imperf., pair.................	*100.00*	☐☐☐☐☐
1843b.		Buff omitted.................	—	☐☐☐☐☐

1980-85

1844	A1231	1c black ('83)	15	15 ☐☐☐☐☐
1844a.		Imperf. pair	*350.00*	☐☐☐☐☐
1844b.		Vertical pair, imperf. between....	—	☐☐☐☐☐
1845	A1232	2c brown black ('82)	15	15 ☐☐☐☐☐
1846	A1233	3c olive green ('83).	15	15 ☐☐☐☐☐
1847	A1234	4c violet ('83).................	15	15 ☐☐☐☐☐
1848	A1235	5c henna brown ('83).	15	15 ☐☐☐☐☐
1849	A1236	6c orange vermilion ('85)	15	15 ☐☐☐☐☐
1849a.		Vertical pair, imperf. between....	—	☐☐☐☐☐
1850	A1237	7c bright carmine ('85)	15	15 ☐☐☐☐☐
1851	A1238	8c olive black ('85).............	15	15 ☐☐☐☐☐
1852	A1239	9c dark green ('85)	16	15 ☐☐☐☐☐
1853	A1240	10c Prussian blue ('84)	18	15 ☐☐☐☐☐
1853a.		Vertical pair, imperf. between....	*1,100.*	☐☐☐☐☐
1853b.		Horizontal pair, imperf. between .	—	☐☐☐☐☐
1854	A1241	11c dark blue ('85).............	20	15 ☐☐☐☐☐
1855	A1242	13c light maroon ('82)...........	24	15 ☐☐☐☐☐
1856	A1243	14c slate green ('85).............	25	15 ☐☐☐☐☐
1856a.		Vertical pair, imperf. horizontally	*150.00*	☐☐☐☐☐
1856b.		Horizontal pair, imperf. between .	10.00	☐☐☐☐☐
1856c.		Vertical pair, imperf. between....	*2,000.*	☐☐☐☐☐
1857	A1244	17c green ('81)	32	15 ☐☐☐☐☐
1858	A1245	18c dark blue ('81).............	32	15 ☐☐☐☐☐
1859	A1246	19c brown	35	15 ☐☐☐☐☐
1860	A1247	20c claret ('82)	40	15 ☐☐☐☐☐
1861	A1248	20c green ('83)	38	15 ☐☐☐☐☐
1862	A1249	20c black('84).................	38	15 ☐☐☐☐☐
1863	A1250	22c dark chalky blue ('85).........	40	15 ☐☐☐☐☐
1863a.		Vertical pair, imperf. horizontally	—	☐☐☐☐☐
1863b.		Vertical pair, imperf. between....	—	☐☐☐☐☐
1863c.		Horizontal pair, imperf. between .	—	☐☐☐☐☐
1864	A1251	30c olive gray ('84)	55	15 ☐☐☐☐☐
1865	A1252	35c gray ('81)	65	15 ☐☐☐☐☐
1866	A1253	37c blue ('82)	70	15 ☐☐☐☐☐
1867	A1254	39c rose lilac ('85)	70	15 ☐☐☐☐☐
1867a.		Vertical pair, imperf. horizontally	*700.00*	☐☐☐☐☐
1867b.		Vertical pair, imperf. between....	*1,100.*	☐☐☐☐☐
1868	A1255	40c dark green ('84).............	70	15 ☐☐☐☐☐
1869	A1256	50c brown ('85)	90	15 ☐☐☐☐☐

1981

1874	A1261	15c gray	28	15 ☐☐☐☐☐
1875	A1262	15c Whitney Moore Young........	28	15 ☐☐☐☐☐

A1231

A1232

A1233

A1234

A1235

A1236

A1237

A1238

A1239

A1240

A1241

A1242

A1243

A1244

A1245

A1246

A1247

A1248

A1249

A1250

A1251

A1252

A1253

A1254

A1255

A1256

Scott No.	Illus. No.	Description	Unused Value	Used Value	//////
1876	A1263	18c Flowers	35	15	□□□□□
1877	A1264	18c Flowers	35	15	□□□□□
1878	A1265	18c Flowers	35	15	□□□□□
1879	A1266	18c Flowers	35	15	□□□□□
1879a.		Block of 4, #1876-1879	1.40	85	□□□□□
1880	A1267	18c Bighorn	35	15	□□□□□
1881	A1268	18c Puma	35	15	□□□□□
1882	A1269	18c Harbor seal	35	15	□□□□□
1883	A1270	18c Bison	35	15	□□□□□
1884	A1271	18c Brown bear	35	15	□□□□□
1885	A1272	18c Polar bear	35	15	□□□□□
1886	A1273	18c Elk (wapiti)	35	15	□□□□□
1887	A1274	18c Moose	35	15	□□□□□
1888	A1275	18c White-tailed deer	35	15	□□□□□
1889	A1276	18c Pronghorn	35	15	□□□□□
1889a.		Booklet pane of 10	9.00	–	□□□□□
1890	A1277	18c Flag	32	15	□□□□□
1890a.		Imperf., pair	100.00		□□□□□
1890b.		Vertical pair, imperf. horizontally	–		□□□□□

Coil stamp, Perf. 10 vertically

1891	A1278	18c Flag	36	15	□□□□□
1891a.		Imperf., pair	20.00		□□□□□

1981

1892	A1279	6c "6" in circle of stars	55	15	□□□□□
1893	A1280	18c Flag	32	15	□□□□□
1893a.		Booklet pane of 8 (2 #1892, 6 #1893)	3.25	–	□□□□□
1893b.		As a, vert. imperf. between	80.00		□□□□□
1893c.		Se-tenant pair, #1892 & 1893	90	–	□□□□□
1894	A1281	20c black, dark blue & red	35	15	□□□□□
1894a.		Vertical pair, imperf.	35.00		□□□□□
1894b.		Vertical pair, imperf. horizontally	650.00		□□□□□
1894c.		Dark blue omitted	225.00		□□□□□
1894d.		Black omitted	300.00		□□□□□
1895	A1281	20c black, dark blue & red	35	15	□□□□□
1895a.		Imperf., pair	10.00		□□□□□
1895b.		Black omitted	65.00		□□□□□
1895c.		Dark blue omitted	–		□□□□□
1895d.		Pair, imperf. between	–		□□□□□
1895e.		Untagged (Bureau precanceled)	48	48	□□□□□
1896	A1281	20c black, dark blue & red	35	15	□□□□□
1896a.		Booklet pane of 6	2.60	–	□□□□□
1896b.		Booklet pane of 10	4.00	–	□□□□□

Omnibus 1880s
USA 1c

A1282

Locomotive 1870s
USA 2c

A1283

Handcar 1880s
USA 3c

A1284

Stagecoach 1890s
USA 4c

A1285

Motorcycle
1913
USA 5c

A1286

Sleigh 1880s
USA 5.2c Auth
Nonprofit
Org

A1287

Bicycle 1870s
USA 5.9c
Auth
Nonprofit
Org

A1288

Baby Buggy 1880s
USA 7.4c

A1289

Mail Wagon 1880s
USA 9.3c
Bulk
Rate

A1290

Hansom Cab 1890s
USA 10.9c
Bulk
Rate

A1291

RR Caboose 1890s
USA 11c
Auth
Bulk Rate

A1292

Electric Auto 1917
USA 17c

A1293

Surrey 1890s
USA 18c

A1294

Fire Pumper
1860s
USA 20c

A1295

A1296

A1207

A1281

A1267   A1268

A1269   A1270

A1271   A1272

A1273   A1274

A1275   A1276

A1277   A1278   A1279   A1280

A1332   A1333   A1334   A1390

155

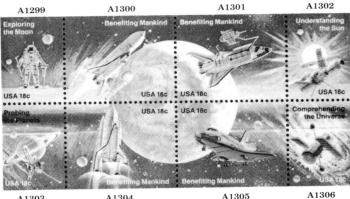

A1299 A1300 A1301 A1302

Exploring the Moon — USA 18c
Benefiting Mankind — USA 18c
Benefiting Mankind — USA 18c
Understanding the Sun — USA 18c

Probing the Planets — USA 18c
USA 18c
USA 18c
Comprehending the Universe — USA 18c

A1303 A1304 A1305 A1306

The Gift of Self

USA 18c

American Red Cross
1881-1981

A1297

Save Wetland Habitats
USA 18c

A1308

Save Grassland Habitats
USA 18c

A1309

Save Mountain Habitats

A1310

Save Woodland Habitats

A1311

SAVINGS AND LOANS

SAVE

USA 18c

A1298

Scott No.	Illus. No.	Description	Unused Value	Used Value	//////
1981-84					
1897	A1282	1c violet ('83)...................	15	15	☐☐☐☐☐
1897b.		Imperf., pair...................	*700.00*		☐☐☐☐☐
1897A	A1283	2c black ('82)...................	15	15	☐☐☐☐☐
1897e.		Imperf., pair...................	*85.00*		☐☐☐☐☐
1898	A1284	3c dark green ('83)...............	15	15	☐☐☐☐☐
1898A	A1285	4c reddish brown ('82)...........	15	15	☐☐☐☐☐
1898b.		Untagged (Bureau precanceled) ..	15	15	☐☐☐☐☐
1898c.		As **b**, imperf., pair	*900.00*		☐☐☐☐☐
1898d.		No. 1898A, imperf., pair		–	☐☐☐☐☐
1899	A1286	5c gray green ('83)	15	15	☐☐☐☐☐
1899a.		Imperf., pair...................	–		☐☐☐☐☐
1900	A1287	5.2c carmine ('83)	15	15	☐☐☐☐☐
1900a.		Untagged (Bureau precanceled) ..	15	15	☐☐☐☐☐
1901	A1288	5.9c blue ('82).................	18	15	☐☐☐☐☐
1901a.		Untagged (Bureau precanceled, lines only)	18	18	☐☐☐☐☐
1901b.		As **a**, imperf., pair	*300.00*		☐☐☐☐☐
1902	A1289	7.4c brown ('84).................	18	15	☐☐☐☐☐
1902a.		Untagged (Bureau precanceled) ..	20	20	☐☐☐☐☐
1903	A1290	9.3c carmine rose...............	25	15	☐☐☐☐☐
1903a.		Untagged (Bureau precanceled, lines only)	22	22	☐☐☐☐☐
1903b.		As **a**, imperf., pair	*165.00*		☐☐☐☐☐
1904	A1291	10.9c purple ('82)...............	24	15	☐☐☐☐☐
1904a.		Untagged (Bureau precanceled, lines only)	24	24	☐☐☐☐☐
1904b.		As **a**, imperf., pair	*225.00*		☐☐☐☐☐
1905	A1292	11c red ('84)...................	24	15	☐☐☐☐☐
1905a.		Untagged (Bureau precanceled, lines only)	24	24	☐☐☐☐☐
1906	A1293	17c ultramarine	32	15	☐☐☐☐☐
1906a.		Untagged (Bureau precanceled, Presorted First Class)	35	35	☐☐☐☐☐
1906b.		Imperf., pair...................	*200.00*		☐☐☐☐☐
1906c.		As **a**, imperf., pair	750.00		☐☐☐☐☐
1907	A1294	18c dark brown	34	15	☐☐☐☐☐
1907a.		Imperf., pair...................	*170.00*		☐☐☐☐☐
1908	A1295	20c vermilion...................	32	15	☐☐☐☐☐
1908a.		Imperf., pair...................	*150.00*		☐☐☐☐☐
1983, Aug. 12					
1909	A1296	$9.35 Eagle....................	24.00	12.50	☐☐☐☐☐
1909a.		Booklet pane of 3..............	72.50	–	☐☐☐☐☐
1981					
1910	A1297	18c Red Cross centennial	32	15	☐☐☐☐☐
1911	A1298	18c Savings & Loan..............	32	15	☐☐☐☐☐

A1307

A1312

A1313

A1314

A1327

A1315

A1316

A1317

A1318

A1319

A1321

A1322

A1320

158

Scott No.	Illus. No.	Description	Unused Value	Used Value	//////
1912	A1299	18c "Exploring the Moon"	32	15	☐☐☐☐☐
1913	A1300	18c Shuttle launch (diagonal)	32	15	☐☐☐☐☐
1914	A1301	18c Shuttle, satellite	32	15	☐☐☐☐☐
1915	A1302	18c "Understanding the Sun"	32	15	☐☐☐☐☐
1916	A1303	18c "Probing the Planets"	32	15	☐☐☐☐☐
1917	A1304	18c Shuttle launch (vertical)	32	15	☐☐☐☐☐
1918	A1305	18c Shuttle in flight	32	15	☐☐☐☐☐
1919	A1306	18c "Comprehending the Universe"	32	15	☐☐☐☐☐
1919a.		Block of 8, #1912-1919	3.00	2.75	☐☐☐☐☐
1919b.		As a, imperf.	8,000.		☐☐☐☐☐
1920	A1307	18c blue & black	32	15	☐☐☐☐☐
1921	A1308	18c Great blue heron	35	15	☐☐☐☐☐
1922	A1309	18c Badger	35	15	☐☐☐☐☐
1923	A1310	18c Grizzly bear	35	15	☐☐☐☐☐
1924	A1311	18c Ruffed grouse	35	15	☐☐☐☐☐
1924a.		Block of 4, #1921-1924	1.40	1.00	☐☐☐☐☐
1925	A1312	18c Man using microscope	32	15	☐☐☐☐☐
1925a.		Vertical pair, imperf. horizontally	2,250.		☐☐☐☐☐
1926	A1313	18c Edna St. Vincent Millay	32	15	☐☐☐☐☐
1926a.		Black (engraved, inscriptions) omitted	650.00	–	☐☐☐☐☐
1927	A1314	18c blue & black	42	15	☐☐☐☐☐
1927a.		Imperf., pair	350.00		☐☐☐☐☐
1928	A1315	18c black & red	42	15	☐☐☐☐☐
1929	A1316	18c black & red	42	15	☐☐☐☐☐
1930	A1317	18c black & red	42	15	☐☐☐☐☐
1931	A1318	18c black & red	42	15	☐☐☐☐☐
1931a.		Block of 4, #1928-1931	1.75	1.00	☐☐☐☐☐
1932	A1319	18c purple	32	15	☐☐☐☐☐
1933	A1320	18c green	32	15	☐☐☐☐☐
1934	A1321	18c gray, green & brown	32	15	☐☐☐☐☐
1934a.		Vertical pair, imperf. between	300.00		☐☐☐☐☐
1934b.		Brown omitted	600.00		☐☐☐☐☐
1935	A1322	18c James Hoban	32	16	☐☐☐☐☐
1936	A1322	20c James Hoban	35	15	☐☐☐☐☐
1937	A1323	18c Battle of Yorktown	35	15	☐☐☐☐☐
1938	A1324	18c Battle of Virginia Capes	35	15	☐☐☐☐☐
1938a.		Pair, #1937-1938	70	15	☐☐☐☐☐
1938b.		As a, black (engraved, inscriptions) omitted	550.00		☐☐☐☐☐
1939	A1325	(20c) Madonna and child	38	15	☐☐☐☐☐
1939a.		Imperf., pair	110.00		☐☐☐☐☐
1939b.		Vertical pair, imperf. horizontally	–		☐☐☐☐☐
1940	A1326	(20c) Felt bear on sled	38	15	☐☐☐☐☐
1940a.		Imperf., pair	250.00		☐☐☐☐☐
1940b.		Vertical pair, imperf. horizontally	–		☐☐☐☐☐
1941	A1327	20c John Hanson	38	15	☐☐☐☐☐
1942	A1328	20c Barrel cactus	35	15	☐☐☐☐☐

 A1323

 A1324

 A1325

 A1326

 A1328

 A1329

A1330

 A1331

 A1335

 A1336

 A1337

160

Scott No.	Illus. No.	Description	Unused Value	Used Value	//////
1943	A1329	20c Agave......................	35	15	☐☐☐☐☐
1944	A1330	20c Beavertail cactus.............	35	15	☐☐☐☐☐
1945	A1331	20c Saguaro	35	15	☐☐☐☐☐
1945a.		Block of 4, #1942-1945	1.50	15	☐☐☐☐☐
1945b.		As a, deep brown omitted	7,500.		☐☐☐☐☐
1945c.		No. 1945 imperf., vertical pair ...	—		☐☐☐☐☐
1946	A1332	(20c) brown	38	15	☐☐☐☐☐

Coil stamp, Perf. 10 vertically

Scott No.	Illus. No.	Description	Unused Value	Used Value	//////
1947	A1332	(20c) brown	60	15	☐☐☐☐☐
1947a.		Imperf., pair..................	1,500.		☐☐☐☐☐

1981

Scott No.	Illus. No.	Description	Unused Value	Used Value	//////
1948	A1333	(20c) brown	38	15	☐☐☐☐☐
1948a.		Booklet pane of 10.............	4.50		☐☐☐☐☐

1982

Scott No.	Illus. No.	Description	Unused Value	Used Value	//////
1949	A1334	20c dark blue (from booklet pane)..	50	15	☐☐☐☐☐
1949a.		Booklet pane of 10.............	5.00	—	☐☐☐☐☐
1949b.		As a, vert. imperf. between	125.00		☐☐☐☐☐
1949c.		Type II	50	15	☐☐☐☐☐
1949d.		As c, booklet pane of 10	5.00	—	☐☐☐☐☐
1950	A1335	20c blue	38	15	☐☐☐☐☐
1951	A1336	20c Love.......................	38	15	☐☐☐☐☐
1951a.		Perf. 11	48	15	☐☐☐☐☐
1951b.		Imperf., pair..................	275.00		☐☐☐☐☐
1951c.		Blue omitted..................	200.00		☐☐☐☐☐
1952	A1337	20c George Washington	38	15	☐☐☐☐☐
1953	A1338	20c Alabama	40	25	☐☐☐☐☐
1954	A1339	20c Alaska	40	25	☐☐☐☐☐
1955	A1340	20c Arizona	40	25	☐☐☐☐☐
1956	A1341	20c Arkansas	40	25	☐☐☐☐☐
1957	A1342	20c California	40	25	☐☐☐☐☐
1958	A1343	20c Colorado	40	25	☐☐☐☐☐
1959	A1344	20c Connecticut.................	40	25	☐☐☐☐☐
1960	A1345	20c Delaware	40	25	☐☐☐☐☐
1961	A1346	20c Florida.....................	40	25	☐☐☐☐☐
1962	A1347	20c Georgia	40	25	☐☐☐☐☐
1963	A1348	20c Hawaii.....................	40	25	☐☐☐☐☐
1964	A1349	20c Idaho......................	40	25	☐☐☐☐☐
1965	A1350	20c Illinois.....................	40	25	☐☐☐☐☐
1966	A1351	20c Indiana	40	25	☐☐☐☐☐
1967	A1352	20c Iowa.......................	40	25	☐☐☐☐☐
1968	A1353	20c Kansas.....................	40	25	☐☐☐☐☐
1969	A1354	20c Kentucky...................	40	25	☐☐☐☐☐
1970	A1355	20c Louisiana...................	40	25	☐☐☐☐☐
1971	A1356	20c Maine	40	25	☐☐☐☐☐
1972	A1357	20c Maryland...................	40	25	☐☐☐☐☐

A1338-A1387—State Birds and Flowers

A1388

A1395

A1389

A1391

A1392

A1393

A1394

162

Scott No.	Illus. No.	Description	Unused Value	Used Value	//////
1973	A1358	20c Massachusetts	40	25	☐☐☐☐☐
1974	A1359	20c Michigan	40	25	☐☐☐☐☐
1975	A1360	20c Minnesota	40	25	☐☐☐☐☐
1976	A1361	20c Mississippi	40	25	☐☐☐☐☐
1977	A1362	20c Missouri	40	25	☐☐☐☐☐
1978	A1363	20c Montana	40	25	☐☐☐☐☐
1979	A1364	20c Nebraska	40	25	☐☐☐☐☐
1980	A1365	20c Nevada	40	25	☐☐☐☐☐
1981	A1366	20c New Hampshire	40	25	☐☐☐☐☐
1982	A1367	20c New Jersey	40	25	☐☐☐☐☐
1983	A1368	20c New Mexico	40	25	☐☐☐☐☐
1984	A1369	20c New York	40	25	☐☐☐☐☐
1985	A1370	20c North Carolina	40	25	☐☐☐☐☐
1986	A1371	20c North Dakota	40	25	☐☐☐☐☐
1987	A1372	20c Ohio.	40	25	☐☐☐☐☐
1988	A1373	20c Oklahoma	40	25	☐☐☐☐☐
1989	A1374	20c Oregon.	40	25	☐☐☐☐☐
1990	A1375	20c Pennsylvania.	40	25	☐☐☐☐☐
1991	A1376	20c Rhode Island.	40	25	☐☐☐☐☐
1992	A1377	20c South Carolina	40	25	☐☐☐☐☐
1993	A1378	20c South Dakota	40	25	☐☐☐☐☐
1994	A1379	20c Tennessee	40	25	☐☐☐☐☐
1995	A1380	20c Texas.	40	25	☐☐☐☐☐
1996	A1381	20c Utah.	40	25	☐☐☐☐☐
1997	A1382	20c Vermont	40	25	☐☐☐☐☐
1998	A1383	20c Virginia	40	25	☐☐☐☐☐
1999	A1384	20c Washington.	40	25	☐☐☐☐☐
2000	A1385	20c West Virginia	40	25	☐☐☐☐☐
2001	A1386	20c Wisconsin	40	25	☐☐☐☐☐
2002	A1387	20c Wyoming.	40	25	☐☐☐☐☐
2002a.		#1953a-2002a, any single, perf. 11	45	30	☐☐☐☐☐
2002b.		Pane of 50, perf. 10½ x 11.	20.00	—	☐☐☐☐☐
2002c.		Pane of 50, perf. 11.	22.50	—	☐☐☐☐☐
2002d.		Pane of 50, imperf.	—		☐☐☐☐☐
2003	A1388	20c vermilion, bright blue & gray black	38	15	☐☐☐☐☐
2003a.		Imperf., pair.	*475.00*		☐☐☐☐☐
2004	A1389	20c red & black	38	15	☐☐☐☐☐

Coil Stamp

2005	A1390	20c sky blue	75	15	☐☐☐☐☐
2005a.		Imperf., pair.	*125.00*		☐☐☐☐☐

1982

2006	A1391	20c "Solar energy".	38	15	☐☐☐☐☐
2007	A1392	20c "Synthetic fuels".	38	15	☐☐☐☐☐
2008	A1393	20c "Breeder reactor"	38	15	☐☐☐☐☐
2009	A1394	20c "Fossil fuels".	38	15	☐☐☐☐☐

A1396

A1399

A1397

A1398

A1400

A1401

A1402

A1403

A1404

A1405

A1406

A1407

164

A1408

A1409

A1411

A1410

A1416

A1412

A1413

A1414

A1415

A1421

A1422

165

A1418

A1417

A1419

A1420

A1423

A1429

A1431

A1432

A1424

A1425

A1426

A1427

A1428

Scott No.	Illus. No.	Description	Unused Value	Used Value	//////
2009a.		Block of 4, #2006-2009	1.55	1.00	☐☐☐☐☐
2010	A1395	20c red & black, *tan*	38	15	☐☐☐☐☐
2011	A1396	20c brown	38	15	☐☐☐☐☐
2012	A1397	20c John, Ethel & Lionel Barrymore	38	15	☐☐☐☐☐
2013	A1398	20c Dr. Mary E. Walker	38	15	☐☐☐☐☐
2014	A1399	20c International Peace Garden	38	15	☐☐☐☐☐
2014a.		Black green & brown (engraved) omitted	*300.00*		☐☐☐☐☐
2015	A1400	20c red & black	38	15	☐☐☐☐☐
2015a.		Vertical pair, imperf. horizontally	*300.00*		☐☐☐☐☐
2016	A1401	20c Jackie Robinson	75	15	☐☐☐☐☐
2017	A1402	20c Touro Synagogue	38	15	☐☐☐☐☐
2017a.		Imperf., pair...................	*800.00*		☐☐☐☐☐
2018	A1403	20c Wolf Trap Farm Park.........	38	15	☐☐☐☐☐
2019	A1404	20c black & brown...............	38	15	☐☐☐☐☐
2020	A1405	20c black & brown...............	38	15	☐☐☐☐☐
2021	A1406	20c black & brown...............	38	15	☐☐☐☐☐
2022	A1407	20c black & brown...............	38	15	☐☐☐☐☐
2022a.		Block of 4, #2019-2022	1.90	1.00	☐☐☐☐☐
2023	A1408	20c St. Francis of Assisi	38	15	☐☐☐☐☐
2024	A1409	20c Ponce de Leon...............	38	15	☐☐☐☐☐
2024a.		Imperf., pair...................	*750.00*		☐☐☐☐☐
2025	A1410	13c Kitten, puppy	24	15	☐☐☐☐☐
2025a.		Imperf., pair...................	*500.00*		☐☐☐☐☐
2026	A1411	20c Madonna and Child	38	15	☐☐☐☐☐
2026a.		Imperf., pair...................	*175.00*		☐☐☐☐☐
2026b.		Horizontal pair, imperf. vertically	—		☐☐☐☐☐
2026c.		Vertical pair, imperf. horizontally	—		☐☐☐☐☐
2027	A1412	20c Children, sleds	45	15	☐☐☐☐☐
2028	A1413	20c Children, snowman..........	45	15	☐☐☐☐☐
2029	A1414	20c Outdoor skating	45	15	☐☐☐☐☐
2030	A1415	20c Children, tree	45	15	☐☐☐☐☐
2030a.		Block of 4, #2027-2030	1.85	1.00	☐☐☐☐☐
2030b.		As **a**, imperf...................	*2,750.*		☐☐☐☐☐
2030c.		As **a**, imperf. horizontally	—		☐☐☐☐☐

1983

Scott No.	Illus. No.	Description	Unused Value	Used Value	//////
2031	A1416	20c Science & industry	38	15	☐☐☐☐☐
2031a.		Black (engraved) omitted	*1,400.*		☐☐☐☐☐
2032	A1417	20c *Intrepid*	38	15	☐☐☐☐☐
2033	A1418	20c Balloons in flight............	38	15	☐☐☐☐☐
2034	A1419	20c Balloons in flight............	38	15	☐☐☐☐☐
2035	A1420	20c *Explorer II*.................	38	15	☐☐☐☐☐
2035a.		Block of 4, #2032-2035	1.55	1.00	☐☐☐☐☐
2035b.		As **a**, imperf...................	*2,500.*		☐☐☐☐☐
2036	A1421	20c Benjamin Franklin	38	15	☐☐☐☐☐
2037	A1422	20c Civilian Conservation Corps ...	38	15	☐☐☐☐☐
2037a.		Imperf., pair...................	*2,250.*		☐☐☐☐☐

USA 20c
Medal of Honor

A1430

CIVIL
SERVICE
1883
1983
USA20c

A1438

Treaty of Paris 1783
US Bicentennial 20 cents

A1437

A1433   **A1434**

Olympics 84
USA
13c

Olympics 84
USA
13c

Olympics 84
USA
13c

Olympics 84
USA
13c

A1435   **A1436**

A1440   **A1441**

USA
20c   Charles Steinmetz

USA
20c   Edwin Armstrong

Nikola Tesla   20c

Philo T. Farnsworth   20c

A1442   **A1443**

A1439

Christmas USA 20c

Raphael, 1483-1983, National Gallery

A1448

Season's Greetings USA 20c

A1449

A1444   **A1445**

First American streetcar, New York City, 1832

Early electric streetcar, Montgomery, Ala., 1886

"Bobtail" horsecar, Sulphur Rock, Ark., 1926

St. Charles streetcar, New Orleans, La., 1923

A1446   **A1447**

Martin Luther

1483-1983 USA 20c

A1450

A1452   **A1453**

Olympics 84 USA 20c

USA 20c

1959-1984 Alaska Statehood

A1451

FEDERAL DEPOSIT INSURANCE CORPORATION

A1456

Olympics 84 USA 20c

A1454   **A1455**

LOVE
LOVE
LOVE
LOVE
LOVE
USA 20c

A1457

A1458

A1461

A1462

A1459

A1460

A1463

A1464

A1466

A1467

A1468

A1473

A1469

A1470

A1474

A1465

A1471

A1472

170

Scott No.	Illus. No.	Description	Unused Value	Used Value	//////
2038	A1423	20c Joseph Priestly	38	15	☐☐☐☐☐
2039	A1424	20c red & black..................	38	15	☐☐☐☐☐
2039a.		Imperf., pair...................	*1,000.*		☐☐☐☐☐
2040	A1425	20c brown	38	15	☐☐☐☐☐
2041	A1426	20c blue	38	15	☐☐☐☐☐
2042	A1427	20c Tennessee Valley Authority....	38	15	☐☐☐☐☐
2043	A1428	20c Physical Fitness..............	38	15	☐☐☐☐☐
2044	A1429	20c Scott Joplin.................	38	15	☐☐☐☐☐
2044a.		Imperf., pair...................	*500.00*		☐☐☐☐☐
2045	A1430	20c Medal of Honor	38	15	☐☐☐☐☐
2045a.		Red omitted...................	*325.00*		☐☐☐☐☐
2046	A1431	20c blue	60	15	☐☐☐☐☐
2047	A1432	20c Nathaniel Hawthorne.........	38	15	☐☐☐☐☐
2048	A1433	13c Discus	28	15	☐☐☐☐☐
2049	A1434	13c High jump..................	28	15	☐☐☐☐☐
2050	A1435	13c Archery	28	15	☐☐☐☐☐
2051	A1436	13c Boxing.....................	28	15	☐☐☐☐☐
2051a.		Block of 4, #2048-2051	1.20	80	☐☐☐☐☐
2052	A1437	20c Treaty of Paris	38	15	☐☐☐☐☐
2053	A1438	20c buff, blue & red..............	38	15	☐☐☐☐☐
2054	A1439	20c yellow & maroon	38	15	☐☐☐☐☐
2055	A1440	20c Charles Steinmetz............	38	15	☐☐☐☐☐
2056	A1441	20c Edwin Armstrong............	38	15	☐☐☐☐☐
2057	A1442	20c Nikola Telsa	38	15	☐☐☐☐☐
2058	A1443	20c Philo T. Farnsworth	38	15	☐☐☐☐☐
2058a.		Block of 4, #2055-2058	1.55	1.00	☐☐☐☐☐
2058b.		As **a,** black omitted	*400.00*		☐☐☐☐☐
2059	A1444	20c First American streetcar.......	38	15	☐☐☐☐☐
2060	A1445	20c Early electric streetcar	38	15	☐☐☐☐☐
2061	A1446	20c "Bobtail" streetcar	38	15	☐☐☐☐☐
2062	A1447	20c St. Charles streetcar	38	15	☐☐☐☐☐
2062a.		Block of 4, #2059-2062	1.55	1.00	☐☐☐☐☐
2062b.		As **a,** black omitted	*550.00*		☐☐☐☐☐
2063	A1448	20c Madonna and Child	38	15	☐☐☐☐☐
2064	A1449	20c Santa Claus	38	15	☐☐☐☐☐
2064a.		Imperf., pair...................	*165.00*		☐☐☐☐☐
2065	A1450	20c Martin Luther...............	38	15	☐☐☐☐☐
2066	A1451	20c Alaska statehood.............	38	15	☐☐☐☐☐

1984

Scott No.	Illus. No.	Description	Unused Value	Used Value	//////
2067	A1452	20c Ice dancing	42	15	☐☐☐☐☐
2068	A1453	20c Downhill skiing..............	42	15	☐☐☐☐☐
2069	A1454	20c Cross-country skiing..........	42	15	☐☐☐☐☐
2070	A1455	20c Hockey	42	15	☐☐☐☐☐
2070a.		Block of 4, #2067-2070	1.70	1.00	☐☐☐☐☐
2071	A1456	20c Federal Deposit Insurance Corp.	38	15	☐☐☐☐☐
2072	A1457	20c Love.......................	38	15	☐☐☐☐☐
2072a.		Horizontal pair, imperf. vertically	*200.00*		☐☐☐☐☐

A1475   **A1478**   **A1479**

A1476   **A1477**

A1480   **A1481**   **A1482**

A1483   **A1484**

A1485   **A1486**

Scott No.	Illus. No.	Description	Unused Value	Used Value	//////
2073	A1458	20c Carter G. Woodson..........	42	15	☐☐☐☐☐
2073a.		Horizontal pair, imperf. vertically	1,200.		☐☐☐☐☐
2074	A1459	20c Soil & water conservation	38	15	☐☐☐☐☐
2075	A1460	20c Credit Union Act	38	15	☐☐☐☐☐
2076	A1461	20c Wild pink	38	15	☐☐☐☐☐
2077	A1462	20c Yellow lady's-slipper	38	15	☐☐☐☐☐
2078	A1463	20c Spreading pogonia	38	15	☐☐☐☐☐
2079	A1464	20c Pacific calypso..............	38	15	☐☐☐☐☐
2079a.		Block of 4, #2076-2079	1.55	1.00	☐☐☐☐☐
2080	A1465	20c Hawaii statehood	38	15	☐☐☐☐☐
2081	A1466	20c Abraham Lincoln, George Washington.................	38	15	☐☐☐☐☐
2082	A1467	20c Diving	55	15	☐☐☐☐☐
2083	A1468	20c Long jump..................	55	15	☐☐☐☐☐
2084	A1469	20c Wrestling...................	55	15	☐☐☐☐☐
2085	A1470	20c Kayaking...................	55	15	☐☐☐☐☐
2085a.		Block of 4, #2082-2085	2.50	1.00	☐☐☐☐☐
2086	A1471	20c Louisiana World Exposition ...	38	15	☐☐☐☐☐
2087	A1472	20c Health Research	38	15	☐☐☐☐☐
2088	A1473	20c Douglas Fairbanks	38	15	☐☐☐☐☐
2089	A1474	20c dark brown	38	15	☐☐☐☐☐
2090	A1475	20c John McCormack............	38	15	☐☐☐☐☐
2091	A1476	20c St. Lawrence Seaway..........	38	15	☐☐☐☐☐
2092	A1477	20c Preserving wetlands	38	15	☐☐☐☐☐
2092a.		Horizontal pair, imperf. vertically	575.00		☐☐☐☐☐
2093	A1478	20c Roanoke Voyages	38	15	☐☐☐☐☐
2094	A1479	20c sage green	38	15	☐☐☐☐☐
2095	A1480	20c orange & dark brown	38	15	☐☐☐☐☐
2096	A1481	20c Smokey the Bear.............	38	15	☐☐☐☐☐
2096a.		Horizontal pair, imperf. between .	300.00		☐☐☐☐☐
2096b.		Vertical pair, imperf. between....	225.00		☐☐☐☐☐
2096c.		Block of 4, imperf. between vertically and horizontally	3,500.		☐☐☐☐☐
2097	A1482	20c Roberto Clemente............	45	15	☐☐☐☐☐
2097a.		Horizontal pair, imperf. vertically	1,600.		☐☐☐☐☐
2098	A1483	20c Beagle, Boston terrier	38	15	☐☐☐☐☐
2099	A1484	20c Chesapeake Bay retriever, cocker spaniel	38	15	☐☐☐☐☐
2100	A1485	20c Alaskan malamute, collie......	38	15	☐☐☐☐☐
2101	A1486	20c Black & tan coonhound, American foxhound	38	15	☐☐☐☐☐
2101a.		Block of 4, #2098-2101	1.55	1.00	☐☐☐☐☐
2102	A1487	20c McGruff, the crime dog	38	15	☐☐☐☐☐
2103	A1488	20c Hispanic Americans..........	38	15	☐☐☐☐☐
2103a.		Vertical pair, imperf. horizontally	1,500.		☐☐☐☐☐
2104	A1489	20c multicolored	38	15	☐☐☐☐☐
2104a.		Horizontal pair, imperf. vertically	600.00		☐☐☐☐☐
2105	A1490	20c deep blue...................	38	15	☐☐☐☐☐

A1487

A1488

A1489

A1490

A1494

A1491

A1492

A1493

A1495

A1496

A1497

A1498

A1499

HOW TO USE THIS BOOK

The number in the first column is its Scott number or identifying number. The letter and number that come next (A41) indicate the design and refer to the illustration so designated. Following that is the denomination of the stamp and its color. Finally, the value, unused and used is shown.

174

Scott No.	Illus. No.	Description	Unused Value	Used Value	//////
2106	A1491	20c brown & maroon	38	15 ☐☐☐☐☐
2107	A1492	20c Madonna and Child	40	15 ☐☐☐☐☐
2108	A1493	20c Santa Claus	40	15 ☐☐☐☐☐
2108a.		Horizontal pair, imperf. vertically	*1,250.*	☐☐☐☐☐
2109	A1494	20c Vietnam Veterans Memorial . . .	38	15 ☐☐☐☐☐

1985

Scott No.	Illus. No.	Description	Unused Value	Used Value	//////
2110	A1495	22c Jerome Kern	40	15 ☐☐☐☐☐
2111	A1496	(22c) green	60	15 ☐☐☐☐☐
2111a.		Vertical pair, imperf.	*75.00*	☐☐☐☐☐
2111b.		Vertical pair, imperf. horizontally	—	☐☐☐☐☐

Coil Stamp, Perf. 10 vertically

Scott No.	Illus. No.	Description	Unused Value	Used Value	//////
2112	A1496	(22c) green	60	15 ☐☐☐☐☐
2112a.		Imperf., pair.	60.00	☐☐☐☐☐

1985

Scott No.	Illus. No.	Description	Unused Value	Used Value	//////
2113	A1497	(22c) green	60	15 ☐☐☐☐☐
2113a.		Booklet pane of 10.	6.50	☐☐☐☐☐
2114	A1498	22c blue, red & black.	40	15 ☐☐☐☐☐
2115	A1498	22c blue, red & black.	40	15 ☐☐☐☐☐
2115a.		Imperf., pair.	17.50	☐☐☐☐☐
2115b.		Inscribed **T** at bottom ('87)	48	15 ☐☐☐☐☐
2115c.		Black field of stars	—	— ☐☐☐☐☐
2116	A1499	22c blue, red & black.	48	15 ☐☐☐☐☐
2116a.		Booklet pane of 5.	2.50	— ☐☐☐☐☐
2117	A1500	22c black & brown.	40	15 ☐☐☐☐☐
2118	A1501	22c Reticulated helmut	40	15 ☐☐☐☐☐
2119	A1502	22c black & brown.	40	15 ☐☐☐☐☐
2120	A1503	22c black & violet	40	15 ☐☐☐☐☐
2121	A1504	22c Lightning whelk	40	15 ☐☐☐☐☐
2121a.		Booklet pane of 10.	4.25	— ☐☐☐☐☐
2121b.		As **a,** violet omitted	*1,100.*	☐☐☐☐☐
2121c.		As **a,** vert. imperf. between	*800.00*	☐☐☐☐☐
2121d.		As **a,** imperf.		— ☐☐☐☐☐
2121e.		Strip of 5, Nos. 2117-2121	2.00	— ☐☐☐☐☐
2122	A1505	$10.75 Eagle & half moon.	20.00	6.75 ☐☐☐☐☐
2122a.		Booklet pane of 3.	62.50	— ☐☐☐☐☐
2122b.		Type II	20.00	— ☐☐☐☐☐
2122c.		As **b,** booklet pane of 3	*62.50*	— ☐☐☐☐☐

1985-87

Scott No.	Illus. No.	Description	Unused Value	Used Value	//////
2123	A1506	3.4c dark bluish green	15	15 ☐☐☐☐☐
2123a.		Untagged (Bureau Precancel)	15	15 ☐☐☐☐☐
2124	A1507	4.9c brown black	15	15 ☐☐☐☐☐
2124a.		Untagged (Bureau Precancel)	16	16 ☐☐☐☐☐
2125	A1508	5.5c deep magenta ('86).	15	15 ☐☐☐☐☐
2125a.		Untagged (Bureau precancel)	15	15 ☐☐☐☐☐

USA 22
Frilled Dogwinkle

A1500

USA 22
Reticulated Helmet

A1501

USA 22
New England Neptune

A1502

USA 22
Calico Scallop

A1503

USA $10.75

A1505

USA 22
Lightning Whelk

A1504

School Bus 1920s
3.4 USA

A1506

Buckboard 1880s
USA 4.9

A1507

Star Route Truck 5.5 USA 1910s

A1508

Tricycle 1880s
6 USA

A1509

Tractor 1920s
7.1 USA

A1510

Ambulance 1860s
8.3 USA

A1511

Tow Truck 1920s
8.5 USA

A1512

Oil Wagon 1890s
10.1 USA

A1513

Stutz Bearcat 1933
11 USA

A1514

Stanley Steamer 1909
USA 12

A1515

Pushcart 1880s
12.5 USA

A1516

Iceboat 1880s
USA 14

A1517

Dog Sled 1920s
17 USA

A1518

Bread Wagon 1880s
25 USA

A1519

A1520

A1527

A1526

A1521

A1522

A1523

A1524

A1525

A1528

A1530

A1529

A1535

A1532

A1536

A1533

A1537

A1538

A1539

A1540

A1541

A1543

A1544

A1545

A1546

Scott No.	Illus. No.	Description	Unused Value	Used Value	//////
2126	A1509	6c red brown	15	15	☐☐☐☐☐
2126a.		Untagged (Bureau Precancel)	15	15	☐☐☐☐☐
2126b.		As a, imperf., pair		225.00	☐☐☐☐☐
2127	A1510	7.1c lake ('87)	15	15	☐☐☐☐☐
2127a.		Untagged (Bureau Precancel)	15	15	☐☐☐☐☐
2128	A1511	8.3c green	18	15	☐☐☐☐☐
2128a.		Untagged (Bureau Precancel)	18	18	☐☐☐☐☐
2129	A1512	8.5c dark Prussian green ('87)	16	15	☐☐☐☐☐
2129a.		Untagged (Bureau Precancel)	16	16	☐☐☐☐☐
2130	A1513	10.1c slate blue	22	15	☐☐☐☐☐
2130a.		Untagged (Bureau Precancel)	22	22	☐☐☐☐☐
2130b.		As a, imperf., pair	15.00		☐☐☐☐☐
2131	A1514	11c dark green	22	15	☐☐☐☐☐
2132	A1515	12c dark blue	24	15	☐☐☐☐☐
2132a.		Untagged (Bureau Precancel)	24	24	☐☐☐☐☐
2132b.		Type II, untagged (Bureau Precancel)	24	24	☐☐☐☐☐
2133	A1516	12.5c olive green	25	15	☐☐☐☐☐
2133a.		Untagged (Bureau Precancel)	25	25	☐☐☐☐☐
2133b.		As a, imperf., pair	75.00		☐☐☐☐☐
2134	A1517	14c sky blue	28	15	☐☐☐☐☐
2134a.		Imperf., pair	150.00		☐☐☐☐☐
2134b.		Type II	28	15	☐☐☐☐☐
2135	A1518	17c sky blue ('86)	30	15	☐☐☐☐☐
2135a.		Imperf., pair	800.00		☐☐☐☐☐
2136	A1519	25c orange brown ('86)	45	15	☐☐☐☐☐
2136a.		Imperf., pair	15.00		☐☐☐☐☐
2136b.		Pair, imperf. between	—		☐☐☐☐☐

1985

2137	A1520	22c Mary McLeod Bethune	40	15	☐☐☐☐☐
2138	A1521	22c Broadbill decoy	42	15	☐☐☐☐☐
2139	A1522	22c Mallard decoy	42	15	☐☐☐☐☐
2140	A1523	22c Canvasback decoy	42	15	☐☐☐☐☐
2141	A1524	22c Redhead decoy	42	15	☐☐☐☐☐
2141a.		Block of 4, #2138-2141	2.00	1.00	☐☐☐☐☐
2142	A1525	22c Winter Special Olympics	40	15	☐☐☐☐☐
2142a.		Vertical pair, imperf. horizontally	800.00		☐☐☐☐☐
2143	A1526	22c Love	40	15	☐☐☐☐☐
2143a.		Imperf., pair	2,250.		☐☐☐☐☐
2144	A1527	22c Rural Electrification Admin.	40	15	☐☐☐☐☐
2145	A1528	22c AMERIPEX '86	40	15	☐☐☐☐☐
2145a.		Red, black & blue omitted	275.00		☐☐☐☐☐
2145b.		Red & black omitted	—		☐☐☐☐☐
2146	A1529	22c Abigail Adams	40	15	☐☐☐☐☐
2146a.		Imperf., pair	350.00		☐☐☐☐☐
2147	A1530	22c Frederic Auguste Bartholdi	40	15	☐☐☐☐☐

A1551   **A1552**   **A1553**   **A1554**

A1555   **A1556**   **A1559**

A1560   **A1561**   **A1562**   **A1563**

A1565   **A1566**   **A1567**

A1569   **A1571**   **A1574**   **A1575**

A1577   **A1577a**   **A1578**   **A1579**

Scott No.	Illus. No.	Description	Unused Value	Used Value	—/—/—/—/—/—
Coil Stamps, Perf. 10 vertically					
2149	A1532	18c George Washington, monument	32	15 □□□□□
2149a.		Untagged (Bureau Precancel)	35	35 □□□□□
2149b.		Imperf., pair...................	*1,250.*	□□□□□
2149c.		As **a**, imperf., pair	*600.00*	□□□□□
2150	A1533	21.1c Envelopes.................	40	15 □□□□□
2150a.		Untagged (Bureau Precancel)	38	38 □□□□□

1985

Scott No.	Illus. No.	Description	Unused Value	Used Value	—/—/—/—/—/—
2152	A1535	22c gray green & rose red	40	15 □□□□□
2153	A1536	22c deep blue & light blue........	40	15 □□□□□
2154	A1537	22c gray green & rose red	40	15 □□□□□
2155	A1538	22c Quarter horse	40	15 □□□□□
2156	A1539	22c Morgan	40	15 □□□□□
2157	A1540	22c Saddlebred.................	40	15 □□□□□
2158	A1541	22c Appaloosa	40	15 □□□□□
2158a.		Block of 4, #2155-2158	2.00	1.00 □□□□□
2159	A1542	22c Public Education............	40	15 □□□□□
2160	A1543	22c YMCA youth camping........	42	15 □□□□□
2161	A1544	22c Boy Scouts.................	42	15 □□□□□
2162	A1545	22c Big Brothers/Big Sisters	42	15 □□□□□
2163	A1546	22c Camp Fire, Inc..............	42	15 □□□□□
2163a.		Block of 4, #2160-2163	2.00	1.00 □□□□□
2164	A1547	22c Help End Hunger	40	15 □□□□□
2165	A1548	22c Genoa Madonna.............	40	15 □□□□□
2165a.		Imperf., pair...................	*130.00*	□□□□□
2166	A1549	22c Poinsettia plants	40	15 □□□□□
2166a.		Imperf., pair...................	*175.00*	□□□□□

1986, Jan. 3

Scott No.	Illus. No.	Description	Unused Value	Used Value	—/—/—/—/—/—
2167	A1550	22c Arkansas statehood..........	40	15 □□□□□
2167a.		Vertical pair, imperf. horizontally	—	□□□□□

1986-90

Scott No.	Illus. No.	Description	Unused Value	Used Value	—/—/—/—/—/—
2168	A1551	1c brownish vermilion	15	15 □□□□□
2169	A1552	2c bright blue ('87).............	15	15 □□□□□
2170	A1553	3c bright blue..................	15	15 □□□□□
2171	A1554	4c blue violet	15	15 □□□□□
2172	A1555	5c dark olive green	15	15 □□□□□
2173	A1556	5c carmine ('90)................	15	15 □□□□□
2176	A1559	10c lake ('87)	18	15 □□□□□
2177	A1560	14c crimson ('87)...............	25	15 □□□□□
2178	A1561	15c claret ('88)	28	15 □□□□□
2179	A1562	17c dull blue green.............	30	15 □□□□□
2180	A1563	21c blue violet ('88).............	38	15 □□□□□
2182	A1565	23c purple ('88)	42	15 □□□□□
2183	A1566	25c blue	45	15 □□□□□
2183a.		Booklet pane of 10 ('88)........	4.75	□□□□□

A1542

A1547

A1548

A1549

A1550

A1585

A1586

A1587

A1594

A1593

A1588-1592

A1599a

Presents of
the United States: II

AMERIPEX 86
International
Stamp Show
Chicago, Illinois
May 22-June 1, 1986

A1599b

Presidents of
the United States: III

AMERIPEX 86
International
Stamp Show
Chicago, Illinois
May 22-June 1, 1986

A1599c

A1599d

A1581-1584

A1600-1603

A1605-1608

Scott No.	Illus. No.	Description	Unused Value	Used Value	//////
2184	A1567	28c myrtle green ('89)	56	15	☐☐☐☐☐
2186	A1569	40c dark blue ('90).............	80	15	☐☐☐☐☐
2188	A1571	45c bright blue ('88).	80	15	☐☐☐☐☐
2191	A1574	56c scarlet	1.00	15	☐☐☐☐☐
2192	A1575	65c dark blue ('88).............	1.20	18	☐☐☐☐☐
2194	A1577	$1 dark Prussian green	1.75	50	☐☐☐☐☐
2194A	A1577a	$1 deep blue ('89)	1.75	50	☐☐☐☐☐
2195	A1578	$2 bright violet	3.50	50	☐☐☐☐☐
2196	A1579	$5 copper red ('87).............	7.75	1.00	☐☐☐☐☐
2197	A1566	25c blue ('88)	45	15	☐☐☐☐☐
2197a.		Booklet pane of 6.............	3.00		☐☐☐☐☐

1986

Scott No.	Illus. No.	Description	Unused Value	Used Value	//////
2198	A1581	22c Handstamped cover	40	15	☐☐☐☐☐
2199	A1582	22c Boy and stamp collection......	40	15	☐☐☐☐☐
2200	A1583	22c 2 stamps, magnifying glass.....	40	15	☐☐☐☐☐
2201	A1584	22c 1986 Presidents' miniature sheet....................	40	15	☐☐☐☐☐
2201a.		Booklet pane of 4, #2198-2201 ...	2.00		☐☐☐☐☐
2201b.		As a, black omitted on #2198, 2201.................	50.00		☐☐☐☐☐
2201c.		As a, blue (litho.) omitted on Nos. 2198-2200..............	—		☐☐☐☐☐
2201d.		As a, buff (litho.) omitted	—		☐☐☐☐☐
2202	A1585	22c Love......................	40	15	☐☐☐☐☐
2203	A1586	22c Sojourner Truty	40	15	☐☐☐☐☐
2204	A1587	22c dark blue, dark red & grayish black	40	15	☐☐☐☐☐
2204a.		Horizontal pair, imperf. vertically	950.00		☐☐☐☐☐
2204b.		Red omitted....................	—		☐☐☐☐☐
2205	A1588	22c Muskellunge	40	15	☐☐☐☐☐
2206	A1589	22c Atlantic cod.................	40	15	☐☐☐☐☐
2207	A1590	22c Largemouth bass.............	40	15	☐☐☐☐☐
2208	A1591	22c Bluefin tuna.................	40	15	☐☐☐☐☐
2209	A1592	22c Catfish....................	40	15	☐☐☐☐☐
2209a.		Booklet pane of 5, #2205-2209 ...	2.75	—	▨☐☐☐☐
2210	A1593	22c Public Hospitals	40	15	☐☐☐☐☐
2210a.		Vertical pair, imperf. horizontally	425.00		☐☐☐☐☐
2210b.		Horizontal pair, imperf. vertically	1,000.		☐☐☐☐☐
2211	A1594	22c Duke Ellington	40	15	☐☐☐☐☐
2211a.		Vertical pair, imperf. horizontally	1,100.	—	☐☐☐☐☐
2216	A1599a	Sheet of 9	3.50		☐☐☐☐☐
2216a.-i.		22c, any single	38	20	☐☐☐☐☐
2216j.		Blue omitted...................	—		☐☐☐☐☐
2216k.		Black inscription omitted	1,250.		☐☐☐☐☐
2216l.		Imperf......................	9,000.		☐☐☐☐☐
2217	A1599b	Sheet of 9	3.50		☐☐☐☐☐
2217a.-i.		22c, any single	38	20	☐☐☐☐☐

A1604a   **A1604**   **A1604b**

A1610-1613

A1609   **A1616**

A1614

A1615

A1618

A1617

A1637

A1619

A1620

A1638

A1639

A1621

A1640

A1641   A1642

A1645

A1643

A1644

Scott No.	Illus. No.	Description	Unused Value	Used Value	//////
2218	A1599c	Sheet of 9	3.50		☐☐☐☐☐
2218a.-i.		22c, any single	38	20	☐☐☐☐☐
2218j.		Brown omitted................	—		☐☐☐☐☐
2218k.		Black inscription omitted	2,000.		☐☐☐☐☐
2219	A1599d	Sheet of 9	3.50		☐☐☐☐☐
2219a.-i.		22c, any single	38	20	☐☐☐☐☐
2220	A1600	22c Elisha Kent Kane	45	15	☐☐☐☐☐
2221	A1601	22c Adolphus W. Greely.	45	15	☐☐☐☐☐
2222	A1602	22c Vihjalmur Stefansson	45	15	☐☐☐☐☐
2223	A1603	22c Robert E. Peary, Matthew Alexander Henson	45	15	☐☐☐☐☐
2223a.		Block of 4, #2220-2223	2.00	1.00	☐☐☐☐☐
2223b.		As a, black (engraved) omitted ...	—		☐☐☐☐☐
2224	A1604	22c scarlet & dark blue	40	15	☐☐☐☐☐

1986-87

2225	A1604a	1c violet	15	15	☐☐☐☐☐
2226	A1604b	2c black ('87)	15	15	☐☐☐☐☐
2228	A1285	4c reddish brown...............	15	15	☐☐☐☐☐
2231	A1511	8.3c green (Bureau precancel)	16	16	☐☐☐☐☐

1986

2235	A1605	22c Navajo art.................	40	15	☐☐☐☐☐
2236	A1606	22c Navajo art.................	40	15	☐☐☐☐☐
2237	A1607	22c Navajo art.................	40	15	☐☐☐☐☐
2238	A1608	22c Navajo art.................	40	15	☐☐☐☐☐
2238a.		Block of 4, #2235-2238	1.65	1.00	☐☐☐☐☐
2238b.		As a, black (engraved) omitted ...	350.00		☐☐☐☐☐
2239	A1609	22c copper red	40	15	☐☐☐☐☐
2240	A1610	22c Highlander figure	40	15	☐☐☐☐☐
2241	A1611	22c Ship figurehead..............	40	15	☐☐☐☐☐
2242	A1612	22c Nautical figure	40	15	☐☐☐☐☐
2243	A1613	22c Cigar store figure.	40	15	☐☐☐☐☐
2243a.		Block of 4, #2240-2243	1.65	1.00	☐☐☐☐☐
2243b.		As a, imperf. vertically	2,000.		☐☐☐☐☐
2244	A1614	22c Madonna..................	40	15	☐☐☐☐☐
2245	A1615	22c Village scene	40	15	☐☐☐☐☐

1987

2246	A1616	22c Michigan statehood	40	15	☐☐☐☐☐
2247	A1617	22c Pan American Games.	40	15	☐☐☐☐☐
2247a.		Silver omitted	1,500.		☐☐☐☐☐
2248	A1618	22c Love......................	40	15	☐☐☐☐☐
2249	A1619	22c Jean Baptiste Pointe de Sable ..	40	15	☐☐☐☐☐
2250	A1620	22c Enrico Caruso	40	15	▨☐☐☐☐
2250a.		Black (engraved) omitted	—		☐☐☐☐☐
2251	A1621	22c Girl Scouts.................	40	15	☐☐☐☐☐

Conestoga Wagon 1800s — USA 3	Milk Wagon 1900s — 5 USA	Elevator 1900s — 5.3 USA Nonprofit Carrier Route Sort	Carreta 1770s — 7.6 USA Nonprofit
A1622	**A1623**	**A1624**	**A1625**

Wheel Chair 1920s — 8.4 USA Nonprofit	Canal Boat 1880s — 10 USA	Patrol Wagon 1880s — USA 13 Presorted First-Class	Coal Car 1870s — 13.2 Bulk Rate USA
A1626	**A1627**	**A1628**	**A1629**

Tugboat 1900s — USA 15	Popcorn Wagon 1902 — 16.7 USA Bulk Rate	Racing Car 1911 — USA 17.5	Cable Car 1880s — USA 20
A1630	**A1631**	**A1632**	**A1633**

Fire Engine 1900s — 20.5 USA ZIP+4 Presort	Railroad Mail Car 1920s — Presorted First-Class 21 USA	Tandem Bicycle 1890s — 24.1 USA ZIP+4
A1634	**A1635**	**A1636**

HOW TO USE THIS BOOK

The number in the first column is its Scott number or identifying number. The letter and number that come next (A41) indicate the design and refer to the illustration so designated. Following that is the denomination of the stamp and its color. Finally, the value, unused and used is shown.

Scott No.	Illus. No.	Description	Unused Value	Used Value	//////
1987-88					
2252	A1622	3c claret ('88)	15	15 ☐☐☐☐☐	
2253	A1623	5c black	15	15 ☐☐☐☐☐	
2254	A1624	5.3c black (Bureau precancel in scarlet) ('88)...............	15	15 ☐☐☐☐☐	
2255	A1625	7.6c brown (Bureau precancel in scarlet) ('88)...............	15	15 ☐☐☐☐☐	
2256	A1626	8.4c deep claret (Bureau precancel in red) ('88)	15	15 ☐☐☐☐☐	
2256a.		Imperf., pair...................	—	☐☐☐☐☐	
2257	A1627	10c sky blue	18	15 ☐☐☐☐☐	
2258	A1628	13c black (Bureau precancel in red) ('88)	22	22 ☐☐☐☐☐	
2259	A1629	13.2c slate green (Bureau precancel in red) ('88)	22	22 ☐☐☐☐☐	
2259a.		Imperf., pair.................	200.00	☐☐☐☐☐	
2260	A1630	15c violet ('88).................	24	15 ☐☐☐☐☐	
2261	A1631	16.7c rose (Bureau precancel in black) ('88).................	28	28 ☐☐☐☐☐	
2261a.		Imperf., pair..................	325.00	☐☐☐☐☐	
2262	A1632	17.5c dark violet	30	15 ☐☐☐☐☐	
2262a.		Untagged (Bureau precancel)	30	30 ☐☐☐☐☐	
2262b.		Imperf., pair...................	1,500.	☐☐☐☐☐	
2263	A1633	20c blue violet ('88).............	35	15 ☐☐☐☐☐	
2263a.		Imperf., pair.................	—	☐☐☐☐☐	
2264	A1634	20.5c rose (Bureau precancel in black) ('88)	38	38 ☐☐☐☐☐	
2265	A1635	21c olive green (Bureau precancel in red) ('88)	38	38 ☐☐☐☐☐	
2265a.		Imperf., pair.................	325.00	☐☐☐☐☐	
2266	A1636	24.1c deep ultramarine (Bureau precancel) ('88)	42	42 ☐☐☐☐☐	
1987					
2267	A1637	22c "Congratulations"............	40	15 ☐☐☐☐☐	
2268	A1638	22c "Get Well"	40	15 ☐☐☐☐☐	
2269	A1639	22c "Thank You"	40	15 ☐☐☐☐☐	
2270	A1640	22c "Love You, Dad"	40	15 ☐☐☐☐☐	
2271	A1641	22c "Best Wishes"...............	40	15 ☐☐☐☐☐	
2272	A1642	22c "Happy Birthday"	40	15 ☐☐☐☐☐	
2273	A1643	22c "Love You, Mother"	40	15 ☐☐☐☐☐	
2274	A1644	22c "Keep in Touch"	40	15 ☐☐☐☐☐	
2274a.		Booklet pane of 10 (#2268-2271, 2273-2274, and 2 each #2267, 2272)	4.25	— ☐☐☐☐☐	
2275	A1645	22c United Way................	40	15 ☐☐☐☐☐	

A1646 A1647 A1648 A1649

A1649a A1649b A1649c A1649d

A1650-1699

HOW TO USE THIS BOOK

The number in the first column is its Scott number or identifying number. The letter and number that come next (A41) indicate the design and refer to the illustration so designated. Following that is the denomination of the stamp and its color. Finally, the value, unused and used is shown.

1987-88

Scott No.	Illus. No.	Description	Unused Value	Used Value	
2276	A1646	22c Flag & fireworks	40	15 ☐☐☐☐☐	
2276a.		Booklet pane of 20.	8.50	– ☐☐☐☐☐	
2277	A1647	(25c) "E" & Earth ('88)	45	15 ☐☐☐☐☐	
2278	A1648	25c Flag & clouds ('88)	40	15 ☐☐☐☐☐	

Coil Stamps, Perf. 10 vertically

Scott No.	Illus. No.	Description	Unused Value	Used Value	
2279	A1647	(25c) "E" & Earth ('88)	45	15 ☐☐☐☐☐	
2279a.		Imperf., pair	160.00	☐☐☐☐☐	
2280	A1649	25c Flag & Yosemite (green trees)			
		('88)	45	15 ☐☐☐☐☐	
2280a.		Imperf., pair	25.00	☐☐☐☐☐	
2280b.		Black trees	–	– ☐☐☐☐☐	
2281	A1649d	25c Honeybee ('88)	45	15 ☐☐☐☐☐	
2281a.		Imperf., pair	32.50	☐☐☐☐☐	
2281b.		Black (engraved) omitted	125.00	☐☐☐☐☐	
2281c.		Black (litho.) omitted	–	☐☐☐☐☐	
2281d.		Pair, imperf. between	–	☐☐☐☐☐	

1987-88

Scott No.	Illus. No.	Description	Unused Value	Used Value	
2282	A1647	(25c) "E" & Earth ('88)	45	15 ☐☐☐☐☐	
2282a.		Booklet pane of 10	4.75	– ☐☐☐☐☐	
2283	A1649a	25c Pheasant ('88)	45	15 ☐☐☐☐☐	
2283a.		Booklet pane of 10	4.75	– ☐☐☐☐☐	
2283b.		25c multicolored, red removed . . .	45	15 ☐☐☐☐☐	
2283c.		As a, booklet pane of 10	4.75	– ☐☐☐☐☐	
2283d.		As a, horizontally imperf. between	–	☐☐☐☐☐	
2284	A1649b	25c Grosbeak ('88)	45	15 ☐☐☐☐☐	
2285	A1649c	25c Owl ('88)	45	15 ☐☐☐☐☐	
2285b.		Booklet pane of 10, 5 each			
		Nos. 2284-2285	4.75	– ☐☐☐☐☐	
2285d.		Pair, Nos. 2284-2285	90	– ☐☐☐☐☐	
2285A	A1648	25c Flag & clouds ('88)	45	15 ☐☐☐☐☐	
2285c.		Booklet pane of 6	2.75	– ☐☐☐☐☐	

1987, June 13

Scott No.	Illus. No.	Description	Unused Value	Used Value	
2286	A1650	22c Barn swallow	40	15 ☐☐☐☐☐	
2287	A1651	22c Monarch butterfly	40	15 ☐☐☐☐☐	
2288	A1652	22c Bighorn sheep	40	15 ☐☐☐☐☐	
2289	A1653	22c Broad-tailed hummingbird	40	15 ☐☐☐☐☐	
2290	A1654	22c Cottontail	40	15 ☐☐☐☐☐	
2291	A1655	22c Osprey	40	15 ☐☐☐☐☐	
2292	A1656	22c Mountain lion	40	15 ☐☐☐☐☐	
2293	A1657	22c Luna moth	40	15 ☐☐☐☐☐	
2294	A1658	22c Mule deer	40	15 ☐☐☐☐☐	
2295	A1659	22c Gray squirrel	40	15 ☐☐☐☐☐	
2296	A1660	22c Armadillo	40	15 ☐☐☐☐☐	
2297	A1661	22c Eastern chipmunk	40	15 ☐☐☐☐☐	

Dec 7, 1787   USA
Delaware 22

A1700

Dec 12, 1787
Pennsylvania

A1701

Dec 18, 1787   USA
New Jersey 22

A1702

January 2, 1788
Georgia

A1703

January 9, 1788
Connecticut

A1704

Feb 6, 1788
Massachusetts

A1705

April 28, 1788   USA
Maryland 22

A1706

May 23, 1788
South Carolina

A1707

June 21, 1788
New Hampshire

A1708

June 25, 1788   USA
Virginia 25

A1709

July 26, 1788   USA
New York 25

A1710

November 21, 1789
North Carolina

A1711

May 29, 1790
Rhode Island

A1712

Scott No.	Illus. No.	Description	Unused Value	Used Value	//////
2298	A1662	22c Moose	40	15	☐☐☐☐☐
2299	A1663	22c Black bear	40	15	☐☐☐☐☐
2300	A1664	22c Tiger swallowtail	40	15	☐☐☐☐☐
2301	A1665	22c Bobwhite	40	15	☐☐☐☐☐
2302	A1666	22c Ringtail	40	15	☐☐☐☐☐
2303	A1667	22c Red-winged blackbird	40	15	☐☐☐☐☐
2304	A1668	22c American lobster	40	15	☐☐☐☐☐
2305	A1669	22c Black-tailed jack rabbit	40	15	☐☐☐☐☐
2306	A1670	22c Scarlet tanager	40	15	☐☐☐☐☐
2307	A1671	22c Woodchuck	40	15	☐☐☐☐☐
2308	A1672	22c Roseate spoonbill	40	15	☐☐☐☐☐
2309	A1673	22c Bald eagle	40	15	☐☐☐☐☐
2310	A1674	22c Alaskan brown bear	40	15	☐☐☐☐☐
2311	A1675	22c Iiwi	40	15	☐☐☐☐☐
2312	A1676	22c Badger	40	15	☐☐☐☐☐
2313	A1677	22c Pronghorn	40	15	☐☐☐☐☐
2314	A1678	22c River otter	40	15	☐☐☐☐☐
2315	A1679	22c Ladybug	40	15	☐☐☐☐☐
2316	A1680	22c Beaver	40	15	☐☐☐☐☐
2317	A1681	22c White-tailed deer	40	15	☐☐☐☐☐
2318	A1682	22c Blue jay	40	15	☐☐☐☐☐
2319	A1683	22c Pika	40	15	☐☐☐☐☐
2320	A1684	22c Bison	40	15	☐☐☐☐☐
2321	A1685	22c Snowy egret	40	15	☐☐☐☐☐
2322	A1686	22c Gray wolf	40	15	☐☐☐☐☐
2323	A1687	22c Mountain goat	40	15	☐☐☐☐☐
2324	A1688	22c Deer mouse	40	15	☐☐☐☐☐
2325	A1689	22c Black-tailed prairie dog	40	15	☐☐☐☐☐
2326	A1690	22c Box turtle	40	15	☐☐☐☐☐
2327	A1691	22c Wolverine	40	15	☐☐☐☐☐
2328	A1692	22c American elk	40	15	☐☐☐☐☐
2329	A1693	22c California sea lion	40	15	☐☐☐☐☐
2330	A1694	22c Mockingbird	40	15	☐☐☐☐☐
2331	A1695	22c Raccoon	40	15	☐☐☐☐☐
2332	A1696	22c Bobcat	40	15	☐☐☐☐☐
2333	A1697	22c Black-footed ferret	40	15	☐☐☐☐☐
2334	A1698	22c Canada goose	40	15	☐☐☐☐☐
2335	A1699	22c Red fox	40	15	☐☐☐☐☐
2335a.		Pane of 50, #2286-2335	20.00		☐☐☐☐☐
2286b-2335b		any single, red omitted	—		☐☐☐☐☐

1987-89

Scott No.	Illus. No.	Description	Unused Value	Used Value	//////
2336	A1700	22c Delaware	40	15	☐☐☐☐☐
2337	A1701	22c Pennsylvania	40	15	☐☐☐☐☐
2338	A1702	22c New Jersey	40	15	☐☐☐☐☐
2338a.		Black (engraved) omitted	—		☐☐☐☐☐
2339	A1703	22c Georgia	40	15	☐☐☐☐☐
2340	A1704	22c Connecticut	40	15	☐☐☐☐☐

A1713

A1714

A1724

A1725

A1715-1718

A1731

A1733

A1732

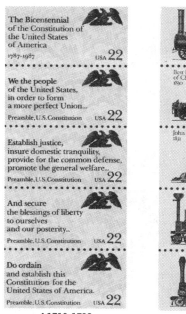

The Bicentennial
of the Constitution of
the United States
of America
1787-1987
USA 22

We the people
of the United States,
in order to form
a more perfect Union...
Preamble, U.S. Constitution   USA 22

Establish justice,
insure domestic tranquility,
provide for the common defense,
promote the general welfare...
Preamble, U.S. Constitution   USA 22

And secure
the blessings of liberty
to ourselves
and our posterity...
Preamble, U.S. Constitution   USA 22

Do ordain
and establish this
Constitution for the
United States of America.
Preamble, U.S. Constitution   USA 22

A1719-1723

Stourbridge Lion
1829   USA 22

Best Friend
of Charleston
1830   USA 22

John Bull
1831   USA 22

Brother Jonathan
1832   USA 22

Gowan & Marx
1839   USA 22

A1726-1730

USA 22   USA 22
Siamese Cat, Exotic Shorthair Cat   Abyssinian Cat, Himalayan Cat

USA 22   USA 22
Maine Coon Cat, Burmese Cat   American Shorthair Cat, Persian Cat

A1736-1739

A1735

A1734

A1740

A1741

A1742

A1743

A1744

A1745-1749

A1754-1757

Scott No.	Illus. No.	Description	Unused Value	Used Value	//////
2341	A1705	22c Massachusetts ('88)	40	15	☐☐☐☐☐
2342	A1706	22c Maryland ('88)	40	15	☐☐☐☐☐
2343	A1707	25c South Carolina ('88)	45	15	☐☐☐☐☐
2344	A1708	25c New Hampshire ('88)	45	15	☐☐☐☐☐
2345	A1709	25c Virginia('88)	45	15	☐☐☐☐☐
2346	A1710	25c New York ('88)	45	15	☐☐☐☐☐
2347	A1711	25c North Carolina ('89)	45	15	☐☐☐☐☐
2348	A1712	25c Rhode Island ('90)	45	15	☐☐☐☐☐

1987

Scott No.	Illus. No.	Description	Unused Value	Used Value	//////
2349	A1713	22c scarlet & black..............	40	15	☐☐☐☐☐
2349a.		Black (engraved) omitted	*450.00*		☐☐☐☐☐
2350	A1714	22c bright green	40	15	☑☐☐☐☐
2351	A1715	22c ultramarine & white	40	15	☐☐☐☐☐
2352	A1716	22c ultramarine & white	40	15	☐☐☐☐☐
2353	A1717	22c ultramarine & white	40	15	☐☐☐☐☐
2354	A1718	22c ultramarine & white	40	15	☐☐☐☐☐
2354a.		Block of 4, Nos. 2351-2354......	1.65	1.00	☐☐☐☐☐
2354b.		As **a**, white omitted	*1,750.*		☐☐☐☐☐
2355	A1719	22c Constitution preamble	40	15	☐☐☐☐☐
2356	A1720	22c Constitution preamble	40	15	☐☐☐☐☐
2357	A1721	22c Constitution preamble	40	15	☐☐☐☐☐
2358	A1722	22c Constitution preamble	40	15	☐☐☐☐☐
2359	A1723	22c Constitution preamble	40	15	☐☐☐☐☐
2359a.		Booklet pane of 5, #2355-2359 ...	2.10	–	☐☐☐☐☐
2360	A1724	22c Signing of the Constitution	40	15	☐☐☐☐☐
2361	A1725	22c Certified Public Accounting....	40	15	☒☐☐☐☐
2361a.		Black (engraved) omitted	*600.00*		☐☐☐☐☐
2362	A1726	22c Stourbridge Lion.............	40	15	☐☐☐☐☐
2363	A1727	22c Best Friend of Charleston......	40	15	☐☐☐☐☐
2364	A1728	22c John Bull...................	40	15	☐☐☐☐☐
2365	A1729	22c Brother Jonathan	40	15	☐☐☐☐☐
2366	A1730	22c Gowan & Marx...............	40	15	☐☐☐☐☐
2366a.		Booklet pane of 5, #2362-2366 ...	2.10	–	☐☐☐☐☐
2367	A1731	22c Madonna...................	40	15	☐☐☐☐☐
2368	A1732	22c Christmas ornaments	40	15	☐☐☐☐☐

1988

Scott No.	Illus. No.	Description	Unused Value	Used Value	//////
2369	A1733	22c 1988 Winter Olympics	40	15	☐☐☐☐☐
2370	A1734	22c Koala & bald eagle...........	40	15	☐☐☐☐☐
2371	A1735	22c James Weldon Johnson	40	15	☐☐☐☐☐
2372	A1736	22c Siamese. exotic shorthair cats ..	40	15	☐☐☐☐☐
2373	A1737	22c Abyssinian, Himalayan cats....	40	15	☐☐☐☐☐
2374	A1738	22c Maine coon, Burmese cats	40	15	☐☐☐☐☐
2375	A1739	22c American shorthair, Persian cats	40	15	☐☐☐☐☐
2375a.		Block of 4, Nos. 2372-2375......	1.65	1.00	☐☐☐☐☐
2376	A1740	22c Knute Rockne..............	40	15	☐☐☐☐☐

A1750-1753

A1758

A1759

A1760

A1761

A1762

A1764

A1763

A1765

A1766

A1767

A1768

A1769-1773

A1774

A1775

A1776

A1777

A1778

A1779

A1781

A1782

A1785

A1790

A1780

A1784   **A1783**

A1786-1789

Scott No.	Illus. No.	Description	Unused Value	Used Value	//////
2377	A1741	25c Francis Ouimet.............	45	15	☐☐☐☐☐
2378	A1742	25c Love......................	45	15	☐☐☐☐☐
2379	A1743	45c Love......................	65	20	☐☐☐☐☐
2380	A1744	25c 1988 Summer Olympics.......	45	15	☐☐☐☐☐
2381	A1745	25c Locomobile................	45	15	☐☐☐☐☐
2382	A1746	25c Pierce-Arrow..............	45	15	☐☐☐☐☐
2383	A1747	25c Cord.....................	45	15	☐☐☐☐☐
2384	A1748	25c Packard	45	15	☐☐☐☐☐
2385	A1749	25c Duesenberg	45	15	☐☐☐☐☐
2385a.		Booklet pane of 5, Nos. 2381-2385......................	2.30	–	☐☐☐☐☐
2386	A1750	25c Nathaniel Palmer	45	15	☐☐☐☐☐
2387	A1751	25c Charles Wilkes	45	15	☐☐☐☐☐
2388	A1752	25c Richard E. Byrd	45	15	☐☐☐☐☐
2389	A1753	25c Lincoln Ellsworth	45	15	☐☐☐☐☐
2389a.		Block of 4, Nos. 2386-2389......	1.85	1.00	☐☐☐☐☐
2389b.		Black (engraved) omitted	2,000.		☐☐☐☐☐
2389c.		As a, imperf. horizontally	–		☐☐☐☐☐
2390	A1754	25c Deer.....................	45	15	☐☐☐☐☐
2391	A1755	25c Horse....................	45	15	☐☐☐☐☐
2392	A1756	25c Camel	45	15	☐☐☐☐☐
2393	A1757	25c Goat.....................	45	15	☐☐☐☐☐
2393a.		Block of 4, Nos. 2390-2393......	1.85	1.00	☐☐☐☐☐
2394	A1758	$8.75 Eagle in flight..............	15.00	7.75	☐☐☐☐☐
2395	A1759	25c "Happy Birthday"	45	15	☐☐☐☐☐
2396	A1760	25c "Best Wishes"..............	45	15	☐☐☐☐☐
2396a.		Booklet pane of 6, 3 #2395 + 3 #2396 with gutter between	2.75	–	☐☐☐☐☐
2397	A1761	25c "Thinking of You"..........	45	15	☐☐☐☐☐
2398	A1762	25c "Love You"	45	15	☐☐☐☐☐
2398a.		Booklet pane of 6, 3 #2397 + 3 #2398 with gutter between	2.75	–	☐☐☐☐☐
2399	A1763	25c Madonna and Child	45	15	☐☐☐☐☐
2399a.		Gold omitted	50.00		☐☐☐☐☐
2400	A1764	25c Sleigh & village scene	45	15	☐☐☐☐☐
1989					
2401	A1765	25c Montana statehood...........	45	15	☐☐☐☐☐
2402	A1766	25c Asa Philip Randolph	45	15	☐☐☐☐☐
2403	A1767	25c North Dakota statehood.......	45	15	☐☐☐☐☐
2404	A1768	25c Washington statehood	45	15	☐☐☐☐☐
2405	A1769	25c *Experiment*	45	15	☐☐☐☐☐
2406	A1770	25c *Phoenix*....................	45	15	☐☐☐☐☐
2407	A1771	25c *New Orleans*	45	15	☐☐☐☐☐
2408	A1772	25c *Washington*.................	45	15	☐☐☐☐☐
2409	A1773	25c *Walk in the Water*	45	15	☐☐☐☐☐
2409a.		Booklet pane of 5, Nos. 2405-2409......................	2.25	–	☐☐☐☐☐

Greetings USA 25

A1792

CHRISTMAS
USA 25

Carraeci, National Gallery

A1791

USA 25

A1793

WORLD STAMP EXPO 89

The classic 1869 U.S. Abraham Lincoln stamp is reborn in these four larger versions commemorating World Stamp Expo'89, held in Washington, D.C. during the 20th Universal Postal Congress of the UPU. These stamps show the issued color and three of the trial proof color combinations.

A1794

USA 25
20th Universal Postal Congress

USA 25
20th Universal Postal Congress

USA 25
20th Universal Postal Congress

USA 25
20th Universal Postal Congress

A1795-1798

LOVE
USA 25

A1800

IDAHO
USA 25 1890

A1799

Ida B. Wells
25
Black Heritage USA

A1801

USA 15

A1802

204

Scott No.	Illus. No.	Description	Unused Value	Used Value	//////
2410	A1774	25c grayish brown, black & carmine rose	45	15 □□□□□
2411	A1775	25c Arturo Toscanini	45	15 □□□□□

1989-90

2412	A1776	25c House of Represetnatives.	45	15 □□□□□
2413	A1777	25c Senate	45	15 □□□□□
2414	A1778	25c Executive Branch	45	15 □□□□□
2415	A1779	25c Supreme Court	45	15 □□□□□

1990

2416	A1780	25c South Dakota statehood.	45	15 □□□□□
2417	A1781	25c Lou Gehrig	45	15 □□□□□
2418	A1782	25c Ernest Hemingway	45	15 □□□□□
2419	A1783	$2.40 Moon landing	3.75	1.90 □□□□□
2419a.		Black (engraved) omitted	—	□□□□□
2419b.		Imperf., pair	—	□□□□□
2420	A1784	25c Letter carriers	45	15 □□□□□
2421	A1785	25c Bill of Rights.	45	15 □□□□□
2421a.		Black (engraved) omitted	*300.00*	□□□□□
2422	A1786	25c Tyrannosaurus Rex.	45	15 □□□□□
2423	A1787	25c Pteranodon	45	15 □□□□□
2424	A1788	25c Stegosaurus	45	15 □□□□□
2425	A1789	25c Brontosaurus.	45	15 □□□□□
2425a.		Block of 4, Nos. 2422-2425.	1.80	1.00 □□□□□
2425b.		As **a**, black (engraved) omitted . . .	—	□□□□□
2426	A1790	25c Southwest carved figure	45	15 □□□□□
2427	A1791	25c Madonna and Child	45	15 □□□□□
2427a.		Booklet pane of 10.	4.50	— □□□□□
2428	A1792	25c Sleigh, presents	45	15 □□□□□
2428a.		Vertical pair, imperf. horizontally	—	□□□□□
2429	A1792	25c Sleigh, presents (from booklet pane)	45	15 □□□□□
2429a.		Booklet pane of 10.	4.50	— □□□□□
2429b.		As **a,** horizontally imperf. between	—	□□□□□
2429c.		As **a,** red omitted	—	□□□□□
2431	A1793	25c Eagle and Shield	50	20 □□□□□
2431a.		Booklet pane of 18.	9.00	□□□□□
2431b.		Vert, pair, no die cutting between.	—	□□□□□
2433	A1794	Sheet of 4	6.00	6.00 □□□□□
2433a.		90c like No. 122.	1.40	1.40 □□□□□
2433b.		90c like No. 132TC (blue frame, brown center)	1.40	1.40 □□□□□
2433c.		90c like No. 132TC (grn frame, blue center).	1.40	1.40 □□□□□
2433d.		90c like No. 132TC (scarlet frame, blue center)	1.40	1.40 □□□□□
2434	A1795	25c Stagecoach.	45	15 □□□□□

A1803

A1808

A1804-07

A1811

A1827

A1829-33

A1834

A1835

Scott No.	Illus. No.	Description	Unused Value	Used Value	//////
2435	A1796	25c Paddlewheel steamer	45	15	☐☐☐☐☐
2436	A1797	25c Biplane	45	15	☐☐☐☐☐
2437	A1798	25c Depot-hack type automobile ...	45	15	☐☐☐☐☐
2437a.		Block of 4, Nos. 2434-2437......	1.80	1.00	☐☐☐☐☐
2437b.		As **a**, dark blue (engraved)			
		omitted	*2,500.*		☐☐☐☐☐
2438		Sheet of 4	2.00	1.75	☐☐☐☐☐
2438a.		A1795 25c Stagecoach.........	45	25	☐☐☐☐☐
2438b.		A1796 25c Paddlewheel steamer..	45	25	☐☐☐☐☐
2438c.		A1797 25c Biplane............	45	25	☐☐☐☐☐
2438d.		A1798 25c Depot-hack type			
		automobile	45	25	☐☐☐☐☐

1990

Scott No.	Illus. No.	Description	Unused Value	Used Value	//////
2439	A1799	25c Idaho statehood	45	15	☐☐☐☐☐
2440	A1800	25c bright blue, dark pink			
		& emerald green	45	15	☐☐☐☐☐
2440a.		Imperf., pair................	—		☐☐☐☐☐
2441	A1800	25c ultramarine, bright pink			
		& dark green	45	15	☐☐☐☐☐
2441a.		Booklet pane of 10............	4.50	—	☐☐☐☐☐
2441b.		As **a**, bright pink omitted	—		☐☐☐☐☐
2442	A1801	25c Ida B. Wells.................	45	15	☐☐☐☐☐
2443	A1802	15c Beach umbrella..............	28	15	☐☐☐☐☐
2443a.		Booklet pane of 10.............	2.80	—	☐☐☐☐☐
2443b.		As **a**, blue omitted	—		☐☐☐☐☐
2444	A1803	25c Wyoming statehood	45	15	☐☐☐☐☐
2445	A1804	25c *The Wizard of Oz*	45	15	☐☐☐☐☐
2446	A1805	25c *Gone with the Wind*	45	15	☐☐☐☐☐
2447	A1806	25c *Beau Geste*.................	45	15	☐☐☐☐☐
2448	A1807	25c *Stagecoach*.................	45	15	☐☐☐☐☐
2448a.		Block of 4, #2445-2448	1.80	1.00	☐☐☐☐☐
2449	A1808	25c Marianne Moore.............	50	15	☐☐☐☐☐

1990-91

Scott No.	Illus. No.	Description	Unused Value	Used Value	//////
2451	A1810	4c claret	15	15	☐☐☐☐☐
2452	A1811	5c red	15	15	☐☐☐☐☐
2468	A1827	$1 blue & scarlet	2.00	50	☐☐☐☐☐

1990

Scott No.	Illus. No.	Description	Unused Value	Used Value	//////
2470	A1829	25c Admiralty Head	50	15	☐☐☐☐☐
2471	A1830	25c Cape Hatteras	50	15	☐☐☐☐☐
2472	A1831	25c West Quoddy Head	50	15	☐☐☐☐☐
2473	A1832	25c American Shoals.............	50	15	☐☐☐☐☐
2474	A1833	25c Sandy Hook	50	15	☐☐☐☐☐
2474a.		Booklet pane of 5, #2470-2474 ...	2.50	—	☐☐☐☐☐
2474b.		As **a**, white (USA 25) omitted....	125.00		☐☐☐☐☐
2475	A1834	25c dark red & dark blue	50	25	☐☐☐☐☐

207

A1855-59   A1860-64

Scott No.	Illus. No.	Description	Unused Value	Used Value	//////
2475a.		Pane of 12.	6.00		☐☐☐☐☐
2476	A1835	$2 Bobcat	4.00	50	☐☐☐☐☐
2496	A1855	25c Jesse Owens.	50	15	☐☐☐☐☐
2497	A1856	25c Ray Ewry.	50	15	☐☐☐☐☐
2498	A1857	25c Hazel Wightman.	50	15	☐☐☐☐☐
2499	A1858	25c Eddie Eagan	50	15	☐☐☐☐☐
2500	A1859	25c Helene Madison	50	15	☐☐☐☐☐
2500a.		Strip of 5, #2496-2500.	2.50	–	☐☐☐☐☐
2501	A1860	25c Assiniboin.	50	15	☐☐☐☐☐
2502	A1861	25c Cheyenne.	50	15	☐☐☐☐☐
2503	A1862	25c Comanche.	50	15	☐☐☐☐☐
2504	A1863	25c Flathead.	50	15	☐☐☐☐☐
2505	A1864	25c Shoshone	50	15	☐☐☐☐☐
2505a.		Booklet pane of 10, 2 each #2501-2505	5.00	–	☐☐☐☐☐
2505b.		As **a,** black (engraved) omitted . . .	–		☐☐☐☐☐
2506	A1865	25c Canoe, Micronesia flag.	50	15	☐☐☐☐☐
2507	A1866	25c Stick chart, canoe, Marshall Islands flag.	50	15	☐☐☐☐☐
2507a.		Pair, #2506-2507	1.00	16	☐☐☐☐☐
2508	A1867	25c Killer whales	50	15	☐☐☐☐☐
2509	A1868	25c Northern sea lions	50	15	☐☐☐☐☐
2510	A1869	25c Sea otter.	50	15	☐☐☐☐☐
2511	A1870	25c Common dolphin	50	15	☐☐☐☐☐
2511a.		Block of 4, #2508-2511	2.00	–	☐☐☐☐☐
2511b.		As **a,** black (engraved) omitted . . .	–		☐☐☐☐☐
2512	A1871	25c Grand Canyon	50	15	☐☐☐☐☐
2513	A1872	25c Dwight D. Eisenhower	50	15	☐☐☐☐☐
2514	A1873	25c Madonna and Child	50	15	☐☐☐☐☐
2514a.		Booklet pane of 10.	5.00		☐☐☐☐☐
2515	A1874	25c Christmas tree.	50	15	☐☐☐☐☐
2516	A1874	25c Christmas tree (from booklet pane)	50	15	☐☐☐☐☐
2516a.		Booklet pane of 10.	5.00		☐☐☐☐☐

1991

Scott No.	Illus. No.	Description	Unused Value	Used Value	//////
2517	A1875	(29c) yellow, black, red & yellow green . ~~Sheet tulip~~ . . .	58	15	☐☐☐☐☐

Coil Stamp, Perf. 10 vertically

2518	A1875	(29c) yellow, black, dull red & dark yellow green	58	15	☐☐☐☐☐

1991

2519	A1875	(29c) yellow, black, dull red & dark green . ~~Booklet~~	58	15	☐☐☐☐☐
2521	A1876	(4c) gold & carmine.	15	15	☐☐☐☐☐
2522	A1877	(29c) black, dark blue & red	58	25	☐☐☐☐☐

F PTM SELF ADHESIVE

A1865-66

A1871

A1867-70

A1872

A1873   **A1874**   **A1875**   **A1876**

A1877

Scott No.	Illus. No.	Description	Unused Value	Used Value	//////
2185	35¢	Dennis Chavez			☐☐☐☐☐
2190	.52	Hubert Humphrey			☐☐☐☐☐
					☐☐☐☐☐
2451	.04	Steam Carriage (engraved)			☐☐☐☐☐
2453	.05	Canoe (engraved)			☐☐☐☐☐
✓		✓ (gravure)			☐☐☐☐☐
2457	.10	Tractor Trailer			☐☐☐☐☐
2464	.23	Lunch wagon			☐☐☐☐☐
2481	.01	Kestrel (bird)			☐☐☐☐☐
2482	.03	Bluebird			☐☐☐☐☐
2487	.19	Fawn			☐☐☐☐☐
2489	.30	Cardinal			☐☐☐☐☐
2493	.29	Wood Duck (black)			☐☐☐☐☐
2494	.29	✓ ✓ (red)			☐☐☐☐☐
					☐☐☐☐☐
2522	F	ATM self adhesive			☐☐☐☐☐
2523	29	Flag / Rushmore (engraved)			☐☐☐☐☐
2523A	29	✓ ✓ (gravure)			☐☐☐☐☐
2525	29	Tulip (Roulette)			☐☐☐☐☐
					☐☐☐☐☐
2527	29	✓ (Booklet)			☐☐☐☐☐
2528	29	Flag / Olympics			☐☐☐☐☐
2529	19	Fishing Boat			☐☐☐☐☐
2530	19	Balloon			☐☐☐☐☐
2531	29	Flag / Parade			☐☐☐☐☐
2531A	29	ATM - Torch self adhesive			☐☐☐☐☐
2532	50	Switzerland			☐☐☐☐☐
2533	29	Vermont			☐☐☐☐☐
2534	29	Savings Bonds			☐☐☐☐☐
2535	29	Love sheet			☐☐☐☐☐
2536A	29	✓ Booklet			☐☐☐☐☐
2537	52	✓			☐☐☐☐☐
2538	29	Wm Saroyan			☐☐☐☐☐

Scott No.	Illus. No.	Description	Unused Value	Used Value	//////
2539	$1	Olympics			☐☐☐☐☐
2540	2⁹⁰	Priority (Eagle)			☐☐☐☐☐
2541	9⁹⁵	US Express Mail			☐☐☐☐☐
2542	$14	International Exp			☐☐☐☐☐
					☐☐☐☐☐
					☐☐☐☐☐
2545	29	Fishing Royal Wulff			☐☐☐☐☐
2546		Jock Scott			☐☐☐☐☐
2547		Apte Tarpon			☐☐☐☐☐
2548		Leftys Deceiver			☐☐☐☐☐
2549		Muddler Minnow			☐☐☐☐☐
2550	29	Cole Porter			☐☐☐☐☐
2551S	29	Desert Storm			☐☐☐☐☐
2551A	✓	✓ ✓ Booklet			☐☐☐☐☐
2553	29	Olympics Pole Vault			☐☐☐☐☐
2554		Discus Throw			☐☐☐☐☐
2555		Sprint			☐☐☐☐☐
2556		Javelin Throw			☐☐☐☐☐
2557		Hurdles			☐☐☐☐☐
2558	29	Numismatics			☐☐☐☐☐
2559 A		World War II Burma Rd			☐☐☐☐☐
B		Peacetime Draft			☐☐☐☐☐
C		Land-Lease Act			☐☐☐☐☐
D		Atlantic Charter			☐☐☐☐☐
E		Arsenal of Dem			☐☐☐☐☐
F		Reuben James			☐☐☐☐☐
G		Civil Defense			☐☐☐☐☐
H		Liberty Ships			☐☐☐☐☐
I		Pearl Harbor			☐☐☐☐☐
J		Dec of War on Japan			☐☐☐☐☐
2560	29	Basketball			☐☐☐☐☐
2561	29	DC Bicentennial			☐☐☐☐☐
					☐☐☐☐☐

Scott No.	Illus. No.	Description	Unused Value	Used Value	//////
2562	29	Comedians Booklet *Laurel & Hardy*			☐☐☐☐☐
2563		Bergen & McCarthy			☐☐☐☐☐
2564		Jack Benny			☐☐☐☐☐
2565		Fanny Bridge			☐☐☐☐☐
2566	✓	✓ Abbott & Costello			☐☐☐☐☐
					☐☐☐☐☐
2568	29	Solar System Mercury			☐☐☐☐☐
2569		Venus			☐☐☐☐☐
2570		Earth			☐☐☐☐☐
2571		Moon			☐☐☐☐☐
2572		Mars			☐☐☐☐☐
2573		Jupiter			☐☐☐☐☐
2574		Saturn			☐☐☐☐☐
2575		Uranus			☐☐☐☐☐
2576		Neptune			☐☐☐☐☐
2577	✓	Pluto			☐☐☐☐☐
2578		Madonna + X-Mas sheet			☐☐☐☐☐
2578A	✓	Booklet			☐☐☐☐☐
2579		Santa Bk Sheet			☐☐☐☐☐
2579A	✓	Booklet			☐☐☐☐☐
					☐☐☐☐☐
					☐☐☐☐☐
2582		Santa Booklet (list)			☐☐☐☐☐
2583	✓	(Pkg)			☐☐☐☐☐
2584	✓	Roof top			☐☐☐☐☐
2585	✓	(sleigh)			☐☐☐☐☐
1055	29¢	Earl Warren			☐☐☐☐☐
1075	75¢	Wendell Willkie			☐☐☐☐☐
4420	29	Winter Olympics Skiing			☐☐☐☐☐
		Hockey			☐☐☐☐☐
		Bobsled			☐☐☐☐☐
		Figure Skating			☐☐☐☐☐
		Speed Skating			☐☐☐☐☐

AP1

AP2

AP3

AP4

AP5

AP6

AP7

AP8

AP9

AP10

AP11

AP12

AP13

AP14

AP15

214

Scott No.	Illus. No.	Description	Unused Value	Used Value	//////
Air Post Stamps					
1918					
C1	AP1	6c orange	62.50	26.00	☐☐☐☐☐
C2	AP1	16c green	90.00	27.50	☐☐☐☐☐
C3	AP1	24c carmine rose & blue	85.00	32.50	☐☐☐☐☐
C3a.		Center inverted	*135,000.*		☐☐☐☐☐
1923					
C4	AP2	8c dark green	25.00	12.00	☐☐☐☐☐
C5	AP3	16c dark blue	85.00	30.00	☐☐☐☐☐
C6	AP4	24c carmine	90.00	24.00	☐☐☐☐☐
1926-27					
C7	AP5	10c dark blue	2.25	25	☐☐☐☐☐
C8	AP5	15c olive brown	2.75	1.90	☐☐☐☐☐
C9	AP5	20c yellow green ('27)	8.00	1.65	☐☐☐☐☐
1927, June 18					
C10	AP6	10c dark blue	6.75	1.65	☐☐☐☐☐
C10a.		Booklet pane of 3	90.00	*50.00*	☐☐☐☐☐
1928, July 25					
C11	AP7	5c carmine & blue	3.50	40	☐☐☐☐☐
C11a.		Vertical pair, imperf. between	*5,500.*		☐☐☐☐☐
1930					
C12	AP8	5c violet	8.00	25	☐☐☐☐☐
C12a.		Horizontal pair, imperf. between	*4,500.*		☐☐☐☐☐
C13	AP9	65c green	275.00	200.00	☐☐☐☐☐
C14	AP10	$1.30 brown	625.00	400.00	☐☐☐☐☐
C15	AP11	$2.60 blue	950.00	600.00	☐☐☐☐☐
1931-32					
C16	AP8	5c violet	4.75	35	☐☐☐☐☐
C17	AP8	8c olive bister ('32)	1.90	20	☐☐☐☐☐
1933, Oct. 2					
C18	AP12	50c green	80.00	65.00	☐☐☐☐☐

Catalogue values for unused stamps in this section, from this point to the end of the section, are for Never Hinged items.

Scott No.	Illus. No.	Description	Unused Value	Used Value	//////
1934, June 30					
C19	AP8	6c dull orange	2.25	15	☐☐☐☐☐
1935, Nov. 22					
C20	AP13	25c blue	1.10	75	☐☐☐☐☐

AP16

AP17

AP19

AP18

AP20

AP21

AP22

AP24

AP23

AP25

AP26

AP27

AP28

AP29

AP30

Scott No.	Illus. No.	Description	Unused Value	Used Value	//////
1937, Feb. 15					
C21	AP14	20c green	8.50	1.25 ☐☐☐☐☐	
C22	AP14	50c carmine	8.00	4.00 ☐☐☐☐☐	
1938, May 14					
C23	AP15	6c dark blue & carmine	40	15 ☐☐☐☐☐	
C23a.		Vertical pair, imperf. horizontally	275.00	☐☐☐☐☐	
C23b.		Horizontal pair, imperf. vertically	*10,000.*	☐☐☐☐☐	
C23c.		6c ultramarine & carmine	150.00	☐☐☐☐☐	
1939, May 16					
C24	AP16	30c dull blue	7.50	1.00 ☐☐☐☐☐	
1941-44					
C25	AP17	6c carmine	15	15 ☐☐☐☐☐	
C25a.		Booklet pane of 3 ('43)	4.00	*1.00* ☐☐☐☐☐	
C25b.		Horizontal pair, imperf. between	*1,500.*	☐☐☐☐☐	
C26	AP17	8c olive green ('44)	16	15 ☐☐☐☐☐	
C27	AP17	10c violet	1.10	20 ☐☐☐☐☐	
C28	AP17	15c brown carmine	2.25	35 ☐☐☐☐☐	
C29	AP17	20c bright green	1.75	30 ☐☐☐☐☐	
C30	AP17	30c blue	2.00	30 ☐☐☐☐☐	
C31	AP17	50c orange	10.00	3.75 ☐☐☐☐☐	
1946, Sept. 25					
C32	AP18	5c carmine	15	15 ☐☐☐☐☐	
1947					
C33	AP19	5c carmine	15	15 ☐☐☐☐☐	
C34	AP20	10c black	25	15 ☐☐☐☐☐	
C35	AP21	15c bright blue green	35	15 ☐☐☐☐☐	
C35a.		Horizontal pair, imperf. between	*1,500.*	☐☐☐☐☐	
C36	AP22	25c blue	85	15 ☐☐☐☐☐	
1948 Coil Stamp, Perf. 10 horizontally					
C37	AP19	5c carmine	80	75 ☐☐☐☐☐	
1948					
C38	AP23	5c bright carmine	15	15 ☐☐☐☐☐	
1949					
C39	AP19	6c carmine	15	15 ☐☐☐☐☐	
C39a.		Booklet pane of 6	9.50	*4.00* ☐☐☐☐☐	
C40	AP24	6c carmine	15	15 ☐☐☐☐☐	
Coil Stamp, Perf. 10 horizontally					
C41	AP19	6c carmine	2.75	15 ☐☐☐☐☐	

AP31

AP32

AP33

AP34

AP35

AP36

AP38

AP37

AP39

AP40

AP42

AP41-Redrawn

AP43

AP44

AP45

AP47

AP46

218

Scott No.	Illus. No.	Description	Unused Value	Used Value	//////
1949					
C42	AP25	10c violet	20	18	☐☐☐☐☐
C43	AP26	15c ultramarine	30	25	☐☐☐☐☐
C44	AP27	25c rose carmine	50	40	☐☐☐☐☐
C45	AP28	6c magenta	15	15	☐☐☐☐☐
1952					
C46	AP29	80c bright red violet	6.00	1.00	☐☐☐☐☐
1953					
C47	AP30	6c carmine	15	15	☐☐☐☐☐
1954					
C48	AP31	4c bright blue	15	15	☐☐☐☐☐
1957, Aug. 1					
C49	AP32	6c blue	15	15	☐☐☐☐☐
1958					
C50	AP31	5c rose red	15	15	☐☐☐☐☐
C51	AP33	7c blue	15	15	☐☐☐☐☐
C51a.		Booklet pane of 6	11.00	*6.00*	☐☐☐☐☐
C52	AP33	7c blue	2.25	15	☐☐☐☐☐
1959					
C53	AP34	7c dark blue	15	15	☐☐☐☐☐
C54	AP35	7c dark blue & red	15	15	☐☐☐☐☐
C55	AP36	7c rose red	15	15	☐☐☐☐☐
C56	AP37	10c violet blue & bright red	24	24	☐☐☐☐☐
1959-66					
C57	AP38	10c black & green ('60)	1.40	70	☐☐☐☐☐
C58	AP39	15c black & orange	35	15	☐☐☐☐☐
C59	AP40	25c black & maroon ('60)	48	15	☐☐☐☐☐
C59a.		Tagged ('66)	50	20	☐☐☐☐☐
1960, Aug. 12					
C60	AP33	7c carmine	15	15	☐☐☐☐☐
C60a.		Booklet pane of 6	14.50	*7.00*	☐☐☐☐☐
Coil Stamp, Perf. 10 horizontally					
C61	AP33	7c carmine	4.00	25	☐☐☐☐☐
1961-67					
C62	AP38	13c black & red	40	15	☐☐☐☐☐
C62a.		Tagged ('67)	70	50	☐☐☐☐☐
C63	AP41	15c black & orange	30	15	☐☐☐☐☐
C63a.		Tagged ('67)	32	15	☐☐☐☐☐
C63b.		As a, horizontally pair, imperf. vertically	*15,000.*		☐☐☐☐☐

AP50

AP48

AP51

AP49

AP52

AP53

AP54

AP55

AP56

AP57

AP58

AP59

AP60

AP61

AP62

AP63

AP70

Scott No.	Illus. No.	Description	Unused Value	Used Value	//////
1962					
C64	AP42	8c carmine	15	15 ☐☐☐☐☐
C64a.		Tagged ('63)	18	15 ☐☐☐☐☐
C64b.		Booklet pane 5 + label	4.75	*2.50* ☐☐☐☐☐
C64c.		As **b**, tagged ('64)	1.75	*50* ☐☐☐☐☐
		Coil Stamp, Perf. 10 horizontally			
C65	AP42	8c carmine	40	15 ☐☐☐☐☐
C65a.		Tagged ('65)	35	15 ☐☐☐☐☐
1963					
C66	AP43	15c carmine, deep claret & blue	60	55 ☐☐☐☐☐
C67	AP44	6c red	15	15 ☐☐☐☐☐
C67a.		Tagged ('67)	2.75	50 ☐☐☐☐☐
C68	AP45	8c carmine & maroon	20	15 ☐☐☐☐☐
1964, Oct. 5					
C69	AP46	8c blue, red & bister	48	15 ☐☐☐☐☐
1967					
C70	AP47	8c brown	24	15 ☐☐☐☐☐
C71	AP48	20c *Columbia Jays.*	80	15 ☐☐☐☐☐
1968, Jan. 5					
C72	AP49	10c carmine	20	15 ☐☐☐☐☐
C72b.		Booklet pane of 8	2.00	75 ☐☐☐☐☐
C72c.		Booklet pane of 5 + label	3.75	75 ☐☐☐☐☐
		Coil Stamp, Perf. 10 vertically			
C73	AP49	10c carmine	30	15 ☐☐☐☐☐
C73a.		Imperf., pair	*600.00*	☐☐☐☐☐
1968					
C74	AP50	10c blue, black & red	25	15 ☐☐☐☐☐
C74a.		Red (tail stripe) omitted	—	☐☐☐☐☐
C75	AP51	20c red, blue & black	48	15 ☐☐☐☐☐
1969, Sept. 9					
C76	AP52	10c Moon landing	20	15 ☐☐☐☐☐
C76a.		Rose red (litho.) omitted	*500.00*	— ☐☐☐☐☐
1971-73					
C77	AP53	9c red	18	15 ☐☐☐☐☐
C78	AP54	11c carmine	20	15 ☐☐☐☐☐
C78a.		Booklet pane of 4 + 2 labels	1.25	75 ☐☐☐☐☐
C78b.		Untagged (Bureau precanceled)		30 ☐☐☐☐☐
C79	AP55	13c carmine ('73)	22	15 ☐☐☐☐☐
C79a.		Booklet pane of 5 + label ('73)	1.35	75 ☐☐☐☐☐
C79b.		Untagged (Bureau precanceled)		28 ☐☐☐☐☐

AP64

AP66

AP68

AP65

AP67

AP69

AP72

AP71

AP73

AP81

AP86

AP87

AP88

AP89

AP90

Scott No.	Illus. No.	Description	Unused Value	Used Value	//////
C80	AP56	17c bluish black, red & dark green ..	40	15	☐☐☐☐☐
C81	AP51	21c red, blue & black............	40	15	☐☐☐☐☐

Coil Stamps, Perf. 10 vertically

C82	AP54	11c carmine	25	15	☐☐☐☐☐
C82a.		Imperf., pair..................	250.00		☐☐☐☐☐
C83	AP55	13c carmine ('73)...............	26	15	☐☐☐☐☐
C83a.		Imperf., pair.................	125.00		☐☐☐☐☐

1972

C84	AP57	11c orange & multicolored	20	15	☐☐☐☐☐
C84a.		Blue & green (litho) omitted	1,400.		☐☐☐☐☐
C85	AP58	11c Skiing....................	22	15	☐☐☐☐☐

1973, July 10

C86	AP59	11c rose lilac & multicolored	22	15	☐☐☐☐☐
C86a.		Vermilion & olive (litho.) omitted	2,250.		☐☐☐☐☐

1974

C87	AP60	18c carmine, black & ultramarine ..	40	25	☐☐☐☐☐
C88	AP61	26c ultramarine, black & carmine ..	48	15	☐☐☐☐☐

1976, Jan. 2

C89	AP62	25c ultramarine, red & black	45	15	☐☐☐☐☐
C90	AP63	31c ultramarine, red & black	55	15	☐☐☐☐☐

1978, Sept. 23

C91	AP64	31c ultramarine & multicolored....	65	30	☐☐☐☐☐
C92	AP65	31c ultramarine & multicolored....	65	30	☐☐☐☐☐
C92a.		Pair, #C91-C92	1.30	85	☐☐☐☐☐
C92b.		As **a**, ultramarine & black (engraved) omitted	1,250.		☐☐☐☐☐
C92c.		As **a**, black (engraved) omitted ...	—		☐☐☐☐☐
C92d.		As **a**, black, yellow, magenta, blue & brown (litho.) omitted	2,000.		☐☐☐☐☐

1979

C93	AP66	21c ultramarine & multicolored....	70	32	☐☐☐☐☐
C94	AP67	21c ultramarine & multicolored....	70	32	☐☐☐☐☐
C94a.		Pair, #C93-C94	1.40	95	☐☐☐☐☐
C94b.		As **a**, ultramarine & black (engraved) omitted	3,500.		☐☐☐☐☐
C95	AP68	25c ultramarine & multicolored....	1.10	35	☐☐☐☐☐
C96	AP69	25c ultramarine & multicolored....	1.10	35	☐☐☐☐☐
C96a.		Pair, #C95-C96	2.25	95	☐☐☐☐☐
C97	AP70	31c High jump.................	65	30	☐☐☐☐☐

Scott No.	Illus. No.	Description	Unused Value	Used Value	//////
1980					
C98	AP71	40c Philip Mazzei	70	15	□□□□□
C98a.		Perf. 10½ x 11	3.00	–	□□□□□
C98b.		Imperf., pair	*3,250.*		□□□□□
C99	AP72	28c Blanche Stuart Scott	55	15	□□□□□
C100	AP73	35c Glenn Curtiss	60	15	□□□□□
1983					
C101	AP81	28c Gymnast	60	28	□□□□□
C102	AP81	28c Hurdler	60	28	□□□□□
C103	AP81	28c Basketball	60	28	□□□□□
C104	AP81	28c Soccer	60	28	□□□□□
C104a.		Block of 4, #C101-C104	2.50	1.75	□□□□□
C104b.		As **a**, imperf. vertically	–		□□□□□
C105	AP81	40c Shot put	90	40	□□□□□
C105a.		Perf. 11x10½	1.00	45	□□□□□
C106	AP81	40c Gymnast	90	40	□□□□□
C106a.		Perf. 11x10½	1.00	45	□□□□□
C107	AP81	40c Swimmer	90	40	□□□□□
C107a.		Perf. 11x10½	1.00	45	□□□□□
C108	AP81	40c Weightlifting	90	40	□□□□□
C108a.		Block of 4, #C105-C108	3.60	2.00	□□□□□
C108b.		As **a**, imperf.	*1,350.*		□□□□□
C108c.		Perf. 11x10½	1.00	45	□□□□□
C108d.		As **a**, perf. 11x10½	4.25	–	□□□□□
C109	AP81	35c Women's fencing	90	35	□□□□□
C110	AP81	35c Cycling	90	35	□□□□□
C111	AP81	35c Women's volleyball	90	35	□□□□□
C112	AP81	35c Pole vaulting	90	35	□□□□□
C112a.		Block of 4, #C109-C112	3.60	1.85	□□□□□
1985					
C113	AP86	33c Alfred V. Verville	60	20	□□□□□
C113a.		Imperf., pair	*1,100.*		□□□□□
C114	AP87	39c Lawrence & Elmer Sperry	70	20	□□□□□
C114a.		Imperf., pair	*1,500.*		□□□□□
C115	AP88	44c Transpacific airmail	80	20	□□□□□
C115a.		Imperf., pair	*1,100.*		□□□□□
C116	AP89	44c Junipero Serra	80	20	□□□□□
C116a.		Imperf., pair	–		□□□□□
1988					
C117	AP90	44c NewSweden	1.25	20	□□□□□
C118	AP91	45c Samuel P. Langley	80	20	□□□□□
C119	AP92	36c Igor Sikorsky	65	20	□□□□□

AP91

AP92

AP93

AP94

AP95-98

AP99

HOW TO USE THIS BOOK

The number in the first column is its Scott number or identifying number. The letter and number that come next (A41) indicate the design and refer to the illustration so designated. Following that is the denomination of the stamp and its color. Finally, the value, unused and used is shown.

Scott No.	Illus. No.	Description	Unused Value	Used Value	//////
1989					
C120	AP93	45c French Revolution	80	22 ☐☐☐☐☐	
C121	AP94	45c Southeast carved figure	80	22 ☐☐☐☐☐	
C122	AP95	45c Spacecraft	90	30 ☐☐☐☐☐	
C123	AP96	45c Air-suspended hover car	90	30 ☐☐☐☐☐	
C124	AP97	45c Moon rover.	90	30 ☐☐☐☐☐	
C125	AP98	45c Space shuttle	90	30 ☐☐☐☐☐	
C125a.		Block of 4, Nos. C122-C125	3.60	2.25 ☐☐☐☐☐	
C125b.		As **a**, light blue (engraved)			
		omitted	3,000.	☐☐☐☐☐	
C126		Sheet of 4	3.60	2.25 ☐☐☐☐☐	
C126a.		AP95 45c Spacecraft	90	50 ☐☐☐☐☐	
C126b.		AP96 45c Air-suspended hover car			
			90	50 ☐☐☐☐☐	
C126c.		AP97 45c Moon rover.	90	50 ☐☐☐☐☐	
C126d.		AP98 45c Space shuttle	90	50 ☐☐☐☐☐	
1990, Oct. 12					
C127	AP99	45c Tropical coast	90	20 ☐☐☐☐☐	
C128	50	Harriet Quimby		☐☐☐☐☐	
C129	40	Wm Piper		☐☐☐☐☐	
C130	50	Antarctic Treaty		☐☐☐☐☐	
C131	50	America crossed sea		☐☐☐☐☐	
				☐☐☐☐☐	
				☐☐☐☐☐	
				☐☐☐☐☐	
				☐☐☐☐☐	
				☐☐☐☐☐	
				☐☐☐☐☐	
				☐☐☐☐☐	
				☐☐☐☐☐	
				☐☐☐☐☐	
				☐☐☐☐☐	
				☐☐☐☐☐	
				☐☐☐☐☐	
				☐☐☐☐☐	
				☐☐☐☐☐	

ASPD1

SD1

SD2

SD3

SD4

SD5

SD6

SD7

SD8

SD9

HOW TO USE THIS BOOK

The number in the first column is its Scott number or identifying number. The letter and number that come next (A41) indicate the design and refer to the illustration so designated. Following that is the denomination of the stamp and its color. Finally, the value, unused and used is shown.

Scott No.	Illus. No.	Description	Unused Value	Used Value	//////
Air Post Special Delivery Stamps					
1934					
CE1	APSD1	16c dark blue	65	85	☐☐☐☐☐
1936					
CE2	APSD1	16c red & blue	40	25	☐☐☐☐☐
CE2a.		Horizontal pair, imperf. vertically	*3,750.*		☐☐☐☐☐
Special Delivery Stamps					
1885					
E1	SD1	10c blue	175.00	27.50	☐☐☐☐☐
1888					
E2	SD2	10c blue	175.00	5.75	☐☐☐☐☐
1893					
E3	SD2	10c orange	110.00	11.00	☐☐☐☐☐
1894					
E4	SD3	10c blue	450.00	14.00	☐☐☐☐☐
1895					
E5	SD3	10c blue	85.00	1.90	☐☐☐☐☐
E5b.		Printed on both sides.	*1,250.*		☐☐☐☐☐
1902					
E6	SD4	10c ultramarine	52.50	1.90	☐☐☐☐☐
1908					
E7	SD5	10c green	45.00	24.00	☐☐☐☐☐
1911					
E8	SD4	10c ultramarine	55.00	2.50	☐☐☐☐☐
E8b.		10c violet blue	55.00	2.50	☐☐☐☐☐
1914					
E9	SD4	10c ultramarine	110.00	3.00	☐☐☐☐☐
1916					
E10	SD4	10c pale ultramarine	200.00	14.00	☐☐☐☐☐
1917					
E11	SD4	10c ultramarine	10.00	25	☐☐☐☐☐
E11b.		10c gray violet	10.00	25	☐☐☐☐☐
E11c.		10c blue	20.00	60	☐☐☐☐☐
1922-25					
E12	SD6	10c gray violet	18.00	15	☐☐☐☐☐
E12a.		10c deep ultramarine	25.00	20	☐☐☐☐☐

Scott No.	Illus. No.	Description	Unused Value	Used Value	//////
E13	SD6	15c deep orange ('25).............	15.00	50	☐☐☐☐☐
E14	SD7	20c black ('25).................	1.65	85	☐☐☐☐☐

1927-31

E15	SD6	10c gray violet.................	60	15	☐☐☐☐☐
E15a.		10c red lilac.................	60	15	☐☐☐☐☐
E15b.		10c gray lilac.................	60	15	☐☐☐☐☐
E15c.		Horizontal pair, imperf. between .	275.00		☐☐☐☐☐
E16	SD6	15c orange ('31).................	70	15	☐☐☐☐☐

1944-51

E17	SD6	13c blue......................	60	15	☐☐☐☐☐
E18	SD6	17c orange yellow..............	2.75	1.75	☐☐☐☐☐
E19	SD7	20c black ('51).................	1.20	15	☐☐☐☐☐

1954-57

E20	SD8	20c deep blue..................	40	15	☐☐☐☐☐
E21	SD8	30c lake ('57)..................	48	15	☐☐☐☐☐

1969-71

E22	SD9	45c carmine & violet blue.........	1.10	15	☐☐☐☐☐
E23	SD9	60c violet blue & carmine ('71).....	85	15	☐☐☐☐☐

_____ ☐☐☐☐☐
_____ ☐☐☐☐☐
_____ ☐☐☐☐☐
_____ ☐☐☐☐☐
_____ ☐☐☐☐☐
_____ ☐☐☐☐☐
_____ ☐☐☐☐☐
_____ ☐☐☐☐☐
_____ ☐☐☐☐☐
_____ ☐☐☐☐☐
_____ ☐☐☐☐☐
_____ ☐☐☐☐☐
_____ ☐☐☐☐☐
_____ ☐☐☐☐☐
_____ ☐☐☐☐☐
_____ ☐☐☐☐☐
_____ ☐☐☐☐☐
_____ ☐☐☐☐☐

RS1

CM1

Scott No.	Illus. No.	Description	Unused Value	Used Value	//////

Registration Stamp
1911

| F1 | RS1 | 10c ultramarine | 55.00 | 2.25 | ☐☐☐☐☐ |

Certified Mail Stamp
1955, June 6

| FA1 | CM1 | 15c red | 28 | 20 | ☐☐☐☐☐ |

D1   D2   D3   D4   D5

Scott No.	Illus. No.	Description	Unused Value	Used Value	//////

Postage Due Stamps
1879

J1	D1	1c brown	30.00	5.00	☐☐☐☐☐
J2	D1	2c brown	200.00	4.00	☐☐☐☐☐
J3	D1	3c brown	25.00	2.50	☐☐☐☐☐
J4	D1	5c brown	300.00	25.00	☐☐☐☐☐
J5	D1	10c brown	350.00	12.50	☐☐☐☐☐
J5a.		Imperf., pair	*1,600.*		☐☐☐☐☐
J6	D1	30c brown	175.00	25.00	☐☐☐☐☐
J7	D1	50c brown	225.00	30.00	☐☐☐☐☐

1884

J15	D1	1c red brown	30.00	2.50	☐☐☐☐☐
J16	D1	2c red brown	37.50	2.50	☐☐☐☐☐
J17	D1	3c red brown	500.00	100.00	☐☐☐☐☐
J18	D1	5c red brown	250.00	12.50	☐☐☐☐☐
J19	D1	10c red brown	225.00	7.00	☐☐☐☐☐

Scott No.	Illus. No.	Description	Unused Value	Used Value	//////
J20	D1	30c red brown	110.00	22.50	☐☐☐☐☐
J21	D1	50c red brown	1,000.	125.00	☐☐☐☐☐

1891
J22	D1	1c bright claret...............	12.50	50	☐☐☐☐☐
J23	D1	2c bright claret...............	15.00	45	☐☐☐☐☐
J24	D1	3c bright claret...............	32.50	4.00	☐☐☐☐☐
J25	D1	5c bright claret...............	35.00	4.00	☐☐☐☐☐
J26	D1	10c bright claret...............	70.00	10.00	☐☐☐☐☐
J27	D1	30c bright claret...............	250.00	85.00	☐☐☐☐☐
J28	D1	50c bright claret...............	275.00	85.00	☐☐☐☐☐

1894
J29	D2	1c vermilion...................	575.00	100.00	☐☐☐☐☐
J30	D2	2c vermilion...................	250.00	50.00	☐☐☐☐☐
J31	D2	1c deep claret.................	20.00	3.00	☐☐☐☐☐
J31b.		Vertical pair, imperf. horizontally	—		☐☐☐☐☐
J32	D2	2c deep claret.................	17.50	1.75	☐☐☐☐☐
J33	D2	3c deep claret.................	75.00	20.00	☐☐☐☐☐
J34	D2	5c deep claret.................	100.00	22.50	☐☐☐☐☐
J35	D2	10c deep claret.................	100.00	17.50	☐☐☐☐☐
J36	D2	30c deep claret.................	225.00	50.00	☐☐☐☐☐
J36a.		30c carmine	225.00	50.00	☐☐☐☐☐
J36b.		30c pale rose.................	210.00	45.00	☐☐☐☐☐
J37	D2	50c deep claret.................	500.00	150.00	☐☐☐☐☐
J37a.		50c pale rose.................	450.00	135.00	☐☐☐☐☐

1895
J38	D2	1c deep claret.................	5.00	30	☐☐☐☐☐
J39	D2	2c deep claret.................	5.00	20	☐☐☐☐☐
J40	D2	3c deep claret.................	35.00	1.00	☐☐☐☐☐
J41	D2	5c deep claret.................	37.50	1.00	☐☐☐☐☐
J42	D2	10c deep claret.................	40.00	2.00	☐☐☐☐☐
J43	D2	30c deep claret.................	300.00	25.00	☐☐☐☐☐
J44	D2	50c deep claret.................	190.00	20.00	☐☐☐☐☐

1910-12
J45	D2	1c deep claret.................	20.00	2.00	☐☐☐☐☐
J45a.		1c rose carmine	17.50	1.75	☐☐☐☐☐
J46	D2	2c deep claret.................	20.00	30	☐☐☐☐☐
J46a.		2c rose carmine	17.50	30	☐☐☐☐☐
J47	D2	3c deep claret.................	350.00	17.50	☐☐☐☐☐
J48	D2	5c deep claret.................	60.00	3.50	☐☐☐☐☐
J48a.		5c rose carmine	—	—	☐☐☐☐☐
J49	D2	10c deep claret.................	75.00	7.50	☐☐☐☐☐
J49a.		10c rose carmine	—	—	☐☐☐☐☐
J50	D2	50c deep claret ('12).............	600.00	75.00	☐☐☐☐☐

Scott No.	Illus. No.	Description	Unused Value	Used Value	//////
1914-15					
J52	D2	1c carmine lake	40.00	7.50	☐☐☐☐☐
J52a.		1c dull rose	40.00	7.50	☐☐☐☐☐
J53	D2	2c carmine lake	32.50	20	☐☐☐☐☐
J53a.		2c dull rose	32.50	20	☐☐☐☐☐
J53b.		2c vermilion	32.50	20	☐☐☐☐☐
J54	D2	3c carmine lake	425.00	20.00	☐☐☐☐☐
J54a.		3c dull rose	425.00	20.00	☐☐☐☐☐
J55	D2	5c carmine lake	25.00	1.50	☐☐☐☐☐
J55a.		5c dull rose	25.00	1.50	☐☐☐☐☐
J56	D2	10c carmine lake	40.00	1.00	☐☐☐☐☐
J56a.		10c dull rose	40.00	1.00	☐☐☐☐☐
J57	D2	30c carmine lake	140.00	12.00	☐☐☐☐☐
J58	D2	50c carmine lake	*5,500.*	375.00	☐☐☐☐☐
1916					
J59	D2	1c rose	1,100.	175.00	☐☐☐☐☐
J60	D2	2c rose	85.00	10.00	☐☐☐☐☐
1917					
J61	D2	1c carmine rose	1.75	15	☐☐☐☐☐
J61a.		1c rose red	1.75	15	☐☐☐☐☐
J61b.		1c deep claret	1.75	15	☐☐☐☐☐
J62	D2	2c carmine rose	1.50	15	☐☐☐☐☐
J62a.		2c rose red	1.50	15	☐☐☐☐☐
J62b.		2c deep claret	1.50	15	☐☐☐☐☐
J63	D2	3c carmine rose	8.50	15	☐☐☐☐☐
J63a.		3c rose red	8.50	15	☐☐☐☐☐
J63b.		3c deep claret	8.50	25	☐☐☐☐☐
J64	D2	5c carmine	8.50	15	☐☐☐☐☐
J64a.		5c rose red	8.50	15	☐☐☐☐☐
J64b.		5c deep claret	8.50	15	☐☐☐☐☐
J65	D2	10c carmine rose	12.50	20	☐☐☐☐☐
J65a.		10c rose red	12.50	15	☐☐☐☐☐
J65b.		10c deep claret	12.50	15	☐☐☐☐☐
J66	D2	30c carmine rose	55.00	40	☐☐☐☐☐
J66a.		30c deep claret	55.00	40	☐☐☐☐☐
J67	D2	50c carmine rose	75.00	15	☐☐☐☐☐
J67a.		50c rose red	75.00	15	☐☐☐☐☐
J67b.		50c deep claret	75.00	15	☐☐☐☐☐
1925					
J68	D2	½c dull red	65	15	☐☐☐☐☐
1930					
J69	D3	½c carmine	3.00	1.00	☐☐☐☐☐
J70	D3	1c carmine	2.50	15	☐☐☐☐☐
J71	D3	2c carmine	3.00	15	☐☐☐☐☐

Scott No.	Illus. No.	Description	Unused Value	Used Value	//////
J72	D3	3c carmine	15.00	1.00	☐☐☐☐☐
J73	D3	5c carmine	14.00	1.50	☐☐☐☐☐
J74	D3	10c carmine	30.00	50	☐☐☐☐☐
J75	D3	30c carmine	85.00	1.00	☐☐☐☐☐
J76	D3	50c carmine	100.00	30	☐☐☐☐☐
J77	D4	$1 carmine	25.00	15	☐☐☐☐☐
J77a.		$1 scarlet	20.00	15	☐☐☐☐☐
J78	D4	$5 carmine	30.00	15	☐☐☐☐☐
J78a.		$5 scarlet	25.00	15	☐☐☐☐☐

1931-56

Scott No.	Illus. No.	Description	Unused Value	Used Value	//////
J79	D3	½c dull carmine	75	15	☐☐☐☐☐
J79a.		½c scarlet	75	15	☐☐☐☐☐
J80	D3	1c dull carmine	15	15	☐☐☐☐☐
J80a.		1c scarlet.	15	15	☐☐☐☐☐
J81	D3	2c dull carmine	15	15	☐☐☐☐☐
J81a.		2c scarlet.	15	15	☐☐☐☐☐
J82	D3	3c dull carmine	25	15	☐☐☐☐☐
J82a.		3c scarlet.	25	15	☐☐☐☐☐
J83	D3	5c dull carmine	35	15	☐☐☐☐☐
J83a.		5c scarlet.	35	15	☐☐☐☐☐
J84	D3	10c dull carmine	1.10	15	☐☐☐☐☐
J84a.		10c scarlet.	1.10	15	☐☐☐☐☐
J85	D3	30c dull carmine	8.50	15	☐☐☐☐☐
J85a.		30c scarlet.	8.50	15	☐☐☐☐☐
J86	D3	50c dull carmine	9.50	15	☐☐☐☐☐
J86a.		50c scarlet.	9.50	15	☐☐☐☐☐
J87	D4	$1 scarlet ('56)	40.00	20	☐☐☐☐☐

1959, June 19

Scott No.	Illus. No.	Description	Unused Value	Used Value	//////
J88	D5	½c carmine rose.	1.25	85	☐☐☐☐☐
J89	D5	1c carmine rose	15	15	☐☐☐☐☐
J89a.		**1 CENT** omitted	*425.00*		☐☐☐☐☐
J89b.		Pair, one without **1 CENT**	—		☐☐☐☐☐
J90	D5	2c carmine rose	15	15	☐☐☐☐☐
J91	D5	3c carmine rose	15	15	☐☐☐☐☐
J91a.		Pair, one without **3 CENTS**	*800.00*		☐☐☐☐☐
J92	D5	4c carmine rose	15	15	☐☐☐☐☐
J93	D5	5c carmine rose	15	15	☐☐☐☐☐
J93a.		Pair, one without **5 CENTS**	—		☐☐☐☐☐
J94	D5	6c carmine rose	15	15	☐☐☐☐☐
J94a.		Pair, one without **6 CENTS**	*800.00*		☐☐☐☐☐
J95	D5	7c carmine rose	15	15	☐☐☐☐☐
J96	D5	8c carmine rose	16	15	☐☐☐☐☐
J96a.		Pair, one without **8 CENTS**	*800.00*		☐☐☐☐☐
J97	D5	10c carmine rose	20	15	☐☐☐☐☐
J98	D5	30c carmine rose	55	15	☐☐☐☐☐
J99	D5	50c carmine rose	90	15	☐☐☐☐☐

Scott No.	Illus. No.	Description	Unused Value	Used Value	//////
J100	D5	$1 carmine rose................	1.50	15	☐☐☐☐☐
J101	D5	$5 carmine rose................	8.00	15	☐☐☐☐☐

1978-85

Scott No.	Illus. No.	Description	Unused Value	Used Value	//////
J102	D5	11c carmine rose	35	15	☐☐☐☐☐
J103	D5	13c carmine rose	30	15	☐☐☐☐☐
J104	D5	17c carmine rose ('85)..........	40	15	☐☐☐☐☐

_____		☐☐☐☐☐
_____		☐☐☐☐☐
_____		☐☐☐☐☐
_____		☐☐☐☐☐
_____		☐☐☐☐☐
_____		☐☐☐☐☐
_____		☐☐☐☐☐
_____		☐☐☐☐☐
_____		☐☐☐☐☐
_____		☐☐☐☐☐
_____		☐☐☐☐☐
_____		☐☐☐☐☐
_____		☐☐☐☐☐
_____		☐☐☐☐☐
_____		☐☐☐☐☐
_____		☐☐☐☐☐
_____		☐☐☐☐☐
_____		☐☐☐☐☐
_____		☐☐☐☐☐
_____		☐☐☐☐☐
_____		☐☐☐☐☐
_____		☐☐☐☐☐
_____		☐☐☐☐☐
_____		☐☐☐☐☐
_____		☐☐☐☐☐
_____		☐☐☐☐☐

SHANGHAI
2¢
CHINA

Scott No.	Illus. No.	Description	Unused Value	Used Value	//////
U.S. Offices in China					
1919					
K1	A140	2c on 1c green	17.50	20.00	□□□□□
K2	A140	4c on 2c rose, type I.............	17.50	20.00	□□□□□
K3	A140	6c on 3c violet, type II..........	32.50	45.00	□□□□□
K4	A140	8c on 4c brown	40.00	45.00	□□□□□
K5	A140	10c on 5c blue	45.00	52.50	□□□□□
K6	A140	12c on 6c red orange	55.00	67.50	□□□□□
K7	A140	14c on 7c black	60.00	72.50	□□□□□
K8	A148	16c on 8c olive bister............	45.00	50.00	□□□□□
K8a.		16c on 8c olive green	40.00	42.50	□□□□□
K9	A148	18c on 9c salmon red............	45.00	55.00	□□□□□
K10	A148	20c on 10c orange yellow	40.00	47.50	□□□□□
K11	A148	24c on 12c brown carmine	47.50	57.50	□□□□□
K11a.		24c on 12c claret brown........	67.50	80.00	□□□□□
K12	A148	30c on 15c gray	57.50	70.00	□□□□□
K13	A148	40c on 20c deep ultramarine......	85.00	115.00	□□□□□
K14	A148	60c on 30c orange red	80.00	95.00	□□□□□
K15	A148	$1 on 50c light violet............	500.00	500.00	□□□□□
K16	A148	$2 on $1 violet brown...........	350.00	400.00	□□□□□
K16a.		Double surcharge.............	*2,500.*	*2,250.*	□□□□□

SHANGHAI

2 Cts.
CHINA

1922, July 3

K17	A140	2c on 1c green	80.00	80.00	□□□□□
K18	A140	4c on 2c carmine, type VII	70.00	70.00	□□□□□

01   08   06

011   012   013   014

Scott No.	Illus. No.	Description	Unused Value	Used Value	//////

Official Stamps
1873

Scott No.	Illus. No.	Description	Unused Value	Used Value	
O1	O1	1c yellow	90.00	40.00	☐☐☐☐☐
O2	O1	2c yellow	70.00	15.00	☐☐☐☐☐
O3	O1	3c yellow	65.00	3.50	☐☐☐☐☐
O4	O1	6c yellow	75.00	12.50	☐☐☐☐☐
O5	O1	10c yellow	150.00	55.00	☐☐☐☐☐
O6	O1	12c yellow	200.00	85.00	☐☐☐☐☐
O7	O1	15c yellow	150.00	55.00	☐☐☐☐☐
O8	O1	24c yellow	175.00	55.00	☐☐☐☐☐
O9	O1	30c yellow	225.00	95.00	☐☐☐☐☐
O10	O1	1c carmine	300.00	100.00	☐☐☐☐☐
O11	O1	2c carmine	200.00	70.00	☐☐☐☐☐
O12	O1	3c carmine	250.00	60.00	☐☐☐☐☐
O12a.		3c violet rose	200.00a	60.00	☐☐☐☐☐
O13	O1	6c carmine	350.00	200.00	☐☐☐☐☐
O14	O1	10c carmine	325.00	160.00	☐☐☐☐☐
O15	O1	1c vermilion	20.00	3.50	☐☐☐☐☐
O16	O1	2c vermilion	17.50	2.00	☐☐☐☐☐
O17	O1	3c vermilion	27.50	2.00	☐☐☐☐☐
O18	O1	6c vermilion	20.00	2.00	☐☐☐☐☐
O19	O1	10c vermilion	19.00	4.00	☐☐☐☐☐
O20	O1	12c vermilion	30.00	3.00	☐☐☐☐☐
O21	O1	15c vermilion	50.00	6.00	☐☐☐☐☐
O22	O1	24c vermilion	37.50	5.00	☐☐☐☐☐
O23	O1	30c vermilion	50.00	6.00	☐☐☐☐☐
O24	O1	90c vermilion	110.00	10.00	☐☐☐☐☐
O25	O1	1c purple	60.00	20.00	☐☐☐☐☐
O26	O1	2c purple	95.00	20.00	☐☐☐☐☐

Scott No.	Illus. No.	Description	Unused Value	Used Value	//////
O27	O1	3c purple	95.00	6.00	☐☐☐☐☐
O28	O1	6c purple	90.00	8.50	☐☐☐☐☐
O29	O1	10c purple	100.00	20.00	☐☐☐☐☐
O30	O1	12c purple	75.00	12.50	☐☐☐☐☐
O31	O1	15c purple	165.00	45.00	☐☐☐☐☐
O32	O1	24c purple	450.00	120.00	☐☐☐☐☐
O33	O1	30c purple	400.00	67.50	☐☐☐☐☐
O34	O1	90c purple	600.00	180.00	☐☐☐☐☐
O35	O1	1c ultramarine	45.00	7.00	☐☐☐☐☐
O35a.		1c dull blue.	52.50	8.50	☐☐☐☐☐
O36	O1	2c ultramarine	32.50	6.00	☐☐☐☐☐
O36a.		2c dull blue.	42.50	7.50	☐☐☐☐☐
O37	O1	3c ultramarine	37.50	4.00	☐☐☐☐☐
O37a.		3c dull blue.	42.50	5.50	☐☐☐☐☐
O38	O1	6c ultramarine	32.50	4.00	☐☐☐☐☐
O38a.		6c dull blue.	42.50	5.00	☐☐☐☐☐
O39	O1	7c ultramarine	225.00	60.00	☐☐☐☐☐
O39a.		7c dull blue.	250.00	70.00	☐☐☐☐☐
O40	O1	10c ultramarine	45.00	11.00	☐☐☐☐☐
O40a.		10c dull blue.	50.00	13.00	☐☐☐☐☐
O41	O1	12c ultramarine	57.50	7.00	☐☐☐☐☐
O42	O1	15c ultramarine	95.00	18.00	☐☐☐☐☐
O43	O1	24c ultramarine	95.00	20.00	☐☐☐☐☐
O43a.		24c dull blue.	110.00	—	☐☐☐☐☐
O44	O1	30c ultramarine	85.00	10.00	☐☐☐☐☐
O45	O1	90c ultramarine	400.00	57.50	☐☐☐☐☐
O45a.		Double impression.		2,000.	☐☐☐☐☐
O47	O6	1c black	7.25	3.00	☐☐☐☐☐
O48	O6	2c black	7.00	2.50	☐☐☐☐☐
O48a.		Double impression.	300.00		☐☐☐☐☐
O49	O6	3c black	2.50	55	☐☐☐☐☐
O49a.		Printed on both sides.		2,750.	☐☐☐☐☐
O50	O6	6c black	8.00	1.40	☐☐☐☐☐
O50a.		Diagonal half used as 3c on cover.		2,750.	☐☐☐☐☐
O51	O6	10c black	40.00	14.50	☐☐☐☐☐
O52	O6	12c black	22.50	3.50	☐☐☐☐☐
O53	O6	15c black	25.00	5.00	☐☐☐☐☐
O53a.		Imperf., pair.	600.00		☐☐☐☐☐
O54	O6	24c black	32.50	6.00	☐☐☐☐☐
O55	O6	30c black	32.50	5.50	☐☐☐☐☐
O56	O6	90c black	47.50	7.50	☐☐☐☐☐
O57	O1	1c dark green	60.00	12.50	☐☐☐☐☐
O58	O1	2c dark green	125.00	20.00	☐☐☐☐☐
O59	O1	3c bright green	50.00	9.00	☐☐☐☐☐
O60	O1	6c bright green	47.50	9.00	☐☐☐☐☐
O61	O1	7c dark green	90.00	15.00	☐☐☐☐☐
O62	O1	10c dark green	75.00	13.50	☐☐☐☐☐
O63	O1	12c dark green	110.00	30.00	☐☐☐☐☐

Scott No.	Illus. No.	Description	Unused Value	Used Value	//////
O64	O1	15c dark green	100.00	20.00	☐☐☐☐☐
O65	O1	24c dark green	250.00	65.00	☐☐☐☐☐
O66	O1	30c dark green	225.00	40.00	☐☐☐☐☐
O67	O1	90c dark green	400.00	100.00	☐☐☐☐☐
O68	O8	$2 green & black	550.00	225.00	☐☐☐☐☐
O69	O8	$5 green & black	4,250.	1,600.	☐☐☐☐☐
O70	O8	$10 green & black	3,000.	1,000.	☐☐☐☐☐
O71	O8	$20 green & black	2,250.	800.00	☐☐☐☐☐
O72	O1	1c brown	22.50	1.75	☐☐☐☐☐
O73	O1	2c brown	25.00	1.75	☐☐☐☐☐
O74	O1	3c brown	16.00	75	☐☐☐☐☐
O75	O1	6c brown	22.50	1.50	☐☐☐☐☐
O76	O1	7c brown	57.50	8.50	☐☐☐☐☐
O77	O1	10c brown	57.50	3.00	☐☐☐☐☐
O78	O1	12c brown	57.50	1.75	☐☐☐☐☐
O79	O1	15c brown	50.00	2.50	☐☐☐☐☐
O80	O1	24c brown	250.00	35.00	☐☐☐☐☐
O81	O1	30c brown	82.50	3.00	☐☐☐☐☐
O82	O1	90c brown	87.50	3.00	☐☐☐☐☐
O83	O1	1c rose	82.50	3.25	☐☐☐☐☐
O84	O1	2c rose	75.00	4.50	☐☐☐☐☐
O85	O1	3c rose	72.50	1.00	☐☐☐☐☐
O86	O1	6c rose	250.00	2.00	☐☐☐☐☐
O87	O1	7c rose	75.00	30.00	☐☐☐☐☐
O88	O1	10c rose	22.50	4.00	☐☐☐☐☐
O89	O1	12c rose	75.00	2.00	☐☐☐☐☐
O90	O1	15c rose	20.00	2.50	☐☐☐☐☐
O91	O1	24c rose	20.00	3.00	☐☐☐☐☐
O92	O1	30c rose	22.50	2.50	☐☐☐☐☐
O93	O1	90c rose	50.00	10.00	☐☐☐☐☐

1879

Scott No.	Illus. No.	Description	Unused Value	Used Value	//////
O94	O1	1c yellow, no gum	1,400.		☐☐☐☐☐
O95	O1	3c yellow	175.00	32.50	☐☐☐☐☐
O96	O1	1c vermilion.................	125.00	70.00	☐☐☐☐☐
O97	O1	2c vermilion.................	2.50	1.00	☐☐☐☐☐
O98	O1	3c vermilion.................	2.00	60	☐☐☐☐☐
O99	O1	6c vermilion.................	3.00	2.50	☐☐☐☐☐
O100	O1	10c vermilion................	32.50	20.00	☐☐☐☐☐
O101	O1	12c vermilion................	65.00	30.00	☐☐☐☐☐
O102	O1	15c vermilion................	150.00	50.00	☐☐☐☐☐
O103	O1	24c vermilion................	1,200.		☐☐☐☐☐
O106	O1	3c bluish purple	50.00	17.50	☐☐☐☐☐
O107	O1	6c bluish purple.............	110.00	70.00	☐☐☐☐☐
O108	O6	3c black	7.50	1.75	☐☐☐☐☐
O109	O1	3c brown	27.50	2.50	☐☐☐☐☐
O110	O1	6c brown	50.00	13.50	☐☐☐☐☐

Scott No.	Illus. No.	Description	Unused Value	Used Value	//////
O111	O1	10c brown	65.00	15.00	☐☐☐☐☐
O112	O1	30c brown	750.00	100.00	☐☐☐☐☐
O113	O1	90c brown	775.00	100.00	☐☐☐☐☐
O114	O1	1c rose red	2.00	1.50	☐☐☐☐☐
O115	O1	2c rose red	3.00	1.50	☐☐☐☐☐
O116	O1	3c rose red	3.00	75	☐☐☐☐☐
O116a.		Imperf., pair	*800.00*		☐☐☐☐☐
O116b.		Double impression	*500.00*		☐☐☐☐☐
O117	O1	6c rose red	2.50	70	☐☐☐☐☐
O118	O1	10c rose red	20.00	10.00	☐☐☐☐☐
O119	O1	12c rose red	15.00	3.00	☐☐☐☐☐
O120	O1	30c rose red	47.50	30.00	☐☐☐☐☐

1911

Scott No.	Illus. No.	Description	Unused Value	Used Value	//////
O121	O11	2c black	9.00	1.10	☐☐☐☐☐
O122	O11	50c dark green	110.00	25.00	☐☐☐☐☐
O123	O11	$1 ultramarine	100.00	7.00	☐☐☐☐☐
O124	O11	1c dark violet	5.50	1.00	☐☐☐☐☐
O125	O11	2c black	30.00	3.50	☐☐☐☐☐
O126	O11	10c carmine	10.00	1.00	☐☐☐☐☐

1983-85

Scott No.	Illus. No.	Description	Unused Value	Used Value	//////
O127	O12	1c red, blue & black	15	15	☐☐☐☐☐
O128	O12	4c red, blue & black	15	20	☐☐☐☐☐
O129	O12	13c red, blue & black	26	50	☐☐☐☐☐
O129A	O12	14c red, blue & black ('85)	28	50	☐☐☐☐☐
O130	O12	17c red, blue & black	34	40	☐☐☐☐☐
O132	O12	$1 red, blue & black	1.75	1.00	☐☐☐☐☐
O133	O12	$5 red, blue & black	9.00	5.00	☐☐☐☐☐

Coil Stamps, Perf. 10 vertically

Scott No.	Illus. No.	Description	Unused Value	Used Value	//////
O135	O12	20c red, blue & black	2.00	*3.00*	☐☐☐☐☐
O135a.		Imperf., pair	*1,500.*		☐☐☐☐☐
O136	O12	22c red, blue & black ('85)	60	*2.00*	☐☐☐☐☐

1985, Feb. 4

Scott No.	Illus. No.	Description	Unused Value	Used Value	//////
O138	O12	(14c) red, blue & black	3.50	5.00	☐☐☐☐☐

1985-88 Coil Stamps, Perf. 10 vertically

Scott No.	Illus. No.	Description	Unused Value	Used Value	//////
O138A	O13	15c red, blue & black ('88)	30	15	☐☐☐☐☐
O138B	O13	20c red, blue & black ('88)	40	15	☐☐☐☐☐
O139	O12	(22c) red, blue & black	3.50	*3.00*	☐☐☐☐☐
O140	O13	(25c) red, blue & black ('88)	50	*2.00*	☐☐☐☐☐
O141	O13	25c red, blue & black ('88)	50	20	☐☐☐☐☐

1989, July 5

Scott No.	Illus. No.	Description	Unused Value	Used Value	//////
O143	O13	1c red, blue & black	15	—	☐☐☐☐☐

Scott No.	Illus. No.	Description	Unused Value	Used Value	//////
1991 Coil Stamp, Perf. 10 vertically					
O144	O14	(29c) red, blue & black	58	25	☐☐☐☐☐
					☐☐☐☐☐
O146	4⁹				☐☐☐☐☐
					☐☐☐☐☐
					☐☐☐☐☐
					☐☐☐☐☐
					☐☐☐☐☐
					☐☐☐☐☐
					☐☐☐☐☐
					☐☐☐☐☐
					☐☐☐☐☐
					☐☐☐☐☐
					☐☐☐☐☐
					☐☐☐☐☐
					☐☐☐☐☐
					☐☐☐☐☐
					☐☐☐☐☐
					☐☐☐☐☐
					☐☐☐☐☐
					☐☐☐☐☐
					☐☐☐☐☐
					☐☐☐☐☐
					☐☐☐☐☐
					☐☐☐☐☐
					☐☐☐☐☐
					☐☐☐☐☐
					☐☐☐☐☐
					☐☐☐☐☐
					☐☐☐☐☐
					☐☐☐☐☐
					☐☐☐☐☐
					☐☐☐☐☐

N1

N2

N3

N4

N5

N6

N7

N8

N9

N10

N11

N12

N13

N14

242

Scott No.	Illus. No.	Description	Unused Value	Used Value	//////
Newspaper Stamps					
1865					
PR1	N1	5c dark blue	185.00	—	☐☐☐☐☐
PR1a.		5c light blue	175.00	—	☐☐☐☐☐
PR2	N2	10c blue green	85.00	—	☐☐☐☐☐
PR2a.		10c green	85.00	—	☐☐☐☐☐
PR2b.		Pelure paper	125.00	—	☐☐☐☐☐
PR3	N3	25c orange red	85.00	—	☐☐☐☐☐
PR3a.		25c carmine red	150.00	—	☐☐☐☐☐
PR3b.		Pelure paper	125.00		☐☐☐☐☐
PR4	N1	5c light blue	50.00	30.00	☐☐☐☐☐
PR4a.		5c dark blue	45.00	30.00	☐☐☐☐☐
PR4b.		Pelure paper	50.00	—	☐☐☐☐☐
1875					
PR9	N4	2c black	12.50	11.00	☐☐☐☐☐
PR10	N4	3c black	16.00	14.50	☐☐☐☐☐
PR11	N4	4c black	14.00	12.50	☐☐☐☐☐
PR12	N4	6c black	18.00	17.00	☐☐☐☐☐
PR13	N4	8c black	25.00	22.50	☐☐☐☐☐
PR14	N4	9c black	55.00	50.00	☐☐☐☐☐
PR15	N4	10c black	25.00	20.00	☐☐☐☐☐
PR16	N5	12c rose	60.00	40.00	☐☐☐☐☐
PR17	N5	24c rose	75.00	45.00	☐☐☐☐☐
PR18	N5	36c rose	85.00	50.00	☐☐☐☐☐
PR19	N5	48c rose	150.00	85.00	☐☐☐☐☐
PR20	N5	60c rose	75.00	45.00	☐☐☐☐☐
PR21	N5	72c rose	180.00	110.00	☐☐☐☐☐
PR22	N5	84c rose	275.00	135.00	☐☐☐☐☐
PR23	N5	96c rose	150.00	100.00	☐☐☐☐☐
PR24	N6	$1.92 dark brown	200.00	125.00	☐☐☐☐☐
PR25	N7	$3 vermilion	275.00	135.00	☐☐☐☐☐
PR26	N8	$6 ultramarine	450.00	165.00	☐☐☐☐☐
PR27	N9	$9 yellow	600.00	225.00	☐☐☐☐☐
PR28	N10	$12 blue green	700.00	300.00	☐☐☐☐☐
PR29	N11	$24 dark gray violet	700.00	325.00	☐☐☐☐☐
PR30	N12	$36 brown rose	800.00	375.00	☐☐☐☐☐
PR31	N13	$48 red brown	1,050.	500.00	☐☐☐☐☐
PR32	N14	$60 violet	1,050.	425.00	☐☐☐☐☐
1879					
PR57	N4	2c black	6.00	4.50	☐☐☐☐☐
PR58	N4	3c black	7.50	5.00	☐☐☐☐☐
PR59	N4	4c black	7.50	5.00	☐☐☐☐☐
PR60	N4	6c black	15.00	11.00	☐☐☐☐☐
PR61	N4	8c black	15.00	11.00	☐☐☐☐☐
PR62	N4	10c black	15.00	11.00	☐☐☐☐☐
PR63	N5	12c red	55.00	25.00	☐☐☐☐☐

Scott No.	Illus. No.	Description	Unused Value	Used Value	//////
PR64	N5	24c red	55.00	22.50	☐☐☐☐☐
PR65	N5	36c red	170.00	95.00	☐☐☐☐☐
PR66	N5	48c red	135.00	60.00	☐☐☐☐☐
PR67	N5	60c red	100.00	60.00	☐☐☐☐☐
PR67a.		Imperf., pair	*600.00*		☐☐☐☐☐
PR68	N5	72c red	210.00	115.00	☐☐☐☐☐
PR69	N5	84c red	165.00	85.00	☐☐☐☐☐
PR70	N5	96c red	110.00	60.00	☐☐☐☐☐
PR71	N6	$1.92 pale brown	90.00	55.00	☐☐☐☐☐
PR72	N7	$3 red vermilion	90.00	55.00	☐☐☐☐☐
PR73	N8	$6 blue	150.00	90.00	☐☐☐☐☐
PR74	N9	$9 orange	110.00	60.00	☐☐☐☐☐
PR75	N10	$12 yellow green	160.00	85.00	☐☐☐☐☐
PR76	N11	$24 dark violet.	200.00	110.00	☐☐☐☐☐
PR77	N12	$36 indian red	250.00	135.00	☐☐☐☐☐
PR78	N13	$48 yellow brown	325.00	165.00	☐☐☐☐☐
PR79	N14	$60 purple	325.00	165.00	☐☐☐☐☐

1885

Scott No.	Illus. No.	Description	Unused Value	Used Value	//////
PR81	N4	1c black	8.50	5.00	☐☐☐☐☐
PR82	N5	12c carmine	27.50	12.50	☐☐☐☐☐
PR83	N5	24c carmine	30.00	15.00	☐☐☐☐☐
PR84	N5	36c carmine	42.50	17.50	☐☐☐☐☐
PR85	N5	48c carmine	60.00	30.00	☐☐☐☐☐
PR86	N5	60c carmine	85.00	40.00	☐☐☐☐☐
PR87	N5	72c carmine	95.00	45.00	☐☐☐☐☐
PR88	N5	84c carmine	200.00	110.00	☐☐☐☐☐
PR89	N5	96c carmine	140.00	85.00	☐☐☐☐☐

1895

Scott No.	Illus. No.	Description	Unused Value	Used Value	//////
PR102	N15	1c black	25.00	7.50	☐☐☐☐☐
PR103	N15	2c black	25.00	7.50	☐☐☐☐☐
PR104	N15	5c black	35.00	12.50	☐☐☐☐☐
PR105	N15	10c black	75.00	32.50	☐☐☐☐☐
PR106	N16	25c carmine	100.00	35.00	☐☐☐☐☐
PR107	N16	50c carmine	235.00	95.00	☐☐☐☐☐
PR108	N17	$2 scarlet	275.00	65.00	☐☐☐☐☐
PR109	N18	$5 ultramarine	375.00	150.00	☐☐☐☐☐
PR110	N19	$10 green	350.00	165.00	☐☐☐☐☐
PR111	N20	$20 slate	675.00	300.00	☐☐☐☐☐
PR112	N21	$50 dull rose	700.00	300.00	☐☐☐☐☐
PR113	N22	$100 purple	775.00	350.00	☐☐☐☐☐

1895-97

Scott No.	Illus. No.	Description	Unused Value	Used Value	//////
PR114	N15	1c black ('96)	3.50	3.00	☐☐☐☐☐
PR115	N15	2c black	4.00	3.50	☐☐☐☐☐
PR116	N15	5c black ('96)	6.00	5.00	☐☐☐☐☐
PR117	N15	10c black	4.00	3.50	☐☐☐☐☐

N15

N16

N17

N18

N19

N20

N21

N22

Scott No.	Illus. No.	Description	Unused Value	Used Value	//////
PR118	N16	25c carmine	8.00	8.00	☐☐☐☐☐
PR119	N16	50c carmine	10.00	12.50	☐☐☐☐☐
PR120	N17	$2 scarlet ('97)	12.00	15.00	☐☐☐☐☐
PR121	N18	$5 dark blue ('96)	20.00	25.00	☐☐☐☐☐
PR121a.		$5 light blue	100.00	45.00	☐☐☐☐☐
PR122	N19	$10 green ('96)	18.00	25.00	☐☐☐☐☐
PR123	N20	$20 slate ('96)	20.00	27.50	☐☐☐☐☐
PR124	N21	$50 dull rose ('97)	25.00	30.00	☐☐☐☐☐
PR125	N22	$100 purple ('96)	30.00	37.50	☐☐☐☐☐

PP1

PP2

PP3

PP4

PP5

PP6

PP7

PP8

PP9

PP10

PP11

PP12

PP13

PPD1

Scott No.	Illus. No.	Description	Unused Value	Used Value	//////

Parcel Post Stamps
1912-13

Q1	PP1	1c carmine rose	2.50	85	□□□□□
Q2	PP2	2c carmine rose	3.00	60	□□□□□
Q3	PP3	3c carmine ('13)	5.75	4.50	□□□□□
Q4	PP4	4c carmine rose	16.00	1.90	□□□□□
Q5	PP5	5c carmine rose	15.00	1.25	□□□□□
Q6	PP6	10c carmine rose	25.00	1.75	□□□□□
Q7	PP7	15c carmine rose	35.00	7.75	□□□□□
Q8	PP8	20c carmine rose	77.50	15.00	□□□□□
Q9	PP9	25c carmine rose	35.00	4.00	□□□□□
Q10	PP10	50c carmine rose ('13)	160.00	27.50	□□□□□
Q11	PP11	75c carmine rose	45.00	22.50	□□□□□
Q12	PP12	$1 carmine rose ('13)	260.00	17.00	□□□□□

Special Handling Stamps
1925-29

QE1	PP13	10c yellow green ('28)	1.00	80	□□□□□
QE2	PP13	15c yellow green ('28)	1.00	70	□□□□□
QE3	PP13	20c yellow green ('28)	1.75	1.00	□□□□□
QE4	PP13	25c yellow green ('29)	13.00	5.50	□□□□□
QE4a.		25c deep green ('25)	22.50	4.50	□□□□□

Parcel Post Postage Due Stamps
1912

JQ1	PPD1	1c dark green	5.00	2.75	□□□□□
JQ2	PPD1	2c dark green	45.00	13.00	□□□□□
JQ3	PPD1	5c dark green	7.00	3.50	□□□□□
JQ4	PPD1	10c dark green	110.00	30.00	□□□□□
JQ5	PPD1	25c dark green	50.00	3.25	□□□□□

CVP1 **CVP2**

Scott No.	Illus. No.	Description	Unused Value	Used Value	//////

Computer Vended Postage

1989, Aug. 23, Washington, DC, Machine 82

1	CVP1	25c 1st Class, any date other than 1st day, or with other serial number	—	—	☐☐☐☐☐
1a.		1st day dated, serial #12501-15500	—	—	☐☐☐☐☐
1b.		1st day dated, serial #00001-12500	—	—	☐☐☐☐☐
2a	CVP1	$1 3rd Class, 1st day dated, serial #15501-18500	—	—	☐☐☐☐☐
3a	CVP2	$1.69 Parcel Post, 1st day dated, serial #18501-21500	—	—	☐☐☐☐☐
4a	CVP1	$2.40 Priority Mail, 1st day dated, serial #21501-24500	—	—	☐☐☐☐☐
4b.		Priority Mail, with bar code (CVP2).....................	—		☐☐☐☐☐
5a	CVP1	$8.75 Express Mail, 1st day dated, serial #24501-27500	—	—	☐☐☐☐☐

Washington, DC, Machine 83

6	CVP1	25c 1st Class, any date other than 1st day, or with other serial number	—	—	☐☐☐☐☐
6a.		1st day dated, serial #12501-15500	—	—	☐☐☐☐☐
6b.		1st day dated, serial #00001-12500	—	—	☐☐☐☐☐
7a	CVP1	$1 3rd Class, 1st day dated, serial #15501-18500	—	—	☐☐☐☐☐
8a	CVP2	$1.69 Parcel Post, 1st day dated, serial #18501-21500	—	—	☐☐☐☐☐
9a	CVP1	$2.40 Priority Mail, 1st day dated, serial #21501-24500	—	—	☐☐☐☐☐
10a	CVP1	$8.75 Express Mail, 1st day dated, serial #24501-27500	—	—	☐☐☐☐☐

1989, Sept. 1, Kensington, MD, Machine 82

11	CVP1	25c 1st Class, any date other than 1st day, or with other serial number	—	—	☐☐☐☐☐
11a.		1st day dated, serial #12501-15500	—	—	☐☐☐☐☐
11b.		1st day dated, serial #00001-12500	—	—	☐☐☐☐☐
12a	CVP1	$1 3rd Class, 1st day dated, serial #15501-18500	—	—	☐☐☐☐☐

Scott No.	Illus. No.	Description	Unused Value	Used Value	//////
13a	CVP2	$1.69 Parcel Post, 1st day dated, serial #18501-21500	—	—	☐☐☐☐☐
14a	CVP1	$2.40 Priority Mail, 1st day dated, serial #21501-24500	—	—	☐☐☐☐☐
15a	CVP1	$8.75 Express Mail, 1st day dated, serial #24501-27500	—	—	☐☐☐☐☐

Kensington, MD, Machine 83

Scott No.	Illus. No.	Description	Unused Value	Used Value	//////
16	CVP1	25c 1st Class, any date other than 1st day....................	—	—	☐☐☐☐☐
16a.		1st day dated, serial #12501-15500	—	—	☐☐☐☐☐
16b.		1st day dated, serial #00001-12500	—	—	☐☐☐☐☐
17a	CVP1	$1 3rd Class, 1st day dated, serial #15501-18500	—	—	☐☐☐☐☐
18a	CVP2	$1.69 Parcel Post, 1st day dated, serial #18501-21500	—	—	☐☐☐☐☐
19a	CVP1	$2.40 Priority Mail, 1st day dated, serial #21501-24500	—	—	☐☐☐☐☐
20a	CVP1	$8.75 Express Mail, 1st day dated, serial #24501-27500	—	—	☐☐☐☐☐

1989, Nov., Washington, DC, Machine 11

Scott No.	Illus. No.	Description	Unused Value	Used Value	//////
21	CVP1	25c 1st Class....................	—		☐☐☐☐☐
24	CVP1	$2.40 Priority Mail	—		☐☐☐☐☐
25	CVP1	$8.75 Express Mail	—		☐☐☐☐☐

Washington, DC, Machine 12

Scott No.	Illus. No.	Description	Unused Value	Used Value	//////
26	CVP1	25c 1st Class....................	—	—	☐☐☐☐☐
29	CVP1	$2.40 Priority Mail, on cover	—	—	☐☐☐☐☐
30	CVP1	$8.75 Express Mail, on cover	—	—	☐☐☐☐☐
		_____	—		☐☐☐☐☐
		_____			☐☐☐☐☐
		_____			☐☐☐☐☐
		_____			☐☐☐☐☐
		_____			☐☐☐☐☐
		_____			☐☐☐☐☐
		_____			☐☐☐☐☐
		_____			☐☐☐☐☐
		_____			☐☐☐☐☐
		_____			☐☐☐☐☐
		_____			☐☐☐☐☐
		_____			☐☐☐☐☐

Scott No.	Illus. No.	Description	Unused Value	Used Value	//////

Special Printings

The Special Printings section include major Scott number stamps which were not issued primarily for postal purposes. These include the reproductions, reprints, reissues and special printings produced for the Post Office Department between 1875 and 1894, certain essays and finished trial color proofs of the 1860's (Nos. 55-62, 66 and 74), and the "Farley" special printings of 1935.

1875

Scott No.	Illus. No.	Description	Unused Value	Used Value	
3	A3	5c red brown	850.00		☐☐☐☐☐ ☐☐☐☐☐
4	A4	10c black	1,000.		

1860

37b	A17	24c red lilac	1,000.		☐☐☐☐☐

1875

40	A5	1c bright blue	500.00		☐☐☐☐☐
41	A10	3c scarlet	2,250.		☐☐☐☐☐
42	A22	5c orange brown	1,000.		☐☐☐☐☐
43	A12	10c blue green	2,000.		☐☐☐☐☐
44	A16	12c greenish black	2,250.		☐☐☐☐☐
45	A17	24c black violet	2,250.		☐☐☐☐☐
46	A18	30c yellow orange	2,250.		☐☐☐☐☐
47	A19	90c deep blue	3,500.		☐☐☐☐☐

1861

55	A24a	1c indigo	20,000.		☐☐☐☐☐
56	A25a	3c brown rose	500.00		☐☐☐☐☐
57	A26a	5c brown	14,000.		☐☐☐☐☐
58	A27a	10c dark green	6,000.		☐☐☐☐☐
59	A28a	12c black	40,000.		☐☐☐☐☐
60	A29	24c dark violet	6,500.		☐☐☐☐☐
61	A30	30c red orange	17,500.		☐☐☐☐☐
62	A31a	90c dull blue	22,500.		☐☐☐☐☐

1861-66

66	A25	3c lake	1,650.		☐☐☐☐☐
74	A25	3c scarlet	5,500.		☐☐☐☐☐

1875

102	A24	1c blue	500.00	800.00	☐☐☐☐☐
103	A32	2c black	2,500.	4,000.	☐☐☐☐☐
104	A25	3c brown red	3,250.	4,250.	☐☐☐☐☐
105	A26	5c brown	1,800.	2,250.	☐☐☐☐☐
106	A27	10c green	2,100.	3,750.	☐☐☐☐☐
107	A28	12c black	3,000.	4,500.	☐☐☐☐☐
108	A33	15c black	3,000.	4,750.	☐☐☐☐☐
109	A29	24c deep violet	4,000.	6,000.	☐☐☐☐☐

Scott No.	Illus. No.	Description	Unused Value	Used Value	//////
110	A30	30c brownish orange	4,500.	6,000.	☐☐☐☐☐
111	A31	90c blue	5,500.	20,000.	☐☐☐☐☐
123	A34	1c buff	325.00	225.00	☐☐☐☐☐
124	A35	2c brown	375.00	325.00	☐☐☐☐☐
125	A36	3c blue	3,000.	10,000.	☐☐☐☐☐
126	A37	6c blue	850.00	550.00	☐☐☐☐☐
127	A38	10c yellow	1,400.	1,200.	☐☐☐☐☐
128	A39	12c green	1,500.	1,200.	☐☐☐☐☐
129	A40	15c brown & blue, type III	1,300.	550.00	☐☐☐☐☐
129a.		Imperf. horizontally, single	1,600.	–	☐☐☐☐☐
130	A41	24c green & violet	1,250.	550.00	☐☐☐☐☐
131	A42	30c blue & carmine	1,750.	1,000.	☐☐☐☐☐
132	A43	90c carmine & black	5,000.	6,000.	☐☐☐☐☐

1880

133	A34	1c buff	200.00	135.00	☐☐☐☐☐
133a.		1c brown orange.	175.00	120.00	☐☐☐☐☐

1875

167	A44a	1c ultramarine	8,000.		☐☐☐☐☐
168	A45a	2c dark brown	3,500.		☐☐☐☐☐
169	A46a	3c blue green	9,500.	–	☐☐☐☐☐
170	A47a	6c dull rose.	8,500.		☐☐☐☐☐
171	A48a	7c reddish vermilion	2,250.		☐☐☐☐☐
172	A49a	10c pale brown.	8,250.		☐☐☐☐☐
173	A50a	12c dark violet.	3,000.		☐☐☐☐☐
174	A51a	15c bright orange	8,000.		☐☐☐☐☐
175	A52	24c dull purple	1,850.	–	☐☐☐☐☐
176	A53	30c greenish black	7,500.		☐☐☐☐☐
177	A54	90c violet carmine	7,500.		☐☐☐☐☐
180	A45a	2c carmine vermilion	17,500.		☐☐☐☐☐
181	A55	5c bright blue	32,500.		☐☐☐☐☐

1880

192	A44a	1c dark ultramarine	10,000.		☐☐☐☐☐
193	A45a	2c black brown.	6,500.		☐☐☐☐☐
194	A46a	3c blue green	15,000.		☐☐☐☐☐
195	A47a	6c dull rose.	11,000.		☐☐☐☐☐
196	A48a	7c scarlet vermilion	2,250.		☐☐☐☐☐
197	A49a	10c deep brown	10,000.		☐☐☐☐☐
198	A50a	12c black purple.	4,500.		☐☐☐☐☐
199	A51a	15c orange	9,750.		☐☐☐☐☐
200	A52	24c dark violet.	3,500.		☐☐☐☐☐
201	A53	30c greenish black	8,500.		☐☐☐☐☐
202	A54	90c dull carmine	9,000.		☐☐☐☐☐
203	A45a	2c scarlet vermilion.	18,000.		☐☐☐☐☐
204	A55	5c deep blue	30,000.		☐☐☐☐☐

Scott No.	Illus. No.	Description	Unused Value	Used Value	//////
1882					
205C	A56	5c gray brown	*20,000.*		☐☐☐☐☐
1883					
211B	A57	2c pale red brown	*600.00*	−	☐☐☐☐☐
211c.		Horizontal pair, imperf. between .	*2,750.*		☐☐☐☐☐
211D	A58	4c deep blue green..............	*15,000.*		☐☐☐☐☐
1935, Mar. 15					
752	A230	3c violet	15	15	☐☐☐☐☐
753	A234	3c dark blue	40	40	☐☐☐☐☐
754	A237	3c deep violet..................	50	50	☐☐☐☐☐
755	A238	3c deep violet..................	50	50	☐☐☐☐☐
756	A239	1c green	20	20	☐☐☐☐☐
757	A240	2c red	22	22	☐☐☐☐☐
758	A241	3c deep violet..................	45	40	☐☐☐☐☐
759	A242	4c brown	90	90	☐☐☐☐☐
760	A243	5c blue	1.40	1.25	☐☐☐☐☐
761	A244	6c dark blue	2.25	2.00	☐☐☐☐☐
762	A245	7c black	1.40	1.25	☐☐☐☐☐
763	A246	8c sage green	1.50	1.40	☐☐☐☐☐
764	A247	9c red orange	1.75	1.50	☐☐☐☐☐
765	A248	10c gray black	3.50	3.00	☐☐☐☐☐
766		Pane of 25	24.00	24.00	☐☐☐☐☐
766a.		A231 1c yellow green...........	65	35	☐☐☐☐☐
767		Pane of 25	22.50	22.50	☐☐☐☐☐
767a.		A232 3c violet	50	35	☐☐☐☐☐
768		Pane of six	18.00	12.50	☐☐☐☐☐
768a.		A234 3c dark blue	2.50	2.00	☐☐☐☐☐
769		Pane of six	12.00	9.00	☐☐☐☐☐
769a.		A239 1c green.................	1.75	1.50	☐☐☐☐☐
770		Pane of six	27.50	22.50	☐☐☐☐☐
770a.		A241 3c deep violet............	3.00	3.00	☐☐☐☐☐
771	APSD1	16c dark blue	2.00	2.00	☐☐☐☐☐
1879 Postage Due Stamps					
J8	D1	1c deep brown	*5,750.*		☐☐☐☐☐
J9	D1	2c deep brown	*3,750.*		☐☐☐☐☐
J10	D1	3c deep brown	*3,500.*		☐☐☐☐☐
J11	D1	5c deep brown	*3,000.*		☐☐☐☐☐
J12	D1	10c deep brown	*1,850.*		☐☐☐☐☐
J13	D1	30c deep brown	*1,850.*		☐☐☐☐☐
J14	D1	50c deep brown	*2,000.*		☐☐☐☐☐
1875 Newspaper Stamps					
PR5	N1	5c dull blue....................	70.00		☐☐☐☐☐
PR5a.		Printed on both sides...........	−		☐☐☐☐☐
PR6	N2	10c dark bluish green	50.00		☐☐☐☐☐

Scott No.	Illus. No.	Description	Unused Value	Used Value	//////
PR6a.		Printed on both sides.	*1,750.*		□□□□□
PR7	N3	25c dark carmine.	80.00		□□□□□

1880

Scott No.	Illus. No.	Description	Unused Value	Used Value	//////
PR8	N1	5c dark blue	125.00		□□□□□
PR33	N4	2c gray black	100.00		□□□□□
PR34	N4	3c gray black	105.00		□□□□□
PR35	N4	4c gray black	110.00		□□□□□
PR36	N4	6c gray black	150.00		□□□□□
PR37	N4	8c gray black	175.00		□□□□□
PR38	N4	9c gray black	200.00		□□□□□
PR39	N4	10c gray black	250.00		□□□□□
PR40	N5	12c pale rose	300.00		□□□□□
PR41	N5	24c pale rose	425.00		□□□□□
PR42	N5	36c pale rose	500.00		□□□□□
PR43	N5	48c pale rose	600.00		□□□□□
PR44	N5	60c pale rose	675.00		□□□□□
PR45	N5	72c pale rose	825.00		□□□□□
PR46	N5	84c pale rose	850.00		□□□□□
PR47	N5	96c pale rose	975.00		□□□□□
PR48	N6	$1.92 dark brown.	3,500.		□□□□□
PR49	N7	$3 vermilion	7,000.		□□□□□
PR50	N8	$6 ultramarine.	8,500.		□□□□□
PR51	N9	$9 yellow	20,000.		□□□□□
PR52	N10	$12 blue green	18,500.		□□□□□
PR53	N11	$24 dark gray violet.	—		□□□□□
PR54	N12	$36 brown rose	—		□□□□□
PR55	N13	$48 red brown	—		□□□□□
PR56	N14	$60 violet.	—		□□□□□

1883

Scott No.	Illus. No.	Description	Unused Value	Used Value	//////
PR80	N4	2c intense black	275.00		□□□□□

1894

Scott No.	Illus. No.	Description	Unused Value	Used Value	//////
PR90	N4	1c intense black	55.00		□□□□□
PR91	N4	2c intense black	55.00		□□□□□
PR92	N4	4c intense black	75.00		□□□□□
PR93	N4	6c intense black	950.00		□□□□□
PR94	N4	10c intense black	125.00		□□□□□
PR95	N5	12c pink	550.00	—	□□□□□
PR96	N5	24c pink	575.00		□□□□□
PR97	N5	36c pink	3,500.		□□□□□
PR98	N5	60c pink	3,500.	—	□□□□□
PR99	N5	96c pink	4,000.		□□□□□
PR100	N7	$3 scarlet	5,500.		□□□□□
PR101	N8	$6 pale blue	6,250.	—	□□□□□

OC1

OC2

Scott No.	Illus. No.	Description	Unused Value	Used Value	//////

Carriers' Stamps
Official Issues

1851
| LO1 | OC1 | (1c) dull blue, rose . . . . | *2,750.* | *3,250.* | ☐☐☐☐☐ |
| LO2 | OC2 | 1c blue . . . . | 15.00 | 20.00 | ☐☐☐☐☐ |

1875
LO3	OC1	(1c) blue, rose, imperf.	40.00		☐☐☐☐☐
LO4	OC1	(1c) blue, perf. 12	*2,500.*		☐☐☐☐☐
LO5	OC2	1c blue, imperf.	20.00		☐☐☐☐☐
LO6	OC2	1c blue, perf. 12	175.00		☐☐☐☐☐

	☐☐☐☐☐
_____	☐☐☐☐☐
_____	☐☐☐☐☐
_____	☐☐☐☐☐
_____	☐☐☐☐☐
_____	☐☐☐☐☐
_____	☐☐☐☐☐
_____	☐☐☐☐☐
_____	☐☐☐☐☐
_____	☐☐☐☐☐
_____	☐☐☐☐☐
_____	☐☐☐☐☐
_____	☐☐☐☐☐
_____	☐☐☐☐☐
_____	☐☐☐☐☐
_____	☐☐☐☐☐
_____	☐☐☐☐☐

C1   C2   C3

C6   C7   C8

C10

C11   C13

C14

C15

C16   C17

C18

C19   C20

C20a   C20b   C20c

Scott No.	Illus. No.	Description	Unused Value	Used Value	/ / / / / /

Semi-Official Issues

Baltimore, MD.
1850-55

Scott No.	Illus. No.	Description	Unused Value	Used Value	/ / / / / /
1LB1	C1	1c red, *bluish*	100.00	60.00	☐☐☐☐☐
1LB2	C1	1c blue, *bluish*	125.00	90.00	☐☐☐☐☐
1LB2a.		Bluish laid paper	—	—	☐☐☐☐☐
1LB3	C1	1c blue	75.00	50.00	☐☐☐☐☐
1LB3a.		Laid paper	150.00	100.00	☐☐☐☐☐
1LB4	C1	1c green	—	600.00	☐☐☐☐☐
1LB5	C1	1c red	350.00	275.00	☐☐☐☐☐

1856

Scott No.	Illus. No.	Description	Unused Value	Used Value	/ / / / / /
1LB6	C2	1c blue	90.00	60.00	☐☐☐☐☐
1LB7	C2	1c red	65.00	40.00	☐☐☐☐☐

1857

Scott No.	Illus. No.	Description	Unused Value	Used Value	/ / / / / /
1LB8	C3	1c black	25.00	20.00	☐☐☐☐☐
1LB8a.		**SENT**	35.00	25.00	☐☐☐☐☐
1LB8b.		Short rays	35.00	25.00	☐☐☐☐☐
1LB9	C3	1c red	40.00	30.00	☐☐☐☐☐
1LB9a.		**SENT**	50.00	40.00	☐☐☐☐☐
1LB9b.		Short rays	50.00	40.00	☐☐☐☐☐

Boston, MA
1849-50

Scott No.	Illus. No.	Description	Unused Value	Used Value	/ / / / / /
3LB1	C6	1c blue	150.00	75.00	☐☐☐☐☐
3LB2	C7	1c blue (shades), slate	125.00	65.00	☐☐☐☐☐

Charleston, SC
1849

Scott No.	Illus. No.	Description	Unused Value	Used Value	/ / / / / /
4LB1	C8	2c black, brown rose	*1,500.*	*1,500.*	☐☐☐☐☐
4LB2	C8	2c black, yellow		*1,500.*	☐☐☐☐☐

1854

Scott No.	Illus. No.	Description	Unused Value	Used Value	/ / / / / /
4LB3	C10	2c black	*650.00*		☐☐☐☐☐

1849-50

Scott No.	Illus. No.	Description	Unused Value	Used Value	/ / / / / /
4LB5	C11	2c black, *bluish,* pelure	*400.00*	*300.00*	☐☐☐☐☐
4LB7	C11	2c black, *yellow*	*400.00*	*400.00*	☐☐☐☐☐

1851-58

Scott No.	Illus. No.	Description	Unused Value	Used Value	/ / / / / /
4LB8	C13	2c black, *bluish.*	175.00	100.00	☐☐☐☐☐
4LB8a.		Period after **Paid**	350.00	150.00	☐☐☐☐☐
4LB8b.		**Cens**	*700.00*		☐☐☐☐☐
4LB8c.		**Conours** and **Bents**		—	☐☐☐☐☐
4LB9	C13	2c black, *bluish,* pelure	*375.00*	425.00	☐☐☐☐☐
4LB11	C14	(2c) black, *bluish*	—	*250.00*	☐☐☐☐☐
4LB12	C14	(2c) black, *bluish,* pelure	—	*250.00*	☐☐☐☐☐

C21

C22

C23

C24

C25

C27

C28

C29

C30

C31

C32

C36

Actual Size
C37

Scott No.	Illus. No.	Description	Unused Value	Used Value	//////
4LB13	C15	(2c) black, *bluish* ('58)	250.00	125.00	☐☐☐☐☐
4LB13a.		Comma after **PAID**	300.00		☐☐☐☐☐
4LB13b.		No period after **Post**	400.00		☐☐☐☐☐
4LB14	C16	2c black, *bluish*	400.00	450.00	☐☐☐☐☐
4LB15	C17	2c black, *bluish*	500.00	500.00	☐☐☐☐☐

1858

| 4LB16 | C18 | 2c black, bluish | *2,750.* | | ☐☐☐☐☐ |

1860

| 4LB17 | C19 | 2c black | | — | ☐☐☐☐☐ |

1859

4LB18	C19	2c black, *bluish*	*2,500.*		☐☐☐☐☐
4LB19	C20	2c black, *bluish*	*1,000.*	—	☐☐☐☐☐
4LB20	C20	2c black, *pink*	150.00	—	☐☐☐☐☐
4LB21	C20	2c black, *yellow*	125.00		☐☐☐☐☐

Cincinnati, OH
1854

| 9LB1 | C20a | 2c brown | *500.00* | 500.00 | ☐☐☐☐☐ |

Cleveland, OH
1854

| 10LB1 | C20b | blue | *500.00* | 500.00 | ☐☐☐☐☐ |
| 10LB2 | C20c | 2c black, *bluish* | *500.00* | 500.00 | ☐☐☐☐☐ |

Louisville, KY
1857-58

5LB1	C21	(2c) bluish green	*35.00*		☐☐☐☐☐
5LB2	C22	(2c) blue ('58)	150.00	150.00	☐☐☐☐☐
5LB3	C22	(2c) black ('58)	*600.00*	*1,750.*	☐☐☐☐☐

New York, NY
1842

| 6LB1 | C23 | 3c black, *grayish* | | *1,250.* | ☐☐☐☐☐ |

1842-45

6LB2	C24	3c black, *rosy buff*	550.00		☐☐☐☐☐
6LB3	C24	3c black, *light blue*	400.00	200.00	☐☐☐☐☐
6LB4	C24	3c black, *green*	*2,000.*		☐☐☐☐☐
6LB5	C24	3c black, *dark blue (shades)*	100.00	75.00	☐☐☐☐☐
6LB5a.		Double impression		*500.00*	☐☐☐☐☐
6LB5b.		3c, black, *blue (shades)*	400.00	*75.00*	☐☐☐☐☐
6LB5c.		As **b**, double impression	—		☐☐☐☐☐
6LB5d.		3c, black, *green (shades)*	400.00	*75.00*	☐☐☐☐☐
6LB5e.		As **d**, double impression	—		☐☐☐☐☐

Scott No.	Illus. No.	Description	Unused Value	Used Value	//////
1846					
6LB7	C25	2c on 3c, on cover	—		☐☐☐☐☐
1849-50					
6LB9	C27	1c black, *rose*	50.00	25.00	☐☐☐☐☐
6LB10	C27	1c black, *yellow*	60.00	25.00	☐☐☐☐☐
6LB11	C27	1c black, *buff*	50.00	25.00	☐☐☐☐☐
6LB11a.		Pair, one stamp sideways	1,000.		☐☐☐☐☐

Philadelphia, PA
1849-50

Scott No.	Illus. No.	Description	Unused Value	Used Value	//////
7LB1	C28	1c black, *rose* (with letters L.P.)	175.00		☐☐☐☐☐
7LB2	C28	1c black, *rose* (with letter S)	500.00		☐☐☐☐☐
7LB3	C28	1c black, *rose* (with letter H)	175.00		☐☐☐☐☐
7LB4	C28	1c black, *rose* (with letters L.S.)	175.00		☐☐☐☐☐
7LB5	C28	1c black, *rose* (with letters J.J.)	2,000.		☐☐☐☐☐
7LB6	C29	1c black, *rose*	150.00	125.00	☐☐☐☐☐
7LB7	C29	1c black, *blue,* glazed	600.00		☐☐☐☐☐
7LB8	C29	1c black, *vermilion,* glazed	500.00		☐☐☐☐☐
7LB9	C29	1c black, *yellow,* glazed	1,350.		☐☐☐☐☐

1850-52

Scott No.	Illus. No.	Description	Unused Value	Used Value	//////
7LB11	C30	1c gold, *black,* glazed	60.00	55.00	☐☐☐☐☐
7LB12	C30	1c blue	200.00	100.00	☐☐☐☐☐
7LB13	C30	1c black	650.00	400.00	☐☐☐☐☐
7LB14	C31	1c blue, *buff*	1,000.		☐☐☐☐☐
7LB16	C31	1c black		1,650.	☐☐☐☐☐

1856(?)

Scott No.	Illus. No.	Description	Unused Value	Used Value	//////
7LB18	C32	1c black	900.00	1,000.	☐☐☐☐☐

St. Louis, MO
1849

Scott No.	Illus. No.	Description	Unused Value	Used Value	//////
8LB1	C36	2c black	2,750.	3,500.	☐☐☐☐☐

1857

Scott No.	Illus. No.	Description	Unused Value	Used Value	//////
8LB2	C37	2c blue		3,500.	☐☐☐☐☐
		————————————————			☐☐☐☐☐
		————————————————			☐☐☐☐☐
		————————————————			☐☐☐☐☐
		————————————————			☐☐☐☐☐
		————————————————			☐☐☐☐☐
		————————————————			☐☐☐☐☐
		————————————————			☐☐☐☐☐

HP1

HP2

HP3

HP4

HP5

HP6

HP7

HP8

HP9

Scott No.	Illus. No.	Description	Unused Value	Used Value	//////

Hunting Permit Stamps

Catalogue values for unused stamps in this section are for Never Hinged items.

1934

RW1	HP1	$1 blue 425.00		85.00	☐☐☐☐☐
RW1a.		Imperf., pair.	—		☐☐☐☐☐
RW1b.		Vertical pair, imperf. horizontally	—		☐☐☐☐☐

1935

| RW2 | | $1 *Canvasback Ducks Taking to Flight* . . . . 400.00 | | 100.00 | ☐☐☐☐☐ |

1936

| RW3 | | $1 *Canada Geese in Flight* . . . . 210.00 | | 50.00 | ☐☐☐☐☐ |

1937

| RW4 | | $1 *Scaup Ducks Taking to Flight* . . . 160.00 | | 27.50 | ☐☐☐☐☐ |

1938

| RW5 | | $1 *Pintail Drake and Duck Alighting* 160.00 | | 35.00 | ☐☐☐☐☐ |

1939

| RW6 | HP2 | $1 chocolate. . . . . 115.00 | | 15.00 | ☐☐☐☐☐ |

1940

| RW7 | | $1 *Black Mallards* . . . . 115.00 | | 15.00 | ☐☐☐☐☐ |

1941

| RW8 | | $1 *Family of Ruddy Ducks* . . . . 115.00 | | 15.00 | ☐☐☐☐☐ |

1942

| RW9 | | $1 *Baldpates*. . . . . 115.00 | | 14.00 | ☐☐☐☐☐ |

1943

| RW10 | | $1 *Wood Ducks* . . . . 47.50 | | 15.00 | ☐☐☐☐☐ |

1944

| RW11 | | $1 *White-fronted Geese*. . . . . 45.00 | | 14.00 | ☐☐☐☐☐ |

1945

| RW12 | | $1 *Shoveller Ducks in Flight* . . . . 30.00 | | 10.00 | ☐☐☐☐☐ |

1946

| RW13 | | $1 *Redhead Ducks*. . . . . 30.00 | | 9.00 | ☐☐☐☐☐ |

1947

| RW14 | | $1 *Snow Geese*. . . . . 30.00 | | 9.00 | ☐☐☐☐☐ |

Scott No.	Illus. No.	Description	Unused Value	Used Value	//////
1948 RW15		$1 *Bufflehead Ducks in Flight*	35.00	9.00	☐☐☐☐☐
1949 RW16	HP3	$2 bright green	37.50	8.00	☐☐☐☐☐
1950 RW17		$2 *Trumpeter Swans in Flight*	45.00	7.00	☐☐☐☐☐
1951 RW18		$2 *Gadwall Ducks*	45.00	5.00	☐☐☐☐☐
1952 RW19		$2 *Harlequin Ducks*	45.00	5.00	☐☐☐☐☐
1953 RW20		$2 *Blue-winged Teal*	45.00	5.00	☐☐☐☐☐
1954 RW21		$2 *Ring-necked Ducks*	45.00	4.75	☐☐☐☐☐
1955 RW22		$2 *Blue Geese*	45.00	4.75	☐☐☐☐☐
1956 RW23		$2 *American Merganser*	45.00	4.75	☐☐☐☐☐
1957 RW24		$2 *American Eider*	45.00	4.75	☐☐☐☐☐
1958 RW25		$2 *Canada Geese*	45.00	4.75	☐☐☐☐☐
1959 RW26	HP4	$3 blue, ocher & black	60.00	4.75	☐☐☐☐☐
1960 RW27	HP5	$3 red brown, dark blue & bister	60.00	4.00	☐☐☐☐☐
1961 RW28		$3 *Mallard Hen and Ducklings*	60.00	4.00	☐☐☐☐☐
1962 RW29	HP6	$3 dark blue, dark red brown & black	70.00	5.50	☐☐☐☐☐
1963 RW30		$3 *Pair of Brant landing*	65.00	5.50	☐☐☐☐☐
1964 RW31		$3 *Hawaiian Nene Geese*	65.00	5.50	☐☐☐☐☐

264

Scott No.	Illus. No.	Description	Unused Value	Used Value	//////
1965					
RW32		$3 *3 Canvasback Drakes*	65.00	5.50	☐☐☐☐☐
1966					
RW33	HP7	$3 ultramarine, slate green & black .	65.00	5.00	☐☐☐☐☐
1967					
RW34		$3 *Old Squaw Ducks*	65.00	5.00	☐☐☐☐☐
1968					
RW35		$3 *Hooded Mergansers*	40.00	5.50	☐☐☐☐☐
1969					
RW36	HP8	$3 gray, brown, indigo & brown red.	40.00	4.50	☐☐☐☐☐
1970					
RW37		$3 *Ross' Geese*	40.00	4.00	☐☐☐☐☐
1971					
RW38		$3 *3 Cinnamon Teal*	27.50	3.75	☐☐☐☐☐
1972					
RW39		$5 *Emperor Geese*	20.00	3.75	☐☐☐☐☐
1973					
RW40		$5 *Steller's Eiders*	17.00	3.75	☐☐☐☐☐
1974					
RW41		$5 *Wood Ducks*	14.00	3.75	☐☐☐☐☐
1975					
RW42		$5 *Weathered canvasback duck decoy and flying ducks*	10.00	3.75	☐☐☐☐☐
1976					
RW43		$5 *Family of Canada Geese*	10.00	3.75	☐☐☐☐☐
1977					
RW44		$5 *Ross' Geese, pair*	10.00	3.75	☐☐☐☐☐
1978					
RW45	HP9	$5 Hooded merganser	9.50	3.75	☐☐☐☐☐
1979					
RW46		$7.50 *Green-winged teal*	12.00	4.00	☐☐☐☐☐
1980					
RW47		$7.50 *Mallards*.	12.00	4.00	☐☐☐☐☐

Scott No.	Illus. No.	Description	Unused Value	Used Value	//////
1981					
RW48		$7.50 *Ruddy Ducks*	12.00	4.00	☐☐☐☐☐
1982					
RW49		$7.50 *Canvasbacks*.	12.00	4.00	☐☐☐☐☐
1983					
RW50		$7.50 *Pintails*	12.00	4.00	☐☐☐☐☐
1984					
RW51		$7.50 *Widgeon*.	12.00	4.00	☐☐☐☐☐
1985					
RW52		$7.50 *Cinnamon Teal*	12.00	4.00	☐☐☐☐☐
1986					
RW53		$7.50 *Fulvous Whistling Duck*	12.00	4.00	☐☐☐☐☐
RW53a.		Black omitted.	—		☐☐☐☐☐
1987					
RW54		$10 *Redheads*.	14.00	4.00	☐☐☐☐☐
1988					
RW55		$10 *Snow Goose*.	14.00	4.00	☐☐☐☐☐
1989					
RW56		$12.50 *Lesser Scaups*.	17.50	3.50	☐☐☐☐☐
1990					
RW57		$12.50 *Black Bellied Whistling Duck*	17.50	3.50	☐☐☐☐☐

_____			☐☐☐☐☐
_____			☐☐☐☐☐
_____			☐☐☐☐☐
_____			☐☐☐☐☐
_____			☐☐☐☐☐
_____			☐☐☐☐☐
_____			☐☐☐☐☐
_____			☐☐☐☐☐
_____			☐☐☐☐☐
_____			☐☐☐☐☐
_____			☐☐☐☐☐
_____			☐☐☐☐☐
_____			☐☐☐☐☐

A5

A6

A7

A8

A9

A10

A11

A12

A13

A14

Marshall Islands

Catalogue values for unused stamps in this section are for Never Hinged items.

1984, May 2

			Unused	Used	
31	A5	20c Outrigger canoe.............	55	55 □□□□□
32	A5	20c Fishnet....................	55	55 □□□□□
33	A5	20c Navigational stick chart	55	55 □□□□□
34	A5	20c Islet	55	55 □□□□□
34a.		Block of 4, Nos. 31-34..........	2.25	2.25 □□□□□

1984-85

35	A6	1c Mili Atoll, astrolabe	15	15 □□□□□
36	A6	3c Likiep, Azimuth compass	15	15 □□□□□
37	A6	5c Ebon, 16th cent. compass.....	15	15 □□□□□
38	A6	10c Jaluit, anchor buoys	20	20 □□□□□
39	A6	13c Ailinginae, Nocturnal.........	26	26 □□□□□
39a.		Booklet pane of 10.............	7.00	– □□□□□
40	A6	14c Wotho Atoll, navigational stick chart	28	28 □□□□□
40a.		Booklet pane of 10.............	7.00	– □□□□□
41	A6	20c Kwajalein and Ebeye, stick chart	40	40 □□□□□
41a.		Booklet pane of 10.............	9.00	– □□□□□
41b.		Booklet pane of 5 each, 13c, 20c..	8.00	– □□□□□
42	A6	22c Enewetak, 18th cent. lode stone storage case	44	44 □□□□□
42a.		Booklet pane of 10.............	9.00	– □□□□□
42b.		Booklet pane of 5 each, 14c, 22c..	8.00	– □□□□□
43	A6	28c Ailinglaplap, printed compass ..	56	56 □□□□□
44	A6	30c Majuro, navigational stick-chart	60	60 □□□□□
45	A6	33c Namu, stick chart	66	66 □□□□□
46	A6	37c Rongelap, quadrant	74	74 □□□□□
47	A6	39c Taka, map compass, 16th cent. sea chart...........	78	78 □□□□□
48	A6	44c Ujelang, chronograph	88	88 □□□□□
49	A6	50c Maloelap and Aur, nocturlabe..	1.00	1.00 □□□□□
49A	A6	$1 Arno, 16th cent. sector compass .	2.00	2.00 □□□□□

1984

50	A7	40c Scott 7	75	75 □□□□□
51	A7	40c Scott 13	75	75 □□□□□
52	A7	40c Scott 4	75	75 □□□□□
53	A7	40c Scott 25	75	75 □□□□□
53a.		Block of 4, Nos. 50-53..........	3.00	3.00 □□□□□
54	A8	20c Common dolphin	50	50 □□□□□
55	A8	20c Risso's dolophin	50	50 □□□□□
56	A8	20c Spotter dolphin	50	50 □□□□□

A15

A16

A17

A18

A19

A20

A21

A22

Scott No.	Illus. No.	Description	Unused Value	Used Value	//////
57	A8	20c Bottlenose dolphin	50	50	☐☐☐☐☐
57a.		Block of 4, Nos. 54-57	2.00	2.00	☐☐☐☐☐
58		Strip of 4	1.90	1.90	☐☐☐☐☐
58a.-d.	A9	20c, any single	45	45	☐☐☐☐☐
58e.		Sheet of 16	8.00		☐☐☐☐☐
59	A10	20c Traditional chief.............	50	50	☐☐☐☐☐
60	A10	20c Amata Kabua	50	50	☐☐☐☐☐
61	A10	20c Chester Nimitz	50	50	☐☐☐☐☐
62	A10	20c Trygve Lie................	50	50	☐☐☐☐☐
62a.		Block of 4, Nos. 59-62.........	2.00	2.00	☐☐☐☐☐

1985

Scott No.	Illus. No.	Description	Unused Value	Used Value	//////
63	A11	22c Forked-tailed Petrel	60	60	☐☐☐☐☐
64	A11	22c Pectoral Sandpiper	60	60	☐☐☐☐☐
64a.		Pair, Nos. 63-64...............	1.20	1.20	☐☐☐☐☐
65	A12	22c Cymatium lotorium	45	45	☐☐☐☐☐
66	A12	22c Chicoreus cornucervi	45	45	☐☐☐☐☐
67	A12	22c Strombus aurisdanae	45	45	☐☐☐☐☐
68	A12	22c Turbo marmoratus	45	45	☐☐☐☐☐
69	A12	22c Chicoreus palmarosae	45	45	☐☐☐☐☐
69a.		Strip of 5, Nos. 65-69	2.25	2.25	☐☐☐☐☐
70	A13	22c Native drum	50	50	☐☐☐☐☐
71	A13	22c Palm branches..............	50	50	☐☐☐☐☐
72	A13	22c Pounding stone	50	50	☐☐☐☐☐
73	A13	22c Ak bird	50	50	☐☐☐☐☐
73a.		Block of 4, Nos. 70-73.........	2.00	2.00	☐☐☐☐☐
74	A14	22c Acanthurus dussumieri	50	50	☐☐☐☐☐
75	A14	22c Adioryx caudimaculatus.......	50	50	☐☐☐☐☐
76	A14	22c Ostracion meleacaris	50	50	☐☐☐☐☐
77	A14	22c Chaetodon ephippium	50	50	☐☐☐☐☐
77a.		Block of 4, Nos. 74-77.........	2.00	2.00	☐☐☐☐☐
78	A15	22c recreational basketball game ...	50	50	☐☐☐☐☐
79	A15	22c Legend teller	50	50	☐☐☐☐☐
80	A15	22c Explaining stick charts	50	50	☐☐☐☐☐
81	A15	22c Jabwa stick dance...........	50	50	☐☐☐☐☐
81a.		Block of 4, Nos. 78-81.........	2.00	2.00	☐☐☐☐☐
82	A16	14c Stock certificate.............	20		☐☐☐☐☐
83	A16	22c *Morning Star* launch..........	35	35	☐☐☐☐☐
84	A16	33c First voyage................	55	55	☐☐☐☐☐
85	A16	44c Pulling ship into lagoon	75	75	☐☐☐☐☐
86	A17	22c Space shuttle, astro telescope, Halley Comet	1.00	1.00	☐☐☐☐☐
87	A17	22c Planet A space probe	1.00	1.00	☐☐☐☐☐
88	A17	22c Giotto spacecraft............	1.00	1.00	☐☐☐☐☐
89	A17	22c INTERCOSMOS project	1.00	1.00	☐☐☐☐☐
90	A17	22c Naval tracking ship, aircraft....	1.00	1.00	☐☐☐☐☐
90a.		Strip of 5, Nos. 86-90	5.00	5.00	☐☐☐☐☐
91	A18	22c Sida fallax	50	50	☐☐☐☐☐

A24

A23

A25

A26

A27

A28

A29

A30

A31

272

Scott No.	Illus. No.	Description	Unused Value	Used Value	//////
92	A18	22c Scaevola frutescens...........	50	50	□□□□□
93	A18	22c Guettarda speciosa...........	50	50	□□□□□
94	A18	22c Cassytha filiformis	50	50	□□□□□
94a.		Block of 4, Nos. 91-94..........	2.00	2.00	□□□□□

1986-87

Scott No.	Illus. No.	Description	Unused Value	Used Value	//////
107	A6	$2 Wotje and Erikub, terrestrial globe, 1571	4.00	4.00	□□□□□
108	A6	$5 Bikini, stick chart.............	10.00	10.00	□□□□□
109	A6	$10 Stick chart of the atolls.......	16.00	16.00	□□□□□

1986

Scott No.	Illus. No.	Description	Unused Value	Used Value	//////
110	A19	14c Triton's trumpet.............	28	28	□□□□□
111	A19	14c Giant clam	28	28	□□□□□
112	A19	14c Small giant clam	28	28	□□□□□
113	A19	14c Coconut crab................	28	28	□□□□□
113a.		Block of 4, Nos. 110-113........	1.15	1.15	□□□□□
114	A20	$1 Douglas C-54 Globester........	2.75	2.75	□□□□□
115	A21	22c King Juda, sailing canoe......	55	55	□□□□□
116	A21	22c USS *Summer*...............	55	55	□□□□□
117	A21	22c Evacuating Bikinians	55	55	□□□□□
118	A21	22c Land reclamation	55	55	□□□□□
118a.		Block of 4, Nos. 115-118........	2.25	2.25	□□□□□
119	A12	22c Ramose murex	40	40	□□□□□
120	A12	22c Orange spider	40	40	□□□□□
121	A12	22c Red-mouth frog shell	40	40	□□□□□
122	A12	22c Laciniate conch.............	40	40	□□□□□
123	A12	22c Giant frog shell	40	40	□□□□□
123a.		Strip of 5, Nos. 119-123	2.00	2.00	□□□□□
124	A22	22c Blue marlin	40	40	□□□□□
125	A22	22c Wahoo..................	40	40	□□□□□
126	A22	22c Dolphin fish	40	40	□□□□□
127	A22	22c Yellowfin tuna	40	40	□□□□□
127a.		Block of 4, Nos. 124-127........	1.60	1.60	□□□□□
128	A23	22c United Nations UR	60	60	□□□□□
129	A23	22c United Nations UL	60	60	□□□□□
130	A23	22c United Nations LR...........	60	60	□□□□□
131	A23	22c United Nations LL...........	60	60	□□□□□
131a.		Block of 4, Nos. 128-131........	2.40	2.40	□□□□□

1987

Scott No.	Illus. No.	Description	Unused Value	Used Value	//////
132	A24	22c James Arnold, 1854	55	55	□□□□□
133	A24	22c General Scott, 1859	55	55	□□□□□
134	A24	22c Charles W. Morgan, 1865......	55	55	□□□□□
135	A24	22c Lucretia, 1884...............	55	55	□□□□□
135a.		Block of 4, Nos. 132-135........	2.25	2.25	□□□□□
136	A25	33c Lindbergh medal, *Spirit of St. Louis*....................	60	60	□□□□□

Scott No.	Illus. No.	Description	Unused Value	Used Value	//////
137	A25	33c Lindbergh in Battle of Marshalls	60	60	☐☐☐☐☐
137a.		Pair, Nos. 136-137.............	1.20	1.20	☐☐☐☐☐
138	A25	39c Bridgeman in Battle of Kwajalein	65	65	☐☐☐☐☐
139	A25	39c Testing Douglas Skyrocket.....	65	65	☐☐☐☐☐
139a.		Pair, Nos. 138-139.............	1.30	1.30	☐☐☐☐☐
140	A25	44c Glenn in Battle of Marshalls ...	70	70	☐☐☐☐☐
141	A25	44c First American to orbit Earth ..	70	70	☐☐☐☐☐
141a.		Pair, Nos. 140-141.............	1.40	1.40	☐☐☐☐☐
142	A26	$1 Map of flight.................	2.00	2.00	☐☐☐☐☐
143	A27	14c We,... Marshall	25	25	☐☐☐☐☐
144	A27	14c National seals	25	25	☐☐☐☐☐
145	A27	14c We,... United States	25	25	☐☐☐☐☐
145a.		Triptych, Nos. 143-145	75	75	☐☐☐☐☐
146	A27	22c All we have....	35	35	☐☐☐☐☐
147	A27	22c Flags......................	35	35	☐☐☐☐☐
148	A27	22c to establish...............	35	35	☐☐☐☐☐
148a.		Triptych, Nos. 146-148	1.05	1.05	☐☐☐☐☐
149	A27	44c With this Constitution....	70	70	☐☐☐☐☐
150	A27	44c Stick chart, Liberty Bell	70	70	☐☐☐☐☐
151	A27	44c to promote...	70	70	☐☐☐☐☐
151a.		Triptych, Nos. 149-151	2.10	2.10	☐☐☐☐☐
152	A12	22c Magnificent cone	40	40	☐☐☐☐☐
153	A12	22c Partridge tun	40	40	☐☐☐☐☐
154	A12	22c Scorpion spider conch	40	40	☐☐☐☐☐
155	A12	22c Hairy triton...............	40	40	☐☐☐☐☐
156	A12	22c Chiragra spider conch........	40	40	☐☐☐☐☐
156a.		Strip of 5, Nos. 152-156	2.00	2.00	☐☐☐☐☐
157	A28	44c Planting coconut.............	75	75	☐☐☐☐☐
158	A28	44c Making copra	75	75	☐☐☐☐☐
159	A28	44c Bottling coconut oil	75	75	☐☐☐☐☐
159a.		Triptych, Nos. 157-159	2.25	2.25	☐☐☐☐☐
160	A29	14c Matthew 2:1	25	25	☐☐☐☐☐
161	A29	22c Luke 2:14..................	35	35	☐☐☐☐☐
162	A29	33c Psalms 33:3................	55	55	☐☐☐☐☐
163	A29	44c Psalms 150:5	70	70	☐☐☐☐☐
1988					
164	A30	44c Pacific reef herons............	70	70	☐☐☐☐☐
165	A30	44c Bar-tailed godwit	70	70	☐☐☐☐☐
166	A30	44c Masked booby...............	70	70	☐☐☐☐☐
167	A30	44c Northern shoveler............	70	70	☐☐☐☐☐
1988-89					
168	A31	1c Damselfish	15	15	☐☐☐☐☐
169	A31	3c Blackface butterflyfish	15	15	☐☐☐☐☐
170	A31	14c Hawkfish	25	25	☐☐☐☐☐
170a.		Booklet pane of 10.............	3.00	–	☐☐☐☐☐

A32

A33

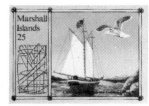

A34

A35

A36

A37

A38

A39

A42

Scott No.	Illus. No.	Description	Unused Value	Used Value	//////
171	A31	15c Balloonfish	25	25	☐☐☐☐☐
171a.		Booklet pane of 10.	2.50	–	☐☐☐☐☐
172	A31	17c Trunk fish	30	30	☐☐☐☐☐
173	A31	22c Lyretail wrasse	35	35	☐☐☐☐☐
173a.		Booklet pane of 10.	4.00	–	☐☐☐☐☐
173b.		Booklet pane of 10 (5 each			
		14c, 22c).	3.60	–	☐☐☐☐☐
174	A31	25c Parrotfish.	40	40	☐☐☐☐☐
174a.		Booklet pane of 10.	4.00	–	☐☐☐☐☐
174b.		Booklet pane of 10 (5 each			
		15c, 25c).	3.25	–	☐☐☐☐☐
175	A31	33c White-spotted boxfish	60	60	☐☐☐☐☐
176	A31	36c Spotted boxfish.	65	65	☐☐☐☐☐
177	A31	39c Surgeonfish	70	70	☐☐☐☐☐
178	A31	44c Long-snouted butterflyfish.	75	75	☐☐☐☐☐
179	A31	45c Trumpetfish	70	70	☐☐☐☐☐
180	A31	56c Sharp-nosed puffer	1.00	1.00	☐☐☐☐☐
181	A31	$1 Seahorse	1.75	1.75	☐☐☐☐☐
182	A31	$2 Ghost pipefish	3.50	3.50	☐☐☐☐☐
183	A31	$5 Big-spotted triggerfish	8.75	8.75	☐☐☐☐☐
187	A31	$10 Blue jack ('89).	15.00	15.00	☐☐☐☐☐

1988

Scott No.	Illus. No.	Description	Unused Value	Used Value	//////
188		Strip of 5	1.25	1.25	☐☐☐☐☐
188a.-e.	A32	15c any single.	25	25	☐☐☐☐☐
189		Strip of 5	2.25	2.25	☐☐☐☐☐
189a.-e.	A33	25c any single.	45	45	☐☐☐☐☐
190		Sheet of 9	4.10	4.10	☐☐☐☐☐
190a.-i.	A34	25c any single.	45	45	☐☐☐☐☐
191	A35	25c *Santa Maria de La Victoria*	40	40	☐☐☐☐☐
192	A35	25c *Charlotte & Scarborough*	40	40	☐☐☐☐☐
193	A35	25c *Flying Fish & Peacock*	40	40	☐☐☐☐☐
194	A35	25c *Planet*.	40	40	☐☐☐☐☐
194a.		Block of 4, Nos. 191-194.	1.60	1.60	☐☐☐☐☐
195	A36	25c Santa Claus in sleigh.	40	40	☐☐☐☐☐
196	A36	25c Reindeer, hut, palm trees.	40	40	☐☐☐☐☐
197	A36	25c Reindeer, palm trees.	40	40	☐☐☐☐☐
198	A36	25c Reindeer, palm tree, fish	40	40	☐☐☐☐☐
199	A36	25c Reindeer, outrigger canoe.	40	40	☐☐☐☐☐
199a.		Strip of 5, Nos. 195-199	2.00	2.00	☐☐☐☐☐
200	A37	25c Nuclear threat diminished	40	40	☐☐☐☐☐
201	A37	25c Signing the Test Ban Treaty. . . .	40	40	☐☐☐☐☐
202	A37	25c Portrait	40	40	☐☐☐☐☐
203	A37	25c US-USSR Hotline	40	40	☐☐☐☐☐
204	A37	25c Peace Corps enactment	40	40	☐☐☐☐☐
204a.		Strip of 5, Nos. 200-204	2.00	2.00	☐☐☐☐☐
205	A38	25c Launch of *Prime*	45		☐☐☐☐☐

A40

A41

A43

A44

A45

A46

A47

A57

A58

Scott No.	Illus. No.	Description	Unused Value	Used Value	//////
206	A38	25c Lifting body reentering atmosphere	45	45	☐☐☐☐☐
207	A38	25c Parachute landing, recovery craft	45	45	☐☐☐☐☐
208	A38	25c Shuttle over island	45	45	☐☐☐☐☐
208a.		Strip of 4, Nos. 205-208	2.00	2.00	☐☐☐☐☐

1989

Scott No.	Illus. No.	Description	Unused Value	Used Value	//////
209	A39	45c Typhoon monument.	70	70	☐☐☐☐☐
210	A39	45c Seaplane base, railway depot . . .	70	70	☐☐☐☐☐
211	A39	45c Fishing boats.	70	70	☐☐☐☐☐
212	A39	45c Honeymooners scuba diving . . .	70	70	☐☐☐☐☐
212a.		Block of 4, Nos. 209-212.	2.80	2.80	☐☐☐☐☐
213	A40	45c Island woman	70	70	☐☐☐☐☐
214	A40	45c Kotzebue, Alaska	70	70	☐☐☐☐☐
215	A40	45c Marshallese Madonna	70	70	☐☐☐☐☐
215a.		Strip of 3, Nos. 213-215	2.25	2.25	☐☐☐☐☐
216	A12	25c Pontifical miter.	40	40	☐☐☐☐☐
217	A12	25c Tapestry turban.	40	40	☐☐☐☐☐
218	A12	25c Flame-mouthed helmet	40	40	☐☐☐☐☐
219	A12	25c Prickly Pacific drupe	40	40	☐☐☐☐☐
220	A12	25c Blood-mouthed conch	40	40	☐☐☐☐☐
220a.		Strip of 5, Nos. 216-220	2.00	2.00	☐☐☐☐☐
221	A41	$1 *In Praise of Sovereigns*	1.75	1.75	☐☐☐☐☐
222	A42	45c Wandering tattler	70	70	☐☐☐☐☐
223	A42	45c Ruddy turnstone.	70	70	☐☐☐☐☐
224	A42	45c Pacific golden plover	70	70	☐☐☐☐☐
225	A42	45c Sanderling	70	70	☐☐☐☐☐
225a.		Block of 4, Nos. 222-225.	3.00	3.00	☐☐☐☐☐
226	A43	45c *Morning Star V,* No. 15.	70	70	☐☐☐☐☐
227	A43	45c Nos. 15-16 on cover	70	70	☐☐☐☐☐
228	A43	45c *Prinz Eitel Friedrich,* cancel. . . .	70	70	☐☐☐☐☐
229	A43	45c Cruiser squadron	70	70	☐☐☐☐☐
229a.		Block of 4, Nos. 226-229.	3.00	3.00	☐☐☐☐☐
230		Sheet of 6	8.50	8.50	☐☐☐☐☐
230a.-f.	A44	25c any single.	1.25	1.25	☐☐☐☐☐
231	A43	$1 German No. 32, cancel	8.50	8.50	☐☐☐☐☐
232	A45	25c Apollo 11 liftoff	60	60	☐☐☐☐☐
233	A45	25c Neil Armstrong.	60	60	☐☐☐☐☐
234	A45	25c Lunar module *Eagle*.	60	60	☐☐☐☐☐
235	A45	25c Michael Collins.	60	60	☐☐☐☐☐
236	A45	25c U.S. flag on Moon.	60	60	☐☐☐☐☐
237	A45	25c Buzz Aldrim	60	60	☐☐☐☐☐
238	A45	$1 First step on Moon.	2.00	2.00	☐☐☐☐☐
238a.		Booklet pane of 7, Nos. 232-238. .	5.75	–	☐☐☐☐☐
239	A46	25c Invasion of Poland (W1)	50	50	☐☐☐☐☐
240	A46	45c Sinking of HMS *Royal Oak* (W2).	90	90	☐☐☐☐☐

A59

A60

A61

A62

A63

A64

A65

A66

Scott No.	Illus. No.	Description	Unused Value	Used Value	//////
241	A46	45c Invasion of Finland (W3)......	90	90	☐☐☐☐☐
242	A46	45c HMS *Exeter* (W4, 4-1)........	90	90	☐☐☐☐☐
243	A46	45c HMS *Ajax* (W4, 4-2)........	90	90	☐☐☐☐☐
244	A46	45c *Admiral Graf Spee* (W4, 4-3)...	90	90	☐☐☐☐☐
245	A46	45c HMNZS *Achilles* (W4, 4-4)....	90	90	☐☐☐☐☐
245a.		Block of 4, #242-245..........	3.60	3.60	☐☐☐☐☐

1990

Scott No.	Illus. No.	Description	Unused Value	Used Value	//////
246	A46	25c Invasion of Denmark (W5, 2-1).	50	50	☐☐☐☐☐
247	A46	25c Invasion of Norway (W5, 2-2)..	50	50	☐☐☐☐☐
247a.		Pair, #246-247...............	1.00	1.00	☐☐☐☐☐
248	A47	25c Katyn Forest massacre (W6)...	50	50	☐☐☐☐☐
249	A46	25c Bombing of Rotterdam (W8, 2-1)...................	50	50	☐☐☐☐☐
250	A46	25c Invasion of Belgium (W8, 2-2)..	50	50	☐☐☐☐☐
250a.		Pair, #249-250...............	1.00	1.00	☐☐☐☐☐
251	A46	45c Winston Churchill (W7).......	90	90	☐☐☐☐☐
252	A46	45c Dunkirk evacuation (W9, 2-1)..	90	90	☐☐☐☐☐
253	A46	45c Dunkirk evacuation (W9, 2-2)..	90	90	☐☐☐☐☐
254	A47	45c Occupation of Paris (W10).....	90	90	☐☐☐☐☐
255	A46	25c Battle of Mers-el-Kebir (W11)..	50	50	☐☐☐☐☐
256	A47	25c Battles for Burma Road(W12)...	50	50	☐☐☐☐☐
257	A46	45c HMS *Georgetown* (W13, 4-1)...	90	90	☐☐☐☐☐
258	A46	45c HMS *Banff* (W13, 4-2)........	90	90	☐☐☐☐☐
259	A46	45c HMS *Buxton* (W13, 4-3)	90	90	☐☐☐☐☐
260	A46	45c HMS *Rockingham* (W13, 4-4)..	90	90	☐☐☐☐☐
260a.		Block of 4, #257-260..........	3.60	3.60	☐☐☐☐☐
261	A46	45c Supermarine Spirfire Mark 1A (W14, 4-1).................	90	90	☐☐☐☐☐
262	A46	45c Hawker Hurricane Mark 1 (W14, 4-2).................	90	90	☐☐☐☐☐
263	A46	45c Messerschmitt Bf109E (W14, 4-3).................	90	90	☐☐☐☐☐
264	A46	45c Junkers JU87B-2 (W14, 4-4)...	90	90	☐☐☐☐☐
264a.		Block of 4, #261-264..........	3.60	3.60	☐☐☐☐☐
265	A46	45c Tripartite Pact (W15).........	90	90	☐☐☐☐☐

1990-91

Scott No.	Illus. No.	Description	Unused Value	Used Value	//////
266	A47	25c Roosevelt elected (W16).......	50	50	☐☐☐☐☐
267	A46	25c HMS *Illustrious* (W17, 4-1)....	50	50	☐☐☐☐☐
268	A46	25c Fairey Swordfish (W17, 4-2)...	50	50	☐☐☐☐☐
269	A46	25c RM *Andrea Doria* (W17, 4-3) ..	50	50	☐☐☐☐☐
270	A46	25c RM *Conte di Cavour* (W17, 4-4)	50	50	☐☐☐☐☐
270a.		Block of 4, #266-270..........	2.00	2.00	☐☐☐☐☐
271	A46	30c Freedom of Speech (W18, 4-1) .	60	60	☐☐☐☐☐
272	A46	30c Freedom from Want (W18, 4-2)	60	60	☐☐☐☐☐
273	A46	30c Freedom of Worship (W18, 4-3)	60	60	☐☐☐☐☐

Scott No.	Illus. No.	Description	Unused Value	Used Value	//////
274	A46	30c Freedom from Fear (W18, 4-4) .	60	60	☐☐☐☐☐
274a.		Block of 4, #271-274	2.40	2.40	☐☐☐☐☐

1989

Scott No.	Illus. No.	Description	Unused Value	Used Value	//////
341	A57	25c Horn	50	50	☐☐☐☐☐
342	A57	25c Singing carol	50	50	☐☐☐☐☐
343	A57	25c Lute	50	50	☐☐☐☐☐
344	A57	25c Lyre	50	50	☐☐☐☐☐
344a.		Block of 4, Nos. 341-344	2.00	2.00	☐☐☐☐☐
345		Sheet of 25	22.50	22.50	☐☐☐☐☐
345a.-y.	A58	45c any single	90	90	☐☐☐☐☐

1990

Scott No.	Illus. No.	Description	Unused Value	Used Value	//////
347	A59	5c Red-tailed tropic bird	15	15	☐☐☐☐☐
349	A59	15c Wandering tattler	30	30	☐☐☐☐☐
353	A59	25c Brown noddy	50	50	☐☐☐☐☐
354	A59	30c Pacific golden plover	60	60	☐☐☐☐☐
355	A59	36c Red footed booby	72	72	☐☐☐☐☐
356	A59	40c White tern	80	80	☐☐☐☐☐
357	A59	50c Great frigate bird	1.00	1.00	☐☐☐☐☐
357a.		Miniature sheet of 4 (#347, 349,			
		353, 357)	1.90	1.90	☐☐☐☐☐
360	A59	$1 Pacific reef heron	2.00	2.00	☐☐☐☐☐
366	A60	25c Lodidean	50	50	☐☐☐☐☐
367	A60	25c Lejonjon	50	50	☐☐☐☐☐
368	A60	25c Etobobo	50	50	☐☐☐☐☐
369	A60	25c Didmakol	50	50	☐☐☐☐☐
369a.		Block of 4, #366-369	2.00	2.00	☐☐☐☐☐
370	A61	25c Penny Black	50	50	☐☐☐☐☐
371	A61	25c Essay by James Chalmers	50	50	☐☐☐☐☐
372	A61	25c Essay by Robert Sievier	50	50	☐☐☐☐☐
373	A61	25c Essay by Charles Whiting	50	50	☐☐☐☐☐
374	A61	25c Essay by George Dickinson	50	50	☐☐☐☐☐
375	A61	25c Engraved model	50	50	☐☐☐☐☐
376	A61	$1 Charles Heath	2.00	2.00	☐☐☐☐☐
376a.		Booklet pane of 7, #370-376	5.00		☐☐☐☐☐
377	A62	25c Pacific green turtle hatchlings . .	50	50	☐☐☐☐☐
378	A62	25c Turtle under water	50	50	☐☐☐☐☐
379	A62	25c Hawksbill hatching eggs	50	50	☐☐☐☐☐
380	A62	25c Hawksbill in water	50	50	☐☐☐☐☐
380a.		Block of 4, #377-380	2.00	2.00	☐☐☐☐☐
381	A63	25c Stick chart, canoe, flag	50	50	☐☐☐☐☐
382	A64	45c German reunificatiion	90	90	☐☐☐☐☐
383	A65	25c Canoe, stick chart	50	50	☐☐☐☐☐
384	A65	25c Missionary preaching	50	50	☐☐☐☐☐
385	A65	25c Sailors dancing	50	50	☐☐☐☐☐
386	A65	25c Youths dancing	50	50	☐☐☐☐☐
386a.		Block of 4, #383-386	2.00	2.00	☐☐☐☐☐

Scott No.	Illus. No.	Description	Unused Value	Used Value	//////
387	A66	25c Harvesting..................	50	50	☐☐☐☐☐
388	A66	25c Peeling, slicing..............	50	50	☐☐☐☐☐
389	A66	25c Preserving	50	50	☐☐☐☐☐
390	A66	25c Kneading dough	50	50	☐☐☐☐☐
390a.		Block of 4, #387-390	2.00	2.00	☐☐☐☐☐
					☐☐☐☐☐
					☐☐☐☐☐
					☐☐☐☐☐
					☐☐☐☐☐
					☐☐☐☐☐
					☐☐☐☐☐
					☐☐☐☐☐
					☐☐☐☐☐
					☐☐☐☐☐
					☐☐☐☐☐
					☐☐☐☐☐
					☐☐☐☐☐
					☐☐☐☐☐
					☐☐☐☐☐
					☐☐☐☐☐
					☐☐☐☐☐
					☐☐☐☐☐
					☐☐☐☐☐
					☐☐☐☐☐
					☐☐☐☐☐
					☐☐☐☐☐
					☐☐☐☐☐
					☐☐☐☐☐
					☐☐☐☐☐
					☐☐☐☐☐
					☐☐☐☐☐

AP1

AP2

AP3

AP4

AP5

HOW TO USE THIS BOOK
The number in the first column is its Scott number or identifying number. The letter and number that come next (A41) indicate the design and refer to the illustration so designated. Following that is the denomination of the stamp and its color. Finally, the value, unused and used is shown.

Scott No.	Illus. No.	Description	Unused Value	Used Value	//////

Air Post Stamps
1985, Feb. 15

Scott No.	Illus. No.	Description	Unused Value	Used Value	//////
C1	A11	44c Booby Gannet, vert.	88	88	☐☐☐☐☐
C2	A11	44c Esquimaux Curlew, vert. . . .⋮. . .	88	88	☐☐☐☐☐
C2a.		Pair, No. C1-C2.	1.80	1.80	☐☐☐☐☐

1986

Scott No.	Illus. No.	Description	Unused Value	Used Value	//////
C3	A20	44c Consolidated PBY-5A Catalin..	75	75	☐☐☐☐☐
C4	A20	44c Grumman SA-16 Albatross. . . .	75	75	☐☐☐☐☐
C5	A20	44c McDonnell Douglas DC-6B. . . .	75	75	☐☐☐☐☐
C6	A20	44c Boeing 727-100.	75	75	☐☐☐☐☐
C6a.		Block of 4, #C3-C6	3.00	3.00	☐☐☐☐☐
C7	A21	44c USS *Saratoga*.	*4.50*	*4.50*	☐☐☐☐☐
C8	AP1	44c Statue of Liberty	85	85	☐☐☐☐☐
C9	AP2	44c Community service	70	70	☐☐☐☐☐
C10	AP2	44c Salute.	70	70	☐☐☐☐☐
C11	AP2	44c Health care	70	70	☐☐☐☐☐
C12	AP2	44c Learning skills.	70	70	☐☐☐☐☐
C12a.		Block of 4, #C9-C12	3.00	3.00	☐☐☐☐☐

1987

Scott No.	Illus. No.	Description	Unused Value	Used Value	//////
C13	AP3	44c Wedge-tailed shearwater	75	75	☐☐☐☐☐
C14	AP3	44c Red-footed booby.	75	75	☐☐☐☐☐
C15	AP3	44c Red-tailed tropic-bird	75	75	☐☐☐☐☐
C16	AP3	44c Great frigatebird	75	75	☐☐☐☐☐
C16a.		Block of 4, #C13-C16	3.00	3.00	☐☐☐☐☐
C17	AP4	44c Amelia Earhart take-off	75	75	☐☐☐☐☐
C18	AP4	44c USCG *Itasca* at Howland Is. . . .	75	75	☐☐☐☐☐
C19	AP4	44c Purported crash landing site . . .	75	75	☐☐☐☐☐
C20	AP4	44c Recovery of Electra	75	75	☐☐☐☐☐
C20a.		Block of 4, Nos. C17-C2	3.00	3.00	☐☐☐☐☐

1988, Dec. 23

Scott No.	Illus. No.	Description	Unused Value	Used Value	//////
C21	A38	45c Astronaut, shuttle over Rongelap	90	90	☐☐☐☐☐

1989, Apr. 24

Scott No.	Illus. No.	Description	Unused Value	Used Value	//////
C22	AP5	12c Dornier Do228	20	20	☐☐☐☐☐
C22a.		Booklet pane of 10.	2.00		☐☐☐☐☐
C23	AP5	36c Boeing 737.	60	60	☐☐☐☐☐
C23a.		Booklet pane of 10.	6.00		☐☐☐☐☐
C24	AP5	39c Hawker Siddeley 748	65	65	☐☐☐☐☐
C24a.		Booklet pane of 10.	6.50		☐☐☐☐☐
C25	AP5	45c Boeing 727.	70	70	☐☐☐☐☐
C25a.		Booklet pane of 10.	7.00		☐☐☐☐☐
C25b.		Booklet pane of 10 (5 each 36c, 45c).	6.50		☐☐☐☐☐

A2

A1

A3

A4

A5

A6

A7

A8

A10

A9

A11

Scott No.	Illus. No.	Description	Unused Value	Used Value	//////

Micronesia, Federated States of

Catalogue values for unused stamps in this section are for Never Hinged items.

1984

1	A1	20c Yap	50	50 ☐☐☐☐☐
2	A1	20c Truk........................	50	50 ☐☐☐☐☐
3	A1	20c Pohnpei.....................	50	50 ☐☐☐☐☐
4	A1	20c Kosrae	50	50 ☐☐☐☐☐
4a.		Block of 4, Nos. 1-4............	2.00	2.00 ☐☐☐☐☐
5	A2	1c Prussian blue.................	15	15 ☐☐☐☐☐
6	A2	2c deep claret...................	15	15 ☐☐☐☐☐
7	A2	3c dark blue	15	15 ☐☐☐☐☐
8	A2	4c green	15	15 ☐☐☐☐☐
9	A3	5c yellow brown.................	15	15 ☐☐☐☐☐
10	A3	10c dark violet..................	16	16 ☐☐☐☐☐
11	A3	13c dark blue	20	20 ☐☐☐☐☐
12	A3	17c brown lake..................	25	25 ☐☐☐☐☐
13	A2	19c dark violet..................	28	28 ☐☐☐☐☐
14	A2	20c olive green..................	30	30 ☐☐☐☐☐
15	A2	30c rose lake....................	45	45 ☐☐☐☐☐
16	A2	37c deep violet..................	55	55 ☐☐☐☐☐
17	A3	50c brown	75	75 ☐☐☐☐☐
18	A3	$1 olive	1.50	1.50 ☐☐☐☐☐
19	A3	$2 Prussian blue	3.00	3.00 ☐☐☐☐☐
20	A3	$5 brown lake	7.00	7.00 ☐☐☐☐☐
21	A4	20c Truk Post Office	48	48 ☐☐☐☐☐
22	A5	20c Child in manger	48	48 ☐☐☐☐☐

1985

23	A6	22c USS *Jamestown*	50	50 ☐☐☐☐☐
24	A7	22c Lelu Protestant Church, Kosrae.	45	45 ☐☐☐☐☐
25	A8	22c Noddy tern	60	60 ☐☐☐☐☐
26	A8	22c Turnstone	60	60 ☐☐☐☐☐
27	A8	22c Golden plover...............	60	60 ☐☐☐☐☐
28	A8	22c Black-bellied plover	60	60 ☐☐☐☐☐
28a.		Block of 4, Nos. 25-28..........	2.50	2.50 ☐☐☐☐☐

1985-88

31	A9	3c Long-billed white-eye..........	15	15 ☐☐☐☐☐
32	A9	14c Truk monarch...............	28	28 ☐☐☐☐☐
33	A3	15c Liduduhriap Waterfall, Pohnpei	30	30 ☐☐☐☐☐
33a.		Booklet pane of 10..............	3.00	— ☐☐☐☐☐
34	A10	22c bright blue green.............	35	35 ☐☐☐☐☐
35	A9	22c Pohnpei mountain starling.....	44	44 ☐☐☐☐☐
36	A3	25c Tonachau Peak, Truk.........	50	50 ☐☐☐☐☐
36a.		Booklet pane of 10..............	5.00	— ☐☐☐☐☐
36b.		Booklet pane of 10, 5 15c + 5 25c.	4.00	— ☐☐☐☐☐

A16

A17

A18

A19

A20

A21

A22

A23

A24

A25

A27

A29

288

Scott No.	Illus. No.	Description	Unused Value	Used Value	//////
37	A10	36c ultramarine	72	72	☐☐☐☐☐
38	A3	45c Sleeping Lady, Kosrae	90	90	☐☐☐☐☐
39	A11	$10 bright ultramarine	15.00	15.00	☐☐☐☐☐

1985, Dec.

45	A16	22c Land of the Sacred Masonry . . .	45	45	☐☐☐☐☐

1986

46	A17	22c International Peace Year	50	50	☐☐☐☐☐
48	A1	22c on 20c No. 1	45	45	☐☐☐☐☐
49	A1	22c on 20c No. 2	45	45	☐☐☐☐☐
50	A1	22c on 20c No. 3	45	45	☐☐☐☐☐
51	A1	22c on 20c No. 4	45	45	☐☐☐☐☐
51a.		Block of 4, Nos. 48-51	1.90	1.90	☐☐☐☐☐
52	A18	22c At ship's helm	50	50	☐☐☐☐☐
53	A19	22c First passport	75	75	☐☐☐☐☐
54	A20	5c Virgin and Child	15	15	☐☐☐☐☐
55	A20	22c Virgin and Child	50	50	☐☐☐☐☐

1987

56	A21	22c International Year of Shelter for the Homeless	45	45	☐☐☐☐☐
57	A21	$1 CAPEX '87	3.00	3.00	☐☐☐☐☐
58	A22	22c Archangel Gabriel	45	35	☐☐☐☐☐

1988

59	A23	22c German	40	40	☐☐☐☐☐
60	A23	22c Spanish	40	40	☐☐☐☐☐
61	A23	22c Japanese	40	40	☐☐☐☐☐
62	A23	22c U.S. Trust Territory	40	40	☐☐☐☐☐
62a.		Block of 4, Nos. 59-62	1.60	1.60	☐☐☐☐☐
63	A24	25c Running	40	40	☐☐☐☐☐
64	A24	25c Women's hurdles	40	40	☐☐☐☐☐
64a.		Pair, Nos. 63-64	80	80	☐☐☐☐☐
65	A24	45c Basketball	70	70	☐☐☐☐☐
66	A24	45c Women's volleyball	70	70	☐☐☐☐☐
66a.		Pair, Nos. 65-66	1.40	1.40	☐☐☐☐☐
67	A25	25c Two girls decorating tree	50	50	☐☐☐☐☐
68	A25	25c Boy, girl, dove	50	50	☐☐☐☐☐
69	A25	25c Boy, girl	50	50	☐☐☐☐☐
70	A25	25c Boy, girl	50	50	☐☐☐☐☐
70a.		Block of 4, Nos. 67-70	2.00	2.00	☐☐☐☐☐
71		Sheet of 18	7.25	7.25	☐☐☐☐☐
71a.-r.	A26	25c any single	40	40	☐☐☐☐☐

1989

72	A27	45c Plumeria	75	75	☐☐☐☐☐
73	A27	45c Hibiscus	75	75	☐☐☐☐☐

A26

A28

HOW TO USE THIS BOOK

The number in the first column is its Scott number or identifying number. The letter and number that come next (A41) indicate the design and refer to the illustration so designated. Following that is the denomination of the stamp and its color. Finally, the value, unused and used is shown.

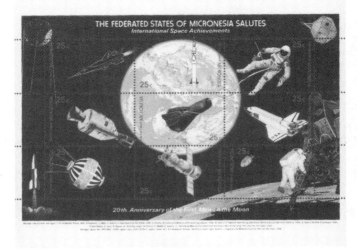

A30

A32

A31

A33

A34

A35

292

Scott No.	Illus. No.	Description	Unused Value	Used Value	//////
74	A27	45c Jasmine	75	75	□□□□□
75	A27	45c Bougainvillea	75	75	□□□□□
75a.		Block of 4, Nos. 72-75.........	3.00	3.00	□□□□□
76	A28	$1 *Pheasant and Chrusanthemum* ..	1.65	1.65	□□□□□
77	A29	25c Whale	40	40	□□□□□
78	A29	25c Hammerhead	40	40	□□□□□
78a.		Pair, Nos. 77-78..............	80	80	□□□□□
79	A29	45c Tiger, vert................	75	75	□□□□□
80	A29	45c Great white, vert.	75	75	□□□□□
80a.		Pair, Nos. 79-80..............	1.50	1.50	□□□□□
81	A30	Sheet of 9	3.50	3.50	□□□□□
81a.-i.		25c any single.................	38	38	□□□□□
82	A31	$2.40 *Earth and Lunar Modul3*	3.25	3.25	□□□□□
83	A32	1c Horse's hoof	15	15	□□□□□
84	A32	3c Rare spotted cowrie	15	15	□□□□□
85	A32	15c Commercial trochus..........	22	22	□□□□□
85a.		Booklet pane of 10.............	2.75	–	□□□□□
87	A32	20c General cone...............	30	30	□□□□□
88	A32	25c Triton's trumpet	38	38	□□□□□
88a.		Booklet pane of 10.............	4.75	–	□□□□□
88B.		Booklet pane of 10 (5 each 15c, 25c)	3.75	–	□□□□□
90	A32	30c Laciniated conch............	45	45	□□□□□
91	A32	36c Red-mouthed olive...........	55	55	□□□□□
93	A32	45c Map cowrie	70	70	□□□□□
95	A32	50c Textile cone...............	75	75	□□□□□
100	A32	$1 Orange spider conch..........	1.50	1.50	□□□□□
101	A32	$2 Golden cowrie	3.00	3.00	□□□□□
102	A32	$5 Episcopal miter..............	7.50	7.50	□□□□□
103		Sheet of 18	9.00	9.00	□□□□□
103a.-r.	A33	25c any single.................	50	50	□□□□□
104	A34	25c Heralding angel.............	50	50	□□□□□
105	A34	45c Three wise men.............	90	90	□□□□□

1990

Scott No.	Illus. No.	Description	Unused Value	Used Value	//////
106	A35	10c Kingfisher (juvenile).........	20	20	□□□□□
107	A35	15c Kingfisher (adult)	30	30	□□□□□
108	A35	20c Pigeon	40	40	□□□□□
109	A35	25c Pigeon, diff.................	50	50	□□□□□
110	A36	45c Wooden whale stamp, *Lyra*	90	90	□□□□□
111	A36	45c Harpoons, *Prudent*	90	90	□□□□□
112	A36	45c Scrimshaw, *Rhone*	90	90	□□□□□
113	A36	45c Scrimshaw on tooth, *Sussex*....	90	90	□□□□□
113a.		Block of 4, #110-113	3.60	3.60	□□□□□
114	A36	$1 Whalers at kill...............	2.00	2.00	□□□□□
115	A37	$1 Great Britain No. 1	2.00	2.00	□□□□□
116	A38	25c Pohnpei Agriculture & Trade School	50	50	□□□□□
117	A38	25c Fr. Hugh Costigan, students....	50	50	□□□□□

A36

A37

A38

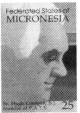

A39

A40

A41

A42

A43

Scott No.	Illus. No.	Description	Unused Value	Used Value	//////
118	A39	25c Fr. Costigan................	50	50	☐☐☐☐☐
119	A38	25c Fr. Costigan, Isaphu Samuel			
		Hadley......................	50	50	☐☐☐☐☐
120	A38	25c New York City Police badge ...	50	50	☐☐☐☐☐
120a.		Strip of 5, #116-120...........	2.50	2.50	☐☐☐☐☐
121	A40	$1 International Garden			
		& Greenery Exposition........	1.80	1.80	☐☐☐☐☐
122	A41	25c Loading mail................	45	45	☐☐☐☐☐
123	A41	45c Japanese mail boat...........	85	85	☐☐☐☐☐
124	A42	25c Stick chart, canoe, Marshall			
		Island flag	50	50	☐☐☐☐☐
125	A42	25c Frigatebird, eagle,			
		USS *Constitution,* U.S. flag	50	50	☐☐☐☐☐
126	A42	25c Canoe, Micronesia flag........	50	50	☐☐☐☐☐
126a.		Strip of 3, #124-126...........	1.50	1.50	☐☐☐☐☐
127	A43	45c Gracillariidae	90	90	☐☐☐☐☐
128	A43	45c Yponomeatidae..............	90	90	☐☐☐☐☐
129	A43	45c Cosmopterigidae.............	90	90	☐☐☐☐☐
130	A43	45c Cosmopterigidae, diff.	90	90	☐☐☐☐☐
130a.		Block of 4, #127-130	3.60	3.60	☐☐☐☐☐

_____				☐☐☐☐☐
_____				☐☐☐☐☐
_____				☐☐☐☐☐
_____				☐☐☐☐☐
_____				☐☐☐☐☐
_____				☐☐☐☐☐
_____				☐☐☐☐☐
_____				☐☐☐☐☐
_____				☐☐☐☐☐
_____				☐☐☐☐☐
_____				☐☐☐☐☐
_____				☐☐☐☐☐
_____				☐☐☐☐☐
_____				☐☐☐☐☐
_____				☐☐☐☐☐
_____				☐☐☐☐☐
_____				☐☐☐☐☐
_____				☐☐☐☐☐

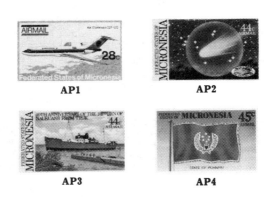

AP1

AP2

AP3

AP4

AP5

HOW TO USE THIS BOOK

The number in the first column is its Scott number or identifying number. The letter and number that come next (A41) indicate the design and refer to the illustration so designated. Following that is the denomination of the stamp and its color. Finally, the value, unused and used is shown.

Scott No.	Illus. No.	Description	Unused Value	Used Value	//////
Air Post Stamps					
1984					
C1	AP1	28c Boeing 727.	55	55 □□□□□
C2	AP1	35c SA-16 Albatross, 1960	70	70 □□□□□
C3	AP1	40c PBY-5A Catalina, 1951	80	80 □□□□□
C4	A4	28c Caroline Is. No. 4	70	70 □□□□□
C5	A4	35c Caroline Is. No. 7	85	85 □□□□□
C6	A4	40c Caroline Is. No. 19	1.00	1.00 □□□□□
C7	A5	28c Illustrated Christmas text.	70	70 □□□□□
C8	A5	35c Decorated palm tree	85	85 □□□□□
C9	A5	40c Feast preparation	1.00	1.00 □□□□□
1985					
C10	A6	33c *L'Astrolabe*	70	70 □□□□□
C11	A6	39c *La Coquille*	80	80 □□□□□
C12	A6	44c *Shenandoah.*	90	90 □□□□□
C13	A7	33c Dublon Protestant Church	70	70 □□□□□
C14	A7	44c Pohnpei Catholic Church	90	90 □□□□□
C15	A8	44c Sooty tern	1.20	1.20 □□□□□
C16	A16	33c Nan Tauas inner courtyard	70	70 □□□□□
C17	A16	39c Outer wall	80	80 □□□□□
C18	A16	44c Tomb.	90	90 □□□□□
1986					
C19	AP2	44c dark blue, blue & black	1.25	1.25 □□□□□
C20	AP3	44c Ship in port	1.25	1.25 □□□□□
C21	A18	33c Forging Hawaiian stamp	70	70 □□□□□
C22	A18	39c Sinking of the Leonora, Kosrae .	85	85 □□□□□
C23	A18	44c Hayes escapes capture	95	95 □□□□□
C24	A18	75c Biography, by Louis Becke.	1.75	1.75 □□□□□
C25	A18	$1 Hayes ransoming chief.	3.50	3.50 □□□□□
C26	A20	33c Virgin and Child	70	70 □□□□□
C27	A20	44c Virgin and Child	90	90 □□□□□
1987					
C28	A21	33c U.S. currency, bicentennial	70	70 □□□□□
C29	A21	39c 1st American in orbit, 25th anniversary	90	90 □□□□□
C30	A21	44c U.S. Constitution, bicentennial .	1.00	1.00 □□□□□
C31	A22	33c Holy Family	70	70 □□□□□
C32	A22	39c Shepherds	80	80 □□□□□
C33	A22	44c Three Wise Men	90	90 □□□□□
1988					
C34	A9	33c Great truk white-eye.	55	55 □□□□□
C35	A9	44c Blue-faced parrotfinch	70	70 □□□□□
C36	A9	$1 Yap monarch	1.75	1.75 □□□□□
C37	A23	44c Traditional skills (boat-building)	85	85 □□□□□

Scott No.	Illus. No.	Description	Unused Value	Used Value	//////
C38	A23	44c Modern Micronesia (tourism) ..	85	85	□□□□□
C38a.		Pair, Nos. C37-C38	1.70	1.70	□□□□□

1989, Jan. 19
C39	AP4	45c Pohnpei....................	75	75	□□□□□
C40	AP4	45c Truk.......................	75	75	□□□□□
C41	AP4	45c Kosrae	75	75	□□□□□
C42	AP4	45c Yap	75	75	□□□□□
C42a.		Block of 4, Nos. C39-C42	3.00	3.00	□□□□□

1990, July 16
C43	AP5	22c Airplane...................	45	45	□□□□□
C44	AP5	36c Airplane...................	72	72	□□□□□
C45	AP5	39c Airplane...................	80	80	□□□□□
C46	AP5	45c Airplane...................	90	90	□□□□□

_____				□□□□□
_____				□□□□□
_____				□□□□□
_____				□□□□□
_____				□□□□□
_____				□□□□□
_____				□□□□□
_____				□□□□□
_____				□□□□□
_____				□□□□□
_____				□□□□□
_____				□□□□□
_____				□□□□□
_____				□□□□□
_____				□□□□□
_____				□□□□□
_____				□□□□□
_____				□□□□□
_____				□□□□□
_____				□□□□□
_____				□□□□□
_____				□□□□□

Scott No.	Illus. No.	Description	Unused Value	Used Value	//////
					☐☐☐☐☐
					☐☐☐☐☐
					☐☐☐☐☐
					☐☐☐☐☐
					☐☐☐☐☐
					☐☐☐☐☐
					☐☐☐☐☐
					☐☐☐☐☐
					☐☐☐☐☐
					☐☐☐☐☐
					☐☐☐☐☐
					☐☐☐☐☐
					☐☐☐☐☐
					☐☐☐☐☐
					☐☐☐☐☐
					☐☐☐☐☐
					☐☐☐☐☐
					☐☐☐☐☐
					☐☐☐☐☐
					☐☐☐☐☐
					☐☐☐☐☐
					☐☐☐☐☐
					☐☐☐☐☐
					☐☐☐☐☐
					☐☐☐☐☐
					☐☐☐☐☐
					☐☐☐☐☐
					☐☐☐☐☐
					☐☐☐☐☐
					☐☐☐☐☐
					☐☐☐☐☐
					☐☐☐☐☐
					☐☐☐☐☐
					☐☐☐☐☐

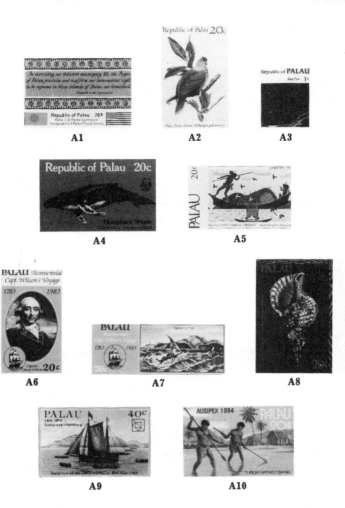

A1

A2

A3

A4

A5

A6

A7

A8

A9

A10

HOW TO USE THIS BOOK

The number in the first column is its Scott number or identifying number. The letter and number that come next (A41) indicate the design and refer to the illustration so designated. Following that is the denomination of the stamp and its color. Finally, the value, unused and used is shown.

Scott No.	Illus. No.	Description	Unused Value	Used Value	
Palau					

Catalogue values for unused stamps in this section are for
Never Hinged items.

1983

1	A1	20c Constitution preamble	65	65	☐☐☐☐☐
2	A1	20c Hunters	65	65	☐☐☐☐☐
3	A1	20c Fish	65	65	☐☐☐☐☐
4	A1	20c Preamble, diff...............	65	65	☐☐☐☐☐
4a.		Block of 4, Nos. 1-4............	2.75	2.75	☐☐☐☐☐
5	A2	20c Palau fruit dove	40	40	☐☐☐☐☐
6	A2	20c Palau morningbird	40	40	☐☐☐☐☐
7	A2	20c Giant white-eye.............	40	40	☐☐☐☐☐
8	A2	20c Palau fantail	40	40	☐☐☐☐☐
8a.		Block of 4, Nos. 5-8	1.65	1.65	☐☐☐☐☐

1983-84

9	A3	1c Sea fan.....................	15	15	☐☐☐☐☐
10	A3	3c Map cowrie	15	15	☐☐☐☐☐
11	A3	5c Jellyfish	15	15	☐☐☐☐☐
12	A3	10c Hawksbill turtle	16	16	☐☐☐☐☐
13	A3	13c Giant Clam	20	20	☐☐☐☐☐
13a.		Booklet pane of 10.............	9.00	—	☐☐☐☐☐
13b.		Booklet pane of 10 (5 #13, 5 #14) .	9.00	—	☐☐☐☐☐
14	A3	20c Parrotfish..................	35	35	☐☐☐☐☐
14b.		Booklet pane of 10.............	10.00	—	☐☐☐☐☐
15	A3	28c Chambered Nautilus.........	45	45	☐☐☐☐☐
16	A3	30c Dappled sea cucumber	50	50	☐☐☐☐☐
17	A3	37c Sea Urchin.................	55	55	☐☐☐☐☐
18	A3	50c Starfish	85	85	☐☐☐☐☐
19	A3	$1 Squid......................	1.60	1.60	☐☐☐☐☐
20	A3	$2 Dugong	4.00	4.00	☐☐☐☐☐
21	A3	$5 Pink sponge................	9.00	9.00	☐☐☐☐☐

1983

24	A4	20c Humpback whale	45	45	☐☐☐☐☐
25	A4	20c Blue whale.................	45	45	☐☐☐☐☐
26	A4	20c Fin whale..................	45	45	☐☐☐☐☐
27	A4	20c Great sperm whale	45	45	☐☐☐☐☐
27a.		Block of 4, Nos. 24-27.........	1.90	1.90	☐☐☐☐☐
28	A5	20c First Child ceremony	65	65	☐☐☐☐☐
29	A5	20c Spearfishing from Red Canoe ..	65	65	☐☐☐☐☐
30	A5	20c Traditional feast at the Bai.....	65	65	☐☐☐☐☐
31	A5	20c Taro gardening	65	65	☐☐☐☐☐
32	A5	20c Spearfishing at New Moon.....	65	65	☐☐☐☐☐
32a.		Strip of 5, Nos. 28-32	3.25	3.25	☐☐☐☐☐
33	A6	20c Capt. Henry Wilson	50	50	☐☐☐☐☐
34	A7	20c Approaching Pelew..........	50	50	☐☐☐☐☐

A12

A11

A13

A14

A15

A16

A17

A18

A19

A20

Scott No.	Illus. No.	Description	Unused Value	Used Value	//////
35	A7	20c Englishman's Camp on Ulong ..	50	50	☐☐☐☐☐
36	A6	20c Prince Lee Boo	50	50	☐☐☐☐☐
37	A6	20c King Abba Thulle............	50	50	☐☐☐☐☐
38	A7	20c Mooring in Koror	50	50	☐☐☐☐☐
39	A7	20c Village scene of Pelew Islands ..	50	50	☐☐☐☐☐
40	A6	20c Ludee.....................	50	50	☐☐☐☐☐
40a.		Block or strip of 8, Nos. 33-40 ...	4.00	4.00	☐☐☐☐☐

1984

Scott No.	Illus. No.	Description	Unused Value	Used Value	//////
41	A8	20c Triton trumpet, d............	40	40	☐☐☐☐☐
42	A8	20c Horned helmet, d............	40	40	☐☐☐☐☐
43	A8	20c Giant clam, d................	40	40	☐☐☐☐☐
44	A8	20c Laciniate conch, d...........	40	40	☐☐☐☐☐
45	A8	20c Royal cloak scallop, d.	40	40	☐☐☐☐☐
46	A8	20c Triton trumpet, v............	40	40	☐☐☐☐☐
47	A8	20c Horned helmet, v............	40	40	☐☐☐☐☐
48	A8	20c Giant clam, v................	40	40	☐☐☐☐☐
49	A8	20c Laciniate conch, v...........	40	40	☐☐☐☐☐
50	A8	20c Royal cloak scallop, v........	40	40	☐☐☐☐☐
50a.		Block of 10, Nos. 41-50.........	4.00	4.00	☐☐☐☐☐
51	A9	40c *Oroolong*, 1783	95	95	☐☐☐☐☐
52	A9	40c *Duff*, 1797	95	95	☐☐☐☐☐
53	A9	40c *Peiho*, 1908	95	95	☐☐☐☐☐
54	A9	40c *Albatross*, 1885	95	95	☐☐☐☐☐
54a.		Block of 4, Nos. 51-54..........	3.80	3.80	☐☐☐☐☐
55	A10	20c Throw spear fishing	45	45	☐☐☐☐☐
56	A10	20c Kite fishing	45	45	☐☐☐☐☐
57	A10	20c Underwater spear fishing	45	45	☐☐☐☐☐
58	A10	20c Net fishing.................	45	45	☐☐☐☐☐
58a.		Block of 4, Nos. 55-58..........	1.90	1.90	☐☐☐☐☐
59	A11	20c Mountain Apple	45	45	☐☐☐☐☐
60	A11	20c Beach Morning Glory.........	45	45	☐☐☐☐☐
61	A11	20c Turmeric	45	45	☐☐☐☐☐
62	A11	20c Plumeria	45	45	☐☐☐☐☐
62a.		Block of 4, Nos. 59-62..........	1.90	1.90	☐☐☐☐☐

1985

Scott No.	Illus. No.	Description	Unused Value	Used Value	//////
63	A12	22c Shearwater chick.............	70	70	☐☐☐☐☐
64	A12	22c Shearwater's head	70	70	☐☐☐☐☐
65	A12	22c Shearwater in flight..........	70	70	☐☐☐☐☐
66	A12	22c Swimming..................	70	70	☐☐☐☐☐
66a.		Block of 4, Nos. 63-66..........	2.80	2.80	☐☐☐☐☐
67	A13	22c Cargo canoe.................	50	50	☐☐☐☐☐
68	A13	22c War canoe	50	50	☐☐☐☐☐
69	A13	22c Bamboo raft	50	50	☐☐☐☐☐
70	A13	22c Racing/sailing canoe..........	50	50	☐☐☐☐☐
70a.		Block of 4, Nos. 67-70..........	2.00	2.00	☐☐☐☐☐
75	A3	14c Trumpet triton	20	20	☐☐☐☐☐

A21

A22

A23

A24

A23a

A25

A26

A27

A28

Scott No.	Illus. No.	Description	Unused Value	Used Value	//////
75a.		Booklet pane of 10.............	6.00	–	☐☐☐☐☐
76	A3	22c Bumphead parrotfish	35	35	☐☐☐☐☐
76a.		Booklet pane of 10.............	10.00	–	☐☐☐☐☐
76b.		Booklet pane of 10 (5 14c, 5 22c) .	9.00	–	☐☐☐☐☐
77	A3	25c Soft coral, damsel fish	40	40	☐☐☐☐☐
79	A3	33c Sea anemone, clownfish	55	55	☐☐☐☐☐
80	A3	39c Green sea turtle..............	65	65	☐☐☐☐☐
81	A3	44c Pacific sailfish..............	70	70	☐☐☐☐☐
85	A3	$10 Spinner dolphins	15.00	15.00	☐☐☐☐☐
86	A14	44c Children.....................	75	75	☐☐☐☐☐
87	A14	44c Children.....................	75	75	☐☐☐☐☐
88	A14	44c Children.....................	75	75	☐☐☐☐☐
89	A14	44c Children.....................	75	75	☐☐☐☐☐
89a.		Block of 4, Nos. 86-89.........	3.00	3.00	☐☐☐☐☐
90	A15	14c Mothers & children	40		☐☐☐☐☐
91	A15	22c Mothers & children	55	55	☐☐☐☐☐
92	A15	33c Mothers & children	85	85	☐☐☐☐☐
93	A15	44c Mothers & children	1.15	1.15	☐☐☐☐☐
94	A16	$1 Martin M-130 China Clipper ...	2.50	2.50	☐☐☐☐☐
95	A17	44c Kaeb canoe, 1758	75	75	☐☐☐☐☐
96	A17	44c USS *Vincennes*, 1835	75	75	☐☐☐☐☐
97	A17	44c SMS *Scharnhorst,* 1910	75	75	☐☐☐☐☐
98	A17	44c Yacht, 1986..................	75	75	☐☐☐☐☐
98a.		Block of 4, Nos. 95-98..........	3.00	3.00	☐☐☐☐☐

1986

Scott No.	Illus. No.	Description	Unused Value	Used Value	//////
99	A18	44c Mangrove flycatcher..........	80	80	☐☐☐☐☐
100	A18	44c Cardinal honeyeater	80	80	☐☐☐☐☐
101	A18	44c Blue-faced parrotfinch	80	80	☐☐☐☐☐
102	A18	44c Dusky and bridled white-eyes ..	80	80	☐☐☐☐☐
102a.		Block of 4, Nos. 99-102.........	3.25	3.25	☐☐☐☐☐
103		Sheet of 40	40.00		☐☐☐☐☐
103a.	A19	14c, any single	30	30	☐☐☐☐☐
104	A20	22c Commercial trochus..........	45	45	☐☐☐☐☐
105	A20	22c Marble cone	45	45	☐☐☐☐☐
106	A20	22c Fluted giant clam	45	45	☐☐☐☐☐
107	A20	22c Bullmouth helmet............	45	45	☐☐☐☐☐
108	A20	22c Golden cowrie...............	45	45	☐☐☐☐☐
108a.		Strip of 5, Nos. 104-108	2.25	2.25	☐☐☐☐☐
109	A21	22c Soldier's helmet	40	40	☐☐☐☐☐
110	A21	22c Plane wreckage	40	40	☐☐☐☐☐
111	A21	22c Woman playing guitar	40	40	☐☐☐☐☐
112	A21	22c Airai vista..................	40	40	☐☐☐☐☐
112a.		Block of 4, Nos. 109-112........	1.65	1.65	☐☐☐☐☐
113	A22	22c Gecko	50	50	☐☐☐☐☐
114	A22	22c Emerald tree skink	50	50	☐☐☐☐☐
115	A22	22c Estuarine crocodile...........	50	50	☐☐☐☐☐
116	A22	22c Leatherback turtle............	50	50	☐☐☐☐☐

A30

22¢

A31

A32

A33

A34

A35

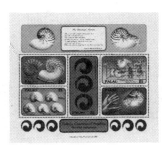

A36

A37

A38

Scott No.	Illus. No.	Description	Unused Value	Used Value	//////
116a.		Block of 4, Nos. 113-116.......	2.00	2.00	☐☐☐☐☐
117	A23	22c Girl playing guitar, boys, goat ..	35	35	☐☐☐☐☐
118	A23	22c Girl carrying bouquet, boys singing......................	35	35	☐☐☐☐☐
119	A23	22c Mother & child..............	35	35	☐☐☐☐☐
120	A23	22c Children, fruit baskets	35	35	☐☐☐☐☐
121	A23	22c Girl, fairy tern...............	35	35	☐☐☐☐☐
121a.		Strip of 5, Nos. 117-121	1.75	1.75	☐☐☐☐☐

1987

Scott No.	Illus. No.	Description	Unused Value	Used Value	//////
121B	A23a	44c Tangadik, soursop............	80	80	☐☐☐☐☐
121C	A23a	44c Dira amartal, sweet orange.....	80	80	☐☐☐☐☐
121D	A23a	44c Ilhuochel, swamp cabbage	80	80	☐☐☐☐☐
121E	A23a	44c Bauosech, fig...............	80	80	☐☐☐☐☐
121f.		Block of 4, Nos. 121B-121E	3.25	3.25	☐☐☐☐☐
122	A24	44c In flight	70	70	☐☐☐☐☐
123	A24	44c Hanging....................	70	70	☐☐☐☐☐
124	A24	44c Eating.....................	70	70	☐☐☐☐☐
125	A24	44c Head	70	70	☐☐☐☐☐
125a.		Block of 4, #122-125	2.80	2.80	☐☐☐☐☐

1987-88

Scott No.	Illus. No.	Description	Unused Value	Used Value	//////
126	A25	1c Ixora casei...................	15	15	☐☐☐☐☐
127	A25	3c Lumnitzera littorea...........	15	15	☐☐☐☐☐
128	A25	5c Sonneratia alba...............	15	15	☐☐☐☐☐
129	A25	10c Tristellateria australasiae	16	16	☐☐☐☐☐
130	A25	14c Bikkia palauensis	20	20	☐☐☐☐☐
130a.		Booklet pane of 10.............	3.00	–	☐☐☐☐☐
131	A25	15c Limnophila aromatica ('88)	22	22	☐☐☐☐☐
131a.		Booklet pane of 10 ('88).	2.25	–	☐☐☐☐☐
132	A25	22c Bruguiera gymnorhiza	35	35	☐☐☐☐☐
132a.		Booklet pane of 10.............	4.00	–	☐☐☐☐☐
132b.		Booklet pane of 10 (5 14c, 5 22c) .	4.00	–	☐☐☐☐☐
133	A25	25c Fagraea ksid ('88)	40	40	☐☐☐☐☐
133a.		Booklet pane of 10 ('88).	4.00	–	☐☐☐☐☐
133b.		Booklet pane of 10 (5 each 15c, 25c) ('88)	4.00	–	☐☐☐☐☐
137	A25	36c Ophiorrhiza palauensis ('88) ...	55	55	☐☐☐☐☐
138	A25	39c Cerbera manghas	60	60	☐☐☐☐☐
140	A25	44c Sandera indica..............	70	70	☐☐☐☐☐
141	A25	45c Maesa canfieldiae ('88)........	72	72	☐☐☐☐☐
142	A25	50c Dolichandrone spathacea......	85	85	☐☐☐☐☐
143	A25	$1 Barringtonia racemosa.........	1.60	1.60	☐☐☐☐☐
144	A25	$2 Nepenthes mirabilis...........	3.25	3.25	☐☐☐☐☐
145	A25	$5 Dendrobium palawense........	8.00	8.00	☐☐☐☐☐
145A	A25	$10 Bouquet ('88)	15.00	15.00	☐☐☐☐☐

A39

A41

A42

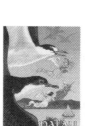

A44

A45

A46

A49

A47

Scott No.	Illus. No.	Description	Unused Value	Used Value	/ / / / / /
1987, June 15					
146	A26	22c Babeldaob Is................	40	40	☐☐☐☐☐
147	A26	22c Floating Garden Isls.	40	40	☐☐☐☐☐
148	A26	22c Rock Is...................	40	40	☐☐☐☐☐
149	A26	22c Koror....................	40	40	☐☐☐☐☐
149a.		Block of 4, Nos. 146-149........	1.60	1.60	☐☐☐☐☐
150	A20	22c Black-striped triton...........	40	40	☐☐☐☐☐
151	A20	22c Tapestry turban..............	40	40	☐☐☐☐☐
152	A20	22c Adusta murex	40	40	☐☐☐☐☐
153	A20	22c Little fox miter	40	40	☐☐☐☐☐
154	A20	22c Cardinal miter...............	40	40	☐☐☐☐☐
154a.		Strip of 5, Nos. 150-154	2.00	2.00	☐☐☐☐☐
155	A27	14c Art. VIII, Sec. 1, Palau	20	20	☐☐☐☐☐
156	A27	14c Presidential seals.............	20	20	☐☐☐☐☐
157	A27	14c Art. II, Sec. 1, U.S..........	20	20	☐☐☐☐☐
157a.		Triptych + label, Nos. 155-157...	60	60	☐☐☐☐☐
158	A27	22c Art. IX, Sec. 1, Palau	35	35	☐☐☐☐☐
159	A27	22c Legislative seals	35	35	☐☐☐☐☐
160	A27	22c Art. I, Sec. 1, U.S..........	35	35	☐☐☐☐☐
160a.		Triptych + label, Nos. 158-160...	1.05	1.05	☐☐☐☐☐
161	A27	44c Art X, Sec. 1, Palau	70	70	☐☐☐☐☐
162	A27	44c Supreme Court seals..........	70	70	☐☐☐☐☐
163	A27	44c Art. III, Sec. 1, U.S.	70	70	☐☐☐☐☐
163a.		Triptych + label, Nos. 161-163...	2.10	2.10	☐☐☐☐☐
164	A28	14c Japan No. 257, Datsun sedan ..	20	20	☐☐☐☐☐
165	A28	22c Japan No. 347, Phosphate mine	35	35	☐☐☐☐☐
166	A28	33c Japan No. B1, DC-2 over Badrulchau	55	55	☐☐☐☐☐
167	A28	44c Japan No. 201, Japanese post office	70	70	☐☐☐☐☐
168	A28	$1 Aviator's grave..............	2.00	2.00	☐☐☐☐☐
173	A30	22c I saw...................	40	40	☐☐☐☐☐
174	A30	22c And what was.....	40	40	☐☐☐☐☐
175	A30	22c 'Twas Joseph...	40	40	☐☐☐☐☐
176	A30	22c Saint Michael................	40	40	☐☐☐☐☐
177	A30	22c And all the bells.............	40	40	☐☐☐☐☐
177a.		Strip of 5, Nos. 173-177	2.00	2.00	☐☐☐☐☐
178	A31	22c Snapping shrimp, goby........	40	40	☐☐☐☐☐
179	A31	22c Mauve vase sponge, sponge crab	40	40	☐☐☐☐☐
180	A31	22c Pope's damselfish, cleaner wrasse	40	40	☐☐☐☐☐
181	A31	22c Clown anemone fish, sea anemone	40	40	☐☐☐☐☐
182	A31	22c Four-color nudibranch, banded coral shrimp	40	40	☐☐☐☐☐
182a.		Strip of 5, Nos. 178-182	2.00	2.00	☐☐☐☐☐

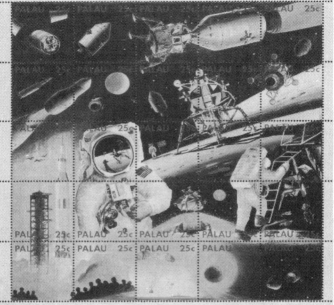

THE SEA OF TRANQUILLITY
'Houston. Tranquillity Base here. The Eagle has landed.'
20th July 1969 - 20:17:43 Greenwich Mean Time

20th Anniversary APOLLO 11 - First Manned Lunar Landing
Astronauts - Neil A. Armstrong, commander; Edwin Aldrin, lunar module pilot;
Michael Collins, command module pilot.

A40

A48

A50

310

Scott No.	Illus. No.	Description	Unused Value	Used Value	//////
1988					
183	A23a	44c Dannas plexippus, Tournefotia argentia	70	70	☐☐☐☐☐
184	A23a	44c Papilio machaon, Citrus reticulata	70	70	☐☐☐☐☐
185	A23a	44c Captopsilia, Crataeva speciosa	70	70	☐☐☐☐☐
186	A23a	44c Colias philodice, Crataeva speciosa	70	70	☐☐☐☐☐
186a.		Block of 4, Nos. 183-186	2.80	2.80	☐☐☐☐☐
187	A32	44c Whimbrel	70	70	☐☐☐☐☐
188	A32	44c Yellow bittern	70	70	☐☐☐☐☐
189	A32	44c Rufous night-heron	70	70	☐☐☐☐☐
190	A32	44c Banded rail	70	70	☐☐☐☐☐
190a.		Block of 4, Nos. 187-190	3.00	3.00	☐☐☐☐☐
191	A20	25c Striped engina	40	40	☐☐☐☐☐
192	A20	25c Ivory cone	40	40	☐☐☐☐☐
193	A20	25c Plaited miter	40	40	☐☐☐☐☐
194	A20	25c Episcopal miter	40	40	☐☐☐☐☐
195	A20	25c Isabelle cowrie	40	40	☐☐☐☐☐
195a.		Strip of 5, Nos. 191-195	2.00	2.00	☐☐☐☐☐
196		Souvenir sheet of 6	2.40	2.40	☐☐☐☐☐
196a.-f.	A33	25c, any single	40	40	☐☐☐☐☐
197	A34	Sheet of 6	4.25	4.25	☐☐☐☐☐
197a.-f.		45c, any single	70	70	☐☐☐☐☐
198	A35	25c Angels, violins	40	40	☐☐☐☐☐
199	A35	25c 3 angles, 3 children	40	40	☐☐☐☐☐
200	A35	25c Nativity	40	40	☐☐☐☐☐
201	A35	25c 2 angels, birds	40	40	☐☐☐☐☐
202	A35	25c 3 children, 2angels, horns	40	40	☐☐☐☐☐
202a.		Strip of 5, Nos. 199-202	2.00	2.00	☐☐☐☐☐
203	A36	Sheet of 5	2.00	2.00	☐☐☐☐☐
203a.-e.		25c, any single	40	40	☐☐☐☐☐
1989					
204	A37	45c Nicobar pigeon	70	70	☐☐☐☐☐
205	A37	45c Ground dove	70	70	☐☐☐☐☐
206	A37	45c Micronesian megapode	70	70	☐☐☐☐☐
207	A37	45c Owl	70	70	☐☐☐☐☐
207a.		Block of 4, Nos. 204-207	3.00	3.00	☐☐☐☐☐
208	A38	45c Gilled auricularia	70	70	☐☐☐☐☐
209	A38	45c Rock mushroom	70	70	☐☐☐☐☐
210	A38	45c Polyporous	70	70	☐☐☐☐☐
211	A38	45c Veiled stinkhorn	70	70	☐☐☐☐☐
211a.		Block of 4, Nos. 208-211	3.00	3.00	☐☐☐☐☐
212	A20	25c Robin redbreast triton	40	40	☐☐☐☐☐
213	A20	25c Hebrew cone	40	40	☐☐☐☐☐
214	A20	25c Tadpole triton	40	40	☐☐☐☐☐
215	A20	25c Lettered cone	40	40	☐☐☐☐☐

A43

HOW TO USE THIS BOOK

The number in the first column is its Scott number or identifying number. The letter and number that come next (A41) indicate the design and refer to the illustration so designated. Following that is the denomination of the stamp and its color. Finally, the value, unused and used is shown.

Scott No.	Illus. No.	Description	Unused Value	Used Value	//////
216	A20	25c Rugose miter...............	40	40	☐☐☐☐☐
216a.		Strip of 5, Nos. 212-216	2.00	2.00	☐☐☐☐☐
217	A39	$1 *A Little Bird, Amidst*			
		Chrysanthemums	1.50	1.50	☐☐☐☐☐
218	A40	Sheet of 25	10.00	10.00	☐☐☐☐☐
218a.-y.		25c, any single	40	40	☐☐☐☐☐
219	A41	$2.40 Buzz Aldrim	3.50	3.50	☐☐☐☐☐
220		Block of 10.....................	4.00	4.00	☐☐☐☐☐
220a.-j.	A42	25c, any single	40	40	☐☐☐☐☐
221	A43	Block of 20.....................	7.50	7.50	☐☐☐☐☐
221a.-t.		25c, any single	35	35	☐☐☐☐☐
222	A44	25c Dusky tern, Audubon's			
		shearwater, angels, island	40	40	☐☐☐☐☐
223	A44	25c Fruit pigeon, angel	40	40	☐☐☐☐☐
224	A44	25c Madonna and child, ground			
		pigeons, fairy terms, rails,			
		sandpipers	40	40	☐☐☐☐☐
225	A44	25c Angel, blue-headed green finch,			
		red flycatcher, honeyeater......	40	40	☐☐☐☐☐
226	A44	25c Angel, black-headed gulls......	40	40	☐☐☐☐☐
226a.		Strip of 5, Nos. 222-226	2.00	2.00	☐☐☐☐☐

1990

Scott No.	Illus. No.	Description	Unused Value	Used Value	//////
227	A45	25c Pink coral	40	40	☐☐☐☐☐
228	A45	25c Pink & violet coral	40	40	☐☐☐☐☐
229	A45	25c Yellow coral	40	40	☐☐☐☐☐
230	A45	25c Red coral....................	40	40	☐☐☐☐☐
230a.		Block of 4, Nos. 227-230........	1.60	1.60	☐☐☐☐☐
231	A46	45c Siberian rubythroat...........	60	60	☐☐☐☐☐
232	A46	45c Palau bush-warbler...........	60	60	☐☐☐☐☐
233	A46	45c Micronesian starling..........	60	60	☐☐☐☐☐
234	A46	45c Cicadabird..................	60	60	☐☐☐☐☐
234a.		Block of 4, #231-234	2.50	2.50	☐☐☐☐☐
235		Sheet of 9	3.00	3.00	☐☐☐☐☐
235a.-i.	A47	25c, any single	32	32	☐☐☐☐☐
236	A48	$1 Great Britain No..............	1.50	1.50	☐☐☐☐☐
237	A49	45c Corymborkis veratrifolia	70	70	☐☐☐☐☐
238	A49	45c Malaxis setipes	70	70	☐☐☐☐☐
239	A49	45c Dipodium freycinetianum	70	70	☐☐☐☐☐
240	A49	45c Bulbophyllum micronesiacum..	70	70	☐☐☐☐☐
241	A49	45c Vanda teres and hookeriana....	70	70	☐☐☐☐☐
241a.		Strip of 5, #237-241.............	3.50	3.50	☐☐☐☐☐
242	A50	45c Wedelia strigulosa...........	70	70	☐☐☐☐☐
243	A50	45c Erthrina variegata...........	70	70	☐☐☐☐☐
244	A50	45c Clerodendrum inerme	70	70	☐☐☐☐☐
245	A50	45c Vigna marina	70	70	☐☐☐☐☐
245a.		Block of 4, #242-245	2.80	2.80	☐☐☐☐☐

Scott No.	Illus. No.	Description	Unused Value	Used Value	//////
					☐☐☐☐☐
					☐☐☐☐☐
					☐☐☐☐☐
					☐☐☐☐☐
					☐☐☐☐☐
					☐☐☐☐☐
					☐☐☐☐☐
					☐☐☐☐☐
					☐☐☐☐☐
					☐☐☐☐☐
					☐☐☐☐☐
					☐☐☐☐☐
					☐☐☐☐☐
					☐☐☐☐☐
					☐☐☐☐☐
					☐☐☐☐☐
					☐☐☐☐☐
					☐☐☐☐☐
					☐☐☐☐☐
					☐☐☐☐☐
					☐☐☐☐☐
					☐☐☐☐☐
					☐☐☐☐☐
					☐☐☐☐☐
					☐☐☐☐☐
					☐☐☐☐☐
					☐☐☐☐☐
					☐☐☐☐☐
					☐☐☐☐☐
					☐☐☐☐☐
					☐☐☐☐☐
					☐☐☐☐☐
					☐☐☐☐☐

SP1

Scott No.	Illus. No.	Description	Unused Value	Used Value	//////
Semi-Postal Stamps					
1988, Aug. 8					
B1	SP1	25c+5c Baseball glove, player......	45	45	☐☐☐☐☐
B2	SP1	25c+5c Running shoe, athlete......	45	45	☐☐☐☐☐
B2a.		Pair, Nos. B1-B2	90	90	☐☐☐☐☐
B3	SP1	45c+5c Goggles, swimmer.........	70	70	☐☐☐☐☐
B4	SP1	45c+5c Gold medal, diver.........	70	70	☐☐☐☐☐
B4a.		Pair, Nos. B3-B4	1.40	1.40	☐☐☐☐☐

     _____ ☐☐☐☐☐
     _____ ☐☐☐☐☐
     _____ ☐☐☐☐☐
     _____ ☐☐☐☐☐
     _____ ☐☐☐☐☐
     _____ ☐☐☐☐☐
     _____ ☐☐☐☐☐
     _____ ☐☐☐☐☐
     _____ ☐☐☐☐☐
     _____ ☐☐☐☐☐
     _____ ☐☐☐☐☐
     _____ ☐☐☐☐☐
     _____ ☐☐☐☐☐
     _____ ☐☐☐☐☐
     _____ ☐☐☐☐☐
     _____ ☐☐☐☐☐
     _____ ☐☐☐☐☐
     _____ ☐☐☐☐☐
     _____ ☐☐☐☐☐
     _____ ☐☐☐☐☐
     _____ ☐☐☐☐☐

AP1

AP2

AP3

AP4

AP5

HOW TO USE THIS BOOK
The number in the first column is its Scott number or identifying number. The letter and number that come next (A41) indicate the design and refer to the illustration so designated. Following that is the denomination of the stamp and its color. Finally, the value, unused and used is shown.

Scott No.	Illus. No.	Description	Unused Value	Used Value	//////
Airpost Stamps					
1984, June 12					
C1	AP1	40c White-tailed tropicbird........	75	75 ☐☐☐☐☐
C2	AP1	40c Fairy tern..................	75	75 ☐☐☐☐☐
C3	AP1	40c Black noddy	75	75 ☐☐☐☐☐
C4	AP1	40c Black-naped tern.............	75	75 ☐☐☐☐☐
C4a.		Block of 4, Nos. C1-C4	3.00	3.00 ☐☐☐☐☐
1985					
C5	A12	44c Audubon's Shearwater	70	70 ☐☐☐☐☐
C6	AP2	44c German flag-raising at Palau ...	90	90 ☐☐☐☐☐
C7	AP2	44c Early German trading post.....	90	90 ☐☐☐☐☐
C8	AP2	44c Abai architecture	90	90 ☐☐☐☐☐
C9	AP2	44c SMS *Cormoran*..............	90	90 ☐☐☐☐☐
C9a.		Block of 4, Nos. C6-C9	3.60	3.60 ☐☐☐☐☐
C10	A16	44c PBY-5a Catalina.............	70	70 ☐☐☐☐☐
C11	A16	44c DC-6B Super Cloudmaster	70	70 ☐☐☐☐☐
C12	A16	44c SA-16 Albatross	70	70 ☐☐☐☐☐
C13	A16	44c Douglas fDC-4	70	70 ☐☐☐☐☐
C13a.		Block of 4, Nos. C10-C13	2.80	2.80 ☐☐☐☐☐
1986					
C14	AP3	44c Presidential seal, inaugural address....................	90	90 ☐☐☐☐☐
C15	AP3	44c War canoe, address excerpt	90	90 ☐☐☐☐☐
C16	AP3	44c Haruo I. Remeliik, Ronald Reagan.....................	90	90 ☐☐☐☐☐
C16a.		Strip of 3, Nos. C14-C16........	2.70	2.70 ☐☐☐☐☐
C17	AP4	44c Statue of Liberty	70	70 ☐☐☐☐☐
1989, May 17					
C18	AP5	36c Cessna 207 Skywagon.........	60	60 ☐☐☐☐☐
C18a.		Booklet pane of 10.............	6.00	— ☐☐☐☐☐
C19	AP5	39c Embraer EMB-110 Bandeirante	65	65 ☐☐☐☐☐
C19a.		Booklet pane of 10.............	6.50	— ☐☐☐☐☐
C20	AP5	45c Boeing 727..................	70	70 ☐☐☐☐☐
C20a.		Booklet pane of 10.............	7.00	— ☐☐☐☐☐
C20b.		Booklet pane of 10 (5 each 36c, 45c)	6.50	— ☐☐☐☐☐

_____	☐☐☐☐☐
_____	☐☐☐☐☐
_____	☐☐☐☐☐
_____	☐☐☐☐☐
_____	☐☐☐☐☐

Scott No.	Illus. No.	Description	Unused Value	Used Value	//////
					☐☐☐☐☐
					☐☐☐☐☐
					☐☐☐☐☐
					☐☐☐☐☐
					☐☐☐☐☐
					☐☐☐☐☐
					☐☐☐☐☐
					☐☐☐☐☐
					☐☐☐☐☐
					☐☐☐☐☐
					☐☐☐☐☐
					☐☐☐☐☐
					☐☐☐☐☐
					☐☐☐☐☐
					☐☐☐☐☐
					☐☐☐☐☐
					☐☐☐☐☐
					☐☐☐☐☐
					☐☐☐☐☐
					☐☐☐☐☐
					☐☐☐☐☐
					☐☐☐☐☐
					☐☐☐☐☐
					☐☐☐☐☐
					☐☐☐☐☐
					☐☐☐☐☐
					☐☐☐☐☐
					☐☐☐☐☐
					☐☐☐☐☐
					☐☐☐☐☐
					☐☐☐☐☐
					☐☐☐☐☐
					☐☐☐☐☐

Scott No.	Illus. No.	Description	Unused Value	Used Value	/ / / / / /
					☐☐☐☐☐
					☐☐☐☐☐
					☐☐☐☐☐
					☐☐☐☐☐
					☐☐☐☐☐
					☐☐☐☐☐
					☐☐☐☐☐
					☐☐☐☐☐
					☐☐☐☐☐
					☐☐☐☐☐
					☐☐☐☐☐
					☐☐☐☐☐
					☐☐☐☐☐
					☐☐☐☐☐
					☐☐☐☐☐
					☐☐☐☐☐
					☐☐☐☐☐
					☐☐☐☐☐
					☐☐☐☐☐
					☐☐☐☐☐
					☐☐☐☐☐
					☐☐☐☐☐
					☐☐☐☐☐
					☐☐☐☐☐
					☐☐☐☐☐
					☐☐☐☐☐
					☐☐☐☐☐
					☐☐☐☐☐
					☐☐☐☐☐
					☐☐☐☐☐
					☐☐☐☐☐
					☐☐☐☐☐
					☐☐☐☐☐
					☐☐☐☐☐
					☐☐☐☐☐

Scott No.	Illus. No.	Description	Unused Value	Used Value	//////
					☐☐☐☐☐
					☐☐☐☐☐
					☐☐☐☐☐
					☐☐☐☐☐
					☐☐☐☐☐
					☐☐☐☐☐
					☐☐☐☐☐
					☐☐☐☐☐
					☐☐☐☐☐
					☐☐☐☐☐
					☐☐☐☐☐
					☐☐☐☐☐
					☐☐☐☐☐
					☐☐☐☐☐
					☐☐☐☐☐
					☐☐☐☐☐
					☐☐☐☐☐
					☐☐☐☐☐
					☐☐☐☐☐
					☐☐☐☐☐
					☐☐☐☐☐
					☐☐☐☐☐
					☐☐☐☐☐
					☐☐☐☐☐
					☐☐☐☐☐
					☐☐☐☐☐
					☐☐☐☐☐
					☐☐☐☐☐
					☐☐☐☐☐
					☐☐☐☐☐
					☐☐☐☐☐
					☐☐☐☐☐
					☐☐☐☐☐

Scott No.	Illus. No.	Description	Unused Value	Used Value	//////
					☐☐☐☐☐
					☐☐☐☐☐
					☐☐☐☐☐
					☐☐☐☐☐
					☐☐☐☐☐
					☐☐☐☐☐
					☐☐☐☐☐
					☐☐☐☐☐
					☐☐☐☐☐
					☐☐☐☐☐
					☐☐☐☐☐
					☐☐☐☐☐
					☐☐☐☐☐
					☐☐☐☐☐
					☐☐☐☐☐
					☐☐☐☐☐
					☐☐☐☐☐
					☐☐☐☐☐
					☐☐☐☐☐
					☐☐☐☐☐
					☐☐☐☐☐
					☐☐☐☐☐
					☐☐☐☐☐
					☐☐☐☐☐
					☐☐☐☐☐
					☐☐☐☐☐
					☐☐☐☐☐
					☐☐☐☐☐
					☐☐☐☐☐
					☐☐☐☐☐
					☐☐☐☐☐
					☐☐☐☐☐
					☐☐☐☐☐
					☐☐☐☐☐

Scott No.	Illus. No.	Description	Unused Value	Used Value	//////
					☐☐☐☐☐
					☐☐☐☐☐
					☐☐☐☐☐
					☐☐☐☐☐
					☐☐☐☐☐
					☐☐☐☐☐
					☐☐☐☐☐
					☐☐☐☐☐
					☐☐☐☐☐
					☐☐☐☐☐
					☐☐☐☐☐
					☐☐☐☐☐
					☐☐☐☐☐
					☐☐☐☐☐
					☐☐☐☐☐
					☐☐☐☐☐
					☐☐☐☐☐
					☐☐☐☐☐
					☐☐☐☐☐
					☐☐☐☐☐
					☐☐☐☐☐
					☐☐☐☐☐
					☐☐☐☐☐
					☐☐☐☐☐
					☐☐☐☐☐
					☐☐☐☐☐
					☐☐☐☐☐
					☐☐☐☐☐
					☐☐☐☐☐
					☐☐☐☐☐
					☐☐☐☐☐
					☐☐☐☐☐
					☐☐☐☐☐

Scott No.	Illus. No.	Description	Unused Value	Used Value	//////
					☐☐☐☐☐
					☐☐☐☐☐
					☐☐☐☐☐
					☐☐☐☐☐
					☐☐☐☐☐
					☐☐☐☐☐
					☐☐☐☐☐
					☐☐☐☐☐
					☐☐☐☐☐
					☐☐☐☐☐
					☐☐☐☐☐
					☐☐☐☐☐
					☐☐☐☐☐
					☐☐☐☐☐
					☐☐☐☐☐
					☐☐☐☐☐
					☐☐☐☐☐
					☐☐☐☐☐
					☐☐☐☐☐
					☐☐☐☐☐
					☐☐☐☐☐
					☐☐☐☐☐
					☐☐☐☐☐
					☐☐☐☐☐
					☐☐☐☐☐
					☐☐☐☐☐
					☐☐☐☐☐
					☐☐☐☐☐
					☐☐☐☐☐
					☐☐☐☐☐
					☐☐☐☐☐
					☐☐☐☐☐
					☐☐☐☐☐

INDEX TO ADVERTISERS

★ ★ ★ ★ ★ ★ ★ ★ ★ ★ ★ ★ ★ ★